LABOUR-MANAGEMENT RELATIONS

LABOUR-MANAGEMENT RELATIONS

A Study of Textile Industry in Jammu and Kashmir

ABDUL GANI

Foreword by
PROF. ABAD AHMAD

CONCEPT PUBLISHING COMPANY, NEW DELHI 110059

The Indian Council of Social Science Research gave the financial support towards the publication of this work. However, the responsibility for the contents of the book — facts, opinions, conclusions, etc. — is entirely that of the author and not of the ICSSR.

ICSSR consultant
PROF. ISHWAR DAYAL

ISBN 81-7022-345-8

First Published 1991

Published and Printed by
Ashok Kumar Mittal
Concept Publishing Company
A/15-16, Commercial Block, Mohan Garden
NEW DELHI 110059 (India)

Lasertypeset by
Microtech Advance Printing Systems (Pvt.) Ltd.
H-13, Bali Nagar
NEW DELHI 110015

DEDICATED
TO
MY PARENTS
FOR WHOM THE QURAN *BIDS ME TO*
PRAY, "MY LORD, SHOW MERCY UNTO
THEM AS THEY NURSED ME MERCIFULLY
WHEN I WAS LITTLE"

FOREWORD

THE EFFORTS to raise the level of living of people in any developing country call for corresponding increase in employment and productivity. The attainment of these goals, in turn, depends on a stable and healthy industrial relations' climate. Systematic research in the field of industrial relations is, therefore, essential for formulating and implementing a sound strategy for socio-economic development.

The problems of industrial relations are being increasingly selected as a focal point of research in India. During the past few years, there has been a notable resurgence of interest in industrial relations, perhaps, due to rapid increase in industrialisation, socio-economic and political upheavals, technological advances and changing composition and values of work-force, etc. The signs of such a renaissance include recent efforts to establish new institutions and centres to advance research in industrial relations, following the path pioneered by some advanced research centres such as the centres at California, Wisconsin, Cornell, etc. A field of study, that had initially belonged to a small number of labour economists, now attracts political scientists, sociologists, psychologists, behavioural scientists, historians and quantitative analysts as well, who have contributed substantially to the understanding of economic, institutional, social, psychological and behavioural dimensions of industrial relations. Quite a large number of research studies have been conducted in various States and industrial centres of the country, dealing with different aspects of industrial relations. It is encouraging to note that considerable work done in this area is exploratory and empirical in nature. The present work by Dr. Gani reflects the same thrust and is, indeed, a welcome one.

The study seeks to examine the labour-management relations in the Textile Industry of Jammu and Kashmir State. After the introductory Chapter in which the significance, objectives and design of the study have been described, the author critically reviews the research available on the subject, identifies the research gaps and outlines the areas for future research. He then presents a comprehensive view of industrial conflicts, giving an analysis of trends, their intensity and workers' participation in them. A detailed study of the working of machinery for handling disputes has been made. The author has examined in depth the working and living conditions of workers, followed by an examination of the degree of their job satisfaction and its associated variables. The study specifically identifies what the operative employees want from their first line supervisors and from the management. Workers' participation in management, the much talked about concept in the academic and political circles these days, is one of the major subject matters of Dr. Gani's work. First, the working and effectiveness of various participative schemes are examined. It is followed by an assessment of the organisational climate for participation, identification of the hurdles to participation and a detailed analysis of the participatory orientation of workers and managers.

The study also covers some important aspects of trade unionism. Attention is focussed on growth and structure of trade unionism, workers' involvement and participation in trade union activities and correlates of union participation. The last chapter recapitulates the major findings of the study, draws conclusions and analysis the implications of these findings. Policy recommendations are offered, which deserve serious attention for improving the state of labour-management relations.

The book taken together presents the essential elements for understanding of the dynamics of labour-management relations in the context of institutional and behavioural factors. The unit by unit analysis of some vital issues is one of the distinguishing features of the book.

The author has combined conceptual analysis with empirical evidence and review of research findings to give a comprehensive picture of the industrial relations. The book will be a valuable contribution to the existing literature on the subject. It will not only be of considerable interest and value to the students, researchers, teachers, labour relations' administrators, practising managers and unionists, but will also prove quite stimulating in future thinking on the subject and for opening new vistas of action and research.

South Campus,
University of Delhi
DELHI

PROF. ABAD AHMAD
Prof. of Management and Director

ACKNOWLEDGEMENTS

AN EMPIRICAL exercise of this nature and magnitude assumes co-operation of a variety of individuals and institutions. I feel lucky to have received guidance, help, comments and criticism from many quarters. I deem it my pleasure to acknowledge with gratitude all of them here. If I miss any or some of them to mention by name, it would be my absent-mindedness but certainly not intentional.

Foremost, I express my profound gratitude to my venerable teacher, Prof. A.R. Mattod for his constant inspiration and vigil. My special thanks are due to Dr. Nisar Ahmad for his seasoned guidance, constant encouragement and keen personal interest in the project. Equally indebted am I to Dr. Fayaz Ahmad for his brotherly assistance and scholarly criticism.

I concede that whatever is really appreciable in this study is as a result my constant interaction with some eminent personalities in the field of labour research in India. I express my unrestrained gratitude to all of them for their scholarly discussions, comments, suggestions and supply of valuable literature. In particular, I am grateful to Dr. B.R. Sharma, Dr. C.K. Johri, Dr. N.R. Sheth, the late Dr. Nitesh R. De and Dr. Prayag Mehta, from whose research experience I have enormously gained and who have alerted me to all such sources that matter in the field of labour research. I would also like to acknowledge my indebtedness to all the writers in India and abroad, whose works have been made use of in this study.

I am grateful to the Ministry of Labour, Government of India, New Delhi; National Labour Institute, New Delhi; Sri Ram Centre, New Delhi; Indian Institute of Public Administration, New Delhi; Central Labour Institute, Bombay; National Documentation Centre, I.C.S.S.R., New Delhi, and Ratan Tata Library, Delhi University, New Delhi, for allowing me use their library facilities and extending all help and co-operation.

I acknowledge my enormous debt to all the executives, workers and trade union leaders, whom I interviewed during my field survey, for their whole-hearted and active co-operation, without which it would have not been possible to complete the survey, which forms the basis of the present work. I would be failing in my duty if I do not put on record the enthusiastic support, co-operation and assistance offered by the Labour Commissioner, Government of Jammu & Kashmir, and his subordinate staff.

I acknowledge my deepest sense of gratitude to Prof. Abad Ahmad, who has not only been a perennial source of inspiration to me but also has written the foreword for the book. In the midst of his multifarious responsibilities, he extended his willing support, for which I cannot adequately express my gratitude to him.

I acknowledge with thanks the publication grant provided by the *I.C.S.S.R.*, New Delhi. I would like to put on record my gratitude to Prof. Ishwar Dayal, who reviewed the manuscript and provided useful suggestions.

The study owes much to the painstaking efforts of a host of friends and admirers. I am grateful to them all for their whole-hearted and active co-operation, detailed comments, constructive criticism and invaluable suggestions on earlier drafts of the manuscript, which have gone a long way in improving the quality of the subsequent drafts. All my colleagues in the faculty of commerce, University of Kashmir have contributed to the completion of this project by way of their co-operation and moral support. To them all, I am highly thankful.

Mr. Ashok Kumar Mittal of Concept Publishing Company has borne the main brunt of publishing the book in a record short time so cheerfully and carefully for which he deserves warm thanks and appreciation.

Finally, a reference here of my deepest sense of gratitude to my dear parents, to whom this work is dedicated, for their affection, encouragement and blessings, looks to me formal but that is truth.

ABDUL GANI

CONTENTS

LIST OF TABLES

1

DESIGN OF RESEARCH AND BACKGROUND OF THE STUDY

HARMONIOUS RELATIONS in every sphere of human activity are a prerequisite for socio-economic progress. Establishing and maintaining smooth and cordial relations between labour and management, in particular, is of utmost importance, especially in the State of Jammu and Kashmir which occupies a low position in the national industrial scenario, where resources are limited, population is growing at an alarming rate and hence industrial progress is the prime need. Mere technical efficiency modern machinery, good plant layout and dynamic organisations etc. are not enough to make a business profitable and lead to economic growth and social improvements. It is harmonious and constructive labour-management relationship in industry, which plays almost a decisive role in this respect.

Unfortunately, increasing complexity of modern industrial system, has widened the hiatus between the employers and the employees more than ever before, the distributional disparities have worsened and discontent and frustration at the lower levels of organisations have heightened.This map is created serious types of industrial conflicts in labour-management relations, resulting in fall of production, increase in prices and creation of adverse balance of payments. Threats to industrial peace are threats to the creation and maximisation of national wealth and can easily be transcribed as threats to the welfare of the people. Therefore, there has always been a need to study the factors, which result in industrial unrest and those which lead to cordial labour management relations, with a view to evolve and implement the policies and strategies relating to industrial relations, keeping the all important aim of socio-economic development of the economy in view.

In India, quite a large number of research studies has been carried out in various States and industrial centres of the country. These studies, which invariably deal with different aspects of industrial relations, have been conducted to meet the needs of individual researchers and found providing agencies. But, unfortunately, no such comprehensive study has, so far, been undertaken in the State of Jammu and Kashmir, except those of Karim (1972) and Mattoo (1976), which too largely deals with the problems of static nature and are general, descriptive, devoid of any empirical basis with limited coverage. There is a conspicuous absence of the study of critical aspects of behavioural dimensions of labour-management relations. The present study has been undertaken to fill this gap and make a modest contribution in this popular field of research.

The study has been undertaken with particular reference to the textile industry of the State. In India, the textile industry, being one of the oldest and largest industries, has been the main focus of attention of researchers in the field of industrial relations, particularly in Bombay, Ahmedabad, Kanpur, Rajasthan and Punjab, leading centres of textile manufacture and witness to some of the earliest industrial conflicts. But the textile industry of Jammu and Kashmir has not at all been touched upon, inspite of its being the oldest, largest, highly dispute prone and most unionised industry in the State. Therefore, the study of labour-management relations in this industry assumes special significance.

OBJECTIVES AND SIGNIFICANCE OF THE STUDY

The study seeks to examine in realistic and comprehensive manner the state of labour-management relations in textile industry of Jammu and Kashmir State and probe objectively into the factors that helps or obstruct the maintenance and development of harmonious relations between labour and management in the industry.

Specifically the study focuses on the following aspects of labour-management relations :

1. The nature, extent and manifestation of industrial conflicts, their associated factors and the working of dispute handling machinery.
2. Working and living conditions of workers, workers' satisfaction with various elements of job, the degree of workers' job satisfaction and its determinants.

3. Workers' expectations from their supervisors and managements with regard to different aspects of their roles at work situations.
4. The nature and extent of workers' participation in decision making, the existing organisational climate for participation, functioning of participatives forums, existing and desired degree of workers' influence in different decision areas and the desired forms of participation in decision making.
5. The growth and structure of trade unionism, the extent of workers' involvement and participation in union activities and the correlates of union involvement.

Along with the examination of above formal aspects of labour-management relations, the study is designed to:

1. examine the attitude and behaviour and assess the reaction and response of the parties in industrial relations system,
2. review the theoretical and empirical literature available on the subject in order to develop a comprehensive base for the study,
3. throw light on the industrial relations system existing in the industry under study and
4. identify the specific roles to be played by workers, supervisors, managements, trade unions and the government officials for the harmonious labour-management relations and on the basis of the findings of the study, offer policy recommendations for achieving the much needed industrial peace.

With a few exceptions, most of the existing studies on industrial relations in India are restricted to a descriptive count of the number of industrial conflicts, their causes and consequences; cold, lifeless and repetitive calculations of the issues underlying these disputes, union membership, wage trends, etc. These fail to fully explain the dynamics of the relationship. However, the present study is an empirical one and of exploratory nature. A study of this type will help the management in developing a deeper insight into the relevant aspect of industrial relations, policies and practices. It can be of positive influence in evolving and implementing policies oriented to better the results. The study, it is hoped, would be useful both to the management and workers as it brings out their view points regarding different issues in industrial relations and can thus pave the way for better understanding and mutual co-operation.

A FRAME OF WORKING HYPOTHESES

To keep the frame of the analysis intact and give a proper direction to the study, the following working hypotheses have been set up:

1. Better the labour-management relations greater will be the productivity and efficiency in the operation of an industry.
2. The regional influence, the size of the work force, approach of the management and attitudes of workers play a significant role in influencing the system of industrial relations in an industry.
3. In a developing economy, such as, ours, economic factors tend to dominate over non-economic factors in causing industrial disputes.
4. Inflation, extent of trade unionism, workers' job dissatisfaction, poor working of participative forums act as positive inducements for conflict proneness.
5. Workers' job satisfaction, participation in decision making, union involvement and participation and their attitude towards various aspects of labour-management relations are influenced by their socio-economic and personal variables.
6. All parties to industrial disputes favour third party intervention and settlement through the machinery, such as, conciliation and arbitration, both compulsory and voluntary, rather than direct negotiations or collective bargaining.

SCOPE OF THE STUDY

As stated earlier, the study has been restricted to the textile industry of Jammu and Kashmir State. The textile industry has been selected deliberately for the purpose of present study for the following reasons :

1. The textile industry is the largest industry in the entire manufacturing sector of the State, both in terms of the number of units and employment.
2. It contributes substantially towards the total value of industrial production, makes maximum use of the locally available inputs and meets the demand not only of the State but also of the national and international consumption.
3. It is highly dispute prone industry in the State, accounting on an average for about 15 per cent of the total disputes raised in the

State, resulting in a huge mandays lost.

4. It has throughout occupied a predominant position in the trade union movement of the State and presently accounts for 12.5 per cent of the total registered trade unions in the State with substantial proportion of union membership.

The textile industry in the State is a typical group having, at one end, well-organised industrial activity with a long history of trade unionism and, at the other unorganised productive activity geographically scattered with no perceivable signs of unionism. The industrial relations scene in the unorganised sector of the industry, consisting of carpets, shawls, garments, handlooms, etc., has neither been uniform nor seriously disturbing because of the absence of awareness on the part of workers and their lack of unity and proper guidance to come together and act jointly. Therefore, the scope of the study has been confined to selected units in the organised sector of the industry only. The following criteria have been taken into account while selecting units for the study:

1. The units should be running and thus the establishments which were closed whether temporarily or permanently were excluded.
2. The units employing less than 100 employees were excluded.
3. As far as possible the units selected should be from both the sectors — public and private — spread over the entire State and represent the main sectors of textile woollen, silk and cotton.
4. The units should as far as possible have contrasted history of labour-management relations.
5. The units should be from the manufacturing sector only in view of the vital role of efficiency, functioning and increase in productivity of manufacturing sector in the economic development and, also, because the schemes of labour welfare, participative management and labour legislation have generally been introduced first in the manufacturing sector.

Keeping in view the above factors and considering the limitation of time and paucity of resources at the disposal of an individual researcher, the study has been restricted to five large and medium scale manufacturing textile units. These employ a total of 3,893 workmen which constitute the universe for the study and are engaged in the spinning, weaving, printing, bleaching, dyeing and furnishing of cotton, silk and woollen textiles. Two sample units, each, represent woollen and silk sectors and one represents the cotton sector of the industry. The details regarding the ownership production line, year of establishment, the employment and the sample size of the organisations adopted for the study are exhibited in Table 1.1.

TABLE 1.1: Organisations covered by the Study and the Number of Respondants Interviewed

Codification of organisation	Location (District)	Production line	Year of establishment	Total employment	No. of workers interviewed (inclusive of trade union leaders)	No. of mgt. personnel interviewed	Total sample
I	Srinagar	Silk spinning and weaving - crape, check, champon, boski, shefan, chinani, etc.	1939	513	56	13	69
II	Jammu	Manufacture of silk yarn, for production of crape, champon, shefan, chinani, boski, etc.	1970	327	36	9	45
III	Srinagar	Spinning, weaving, dyeing, finishing of worsted suiting and shirtings, manufacture of woollen and worsted yarn.	1970	321	35	8	43
IV	Srinagar	Production of shaddy yarn, blankets, woollen tweeds, worsted carpets, spinning, weaving, dyeing and finishing of woollen fabrics.	1934	245	25	6	31
V	Kathua	Spinning of cotton and synethetic yarn.	1963	2,487	98	24	122
		Total		3,893	250	60	310

REFERENCE PERIOD

The study limits itself to the period since 1971. The selection of this period has not been a matter of arbitrary choice but has been governed by two main factors. First, it has been during this period that substantial development has taken place in the State in various sectors of industrial activity in general and in the textile sector in particular. Secondly, most of the labour enactments, regulating labour-management relations, have been introduced in the State right from 1971. Efforts have been made to cover the period from 1971 to 1986. However, for the purposes of comparison, wherever necessary, reference has been made to the data and incidents prior to 1971. Where information was not available for the entire reference period, reliance was placed on the available data only.

MATERIALS AND METHODS

Research Approach

With a view to substantiate the above hypotheses the following research approach has been employed:

1. Literature survey to critically review the available research on various aspects of industrial relations.
2. Field study to observe in proper perspective the situation with regard to the labour conditions and other aspects of employment relationship in the organisations under study.
3. Interviewing workers, trade unionists, management representatives and government officials, concerned with the labour administration, through personal interviews on scheduled questionnaires.
4. Study of records, annual reports, statistical handbooks, committee and survey reports and other official documents in sample units and in concerned government agencies.

Materials: Source and Scope

The study involves the data collected from the primary as well as the secondary sources. The data pertaining to the sample organisations, such as the historical development, the production line, nature of workforce, wage rates, individual grievances, working of bipartite committees, trade unions, industrial relations climate, industrial disputes, dispute handling procedure, personnel policies, performance in terms of both financial and non-financial parameters, have been obtained from various records and documents of the sample organisations and also through discussion with the concerned authorities.

The data on other matters, such as trade unions, wage structure, participative schemes, industrial conflicts and conflict resolution mechanism etc., pertaining to the industry under study and other industries/States and also for studies related to various aspects of labour-management relations, have been obtained from the office of the Labour Commissioner, Government of Jammu and Kashmir, Srinagar/Jammu; Ministry of Labour and Employment, New Delhi; Sri Ram Centre for Industrial Relations and Human Resources, New Delhi; National Labour Institute, New Delhi; National Documentation Centre, I.C.S.S.R., New Delhi; Ratna Tata Library, Delhi University, Delhi; Indian Institute of Public Administration, New Delhi; Central Labour Institute, Bombay, and from various other books, journals and Government reports.

Questionnaire : Development and Administration

The primary data have been collected primarily from workers and management personnel, constituting the major source of data for the study. For this purpose two separate comprehensive questionnaires, intended to be the principal instruments for obtaining necessary information, were prepared for (1) workers and (2) management personnel (See Appendix I and Appendix II, respectively). The questionnaires were pre-tested with workers and management personnel in one of the units under study in Srinagar. The questions which were reported as inappropriate and difficult to understand or which had poor responses were revised and reframed to meet the requirements. Further, during the pre-testing stage, the respondents were found hesitant to respond to open end and direct questions, but highly responsive to indirect structured questionnaire. As such, it was thought expedient to use well structured interview schedule. This helped in keeping the frame of the study intact and achieving qualitativeness in the interpretation of data.

Likert-type technique was used to prepare scales for selection of items to measure attitudes of workers and management personnel towards various aspects of labour-management relations. Items which did not show a substantial correlation with the total scores were eliminated to ensure that the questionnaires are "internally consistent", i.e., every item is related to the same general attitude.

Interview schedule for workers was designed to seek data on the workers' (inclusive of trade union leaders) socio-economic background, their perception/views regarding the nature and extent of industrial conflicts and settlement, their aspirations and job satisfaction, workers' participation in decision-making and trade union activities, etc.

The interview schedule for management personnel was designed to elicit information regarding the perception/views of management personnel towards industrial conflicts, conflict resolution, workers' participation in decision-making, trade unions, etc.

The information obtained from each sampled respondent in every organisation studied was secured directly through personal interviews using the questionnaire schedules. However, some of the management representatives and trade union leaders filled up the questionnaires themselves. Before the interviews, the respondents were explained in detail the different aspects of the interview schedules and their background. Since majority of the respondents were illiterate, the language difficulties were sorted out by explaining the statements in the language of common parlance. Repeated interviews were conducted, wherever necessary. To get true responses of respondents, as far as possible, there were inbuilt checks in the questionnaires, which pointed out the wrong responses. On these items also repeated interviews were held after clarifying the doubts and misgivings.

In order to secure their co-operation, the purpose of the study was explained to them and they were assured that their views and personal information would be kept strictly confidential. They were encouraged to express themselves as honestly and frankly as possible. Every possible effort has been made to supplement quantitative and qualitative data through the information received by informal interviews as well as personal observations. Wherever possible, incidents and verbal statements of respondents have been used to support the emerging conclusions in the analyses of the issues.

Sample Design

As reported earlier, the study has been restricted to five large and medium scale textile units employing 3,893 employees. Since the total number of employees in the units was too large to be covered by an individual researcher, it was decided to employ sample method of study. Keeping in view the characteristics of the population and the variables to be studied, the stratified random sampling procedure was used.

The population was stratified as (1) workers and (2) management personnel. With a view to give sufficient representation to each organisation studied and the two classes of employees and to have a manageable one the size of the sample was restricted to 250 workers and 60 management personnel (for the sample composition see Table 1.1).

Workers for the sample include different categories of operatives and non-operatives and some office-bearers of trade unions and bipartite committees. Similarly, the sample of management personnel includes top management personnel, management personnel of all important functions at different hierarchies, office-bearers of personnel departments, higher level supervisory staff and also a few management nominees representing different joint committees/forums.

After determining the sample size for each organisation, the technique of stratified proportionate representative sampling has been used for drawing the sample of workers from each organisation using job as the criterion for stratification. The universe was stratified according to the job status of its constituents because the respondents displayed basic differences in terms of the degree and the nature of skill possessed, wage rates, task assignment and the managements' perception of their job importance. For operational purpose, the departments performing different jobs, such as, spinning, weaving, printing, bleaching, dyeing and finishing, have been used as different strata. The size of the sample drawn from each stratum has been randomly selected from the list of workers prepared for each department separately. The attendance roll of the concerned departments, in each organisation, has been utilised for selecting the required number of respondents. Similar procedure for selecting the sample of management personnel has adopted.

Data Processing and Statistical Analysis

The data collected, both from the primary and secondary sources have been arranged in logical order and processed both manually and by computer. Minor tables were prepared manually while as cross tables involving large scale calculations were prepared with the help of computer. As a pre-condition of data processing by computer, the verbal responses were translated into numerical symbols and properly coded.

The data collected have been statistically analysed using, besides the absolute numbers, the methods of percentage comparison, index numbers, summary statistics such as, averages, coefficient of variation, ranking based on overall scores and comparison of mean scores based on the scoring scale depending upon the desirability of different dimensions studied. The χ^2 test has been used to study the divergence of actual and expected frequencies to find out the association between the attributes in question. Wherever necessary, *t*-test has been applied to find out the level of significance of difference in mean scores. Apart from organisation-wise analysis, inter-organisational, inter-State, inter-industry and inter-sector comparisons have been made and specific conclusions drawn.

Since the study mainly focuses on the attitude analysis, the need was felt to quantify the data which were otherwise qualitative in nature. In the present study summated Rating Scoring Scale developed by Rensis Likert (1932) popularly known as Likert-type technique was applied for the purpose. In such a scale the subjects were asked to respond to each item on a particular issue under study in terms of several degrees of agreement or disagreement, for example

(1) completely satisfied,
(2) considerable satisfied,
(3) moderately satisfied,
(4) slightly satisfied and
(5) not at all satisfied.

The responses to various items were scored in such a way that a response indicative of the most favourable attitude was given the highest score and *vice versa* (5 = High; 1 = Low). Though, in most of the cases a five-point continuum was used, a three-point or four-point continuum was also applied wherever necessary.

The technique of choice scoring has been used to assess the order of preference, or in other words, the degree of popularity of a particular variable. If the respondents ranked a certain specimen as number one, at the top of five given specimens, he evidently preferred it to other four and so no. In such cases weight of five to the 1st, four to the 2nd, three to the 3rd, two to the 4th and one to the 5th has been given on a five-point continuum. In case of three-point scale, scores of 3, 2 and 1 have been assigned according to the order in which the items in question were ranked. Similarly, the other scoring scales have been applied as per the requirements.

LIMITATIONS OF THE STUDY

Any study analysing human factor in the work setting cannot claim perfection in view of the nature of the subject itself and the present one is no exception to it. During the study a number of limitations and constraints were faced and it is necessary to point them out at the very outset.

It is an industry-cum-region study. Its scope is limited and excludes deeper enquiry into other aspects of industrial relations, such as wage structure, employment, job security and other personnel issues such as, promotion, training, selection, absenteeism, labour turnover, retrenchment, etc.

The main limitation of the study relates to the inadequate and incompleteness of the statistical data. Almost the entire secondary data both published and unpublished, used in the present study have been obtained from the office of the Labour Commissioner, Srinagar/ Jammu, which collects, compiles and publishes labour statistics pertaining to the State of Jammu and Kashmir. The general limitations of the kind of secondary data originating from government offices, particularly their incompleteness and inaccuracy, cannot be ruled out.

The non-availability of adequate and reliable statistical information for some years and for some vital issues has made it difficult to study all the important issues in industrial relations in proper perspective. For example, the detailed statistics relating to real wages, earnings and consumer price index for the State as a whole and its break up sector-wise and industry-wise are not available. The statistics relating to industrial disputes and their settlement are available for the State as a whole and no data regarding the sector-wise and industry-wise disputes, their causative factors, their impact, collective agreements, the implementation of settlements participative forums, etc., are available. The information about the arbitration and adjudication awards was not provided in spite of repeated requests. All this has made the study of various vital issues in labour-management relations very difficult.

In the present study it was envisaged to assess the degree of unionisation and the extent of industrial conflicts, explain their growth factors and find the relationship between the degree of unionisation and incidence of industrial conflicts in the State and in the industry under study. But again the non-availablity of data relating to various variables have stood in the way of such an important analysis. The statistical information regarding the union membership as used in the study is claimed membership which is most likely to be exaggerated, since they are based on voluntary disclosure and the concerned government agency does not have any practice of verifying the union membership.

The working of all the sample units was not found uniform and the records and relevant data on some vital aspects were kept in haphazard manner and differed widely, making any generalisation difficult. Some of the organisations did not provide data regarding the financial and production aspects, in spite of the undertaking given by the investigator that the names of the companies and the identity of the respondents would not be disclosed.

The limitations of the primary data again cannot be ruled out. The general limitations of such data, obtained through attitude survey, relate to partial and non-response of the respondents which owing to the factors, such as, unwillingness to disclose certain information, particularly, pertaining to the personal variables, must have occurred in spite of the best efforts of the investigator. Because human beings are wise enough to manipulate their answers in consonance with the social values. Therefore, some element of bias in the opinion/perception of the respondents cannot be ruled out. However, in spite of the non-co-operative attitude of the management, at times in some organisations and the reluctance on the part of some workers to respond freely, every possible effort was made to find out the attitude/perception of the workers and management regarding various aspects of labour-management relations in an objective manner. The best use of the data available has been made to make the study purposeful. As reported earlier, to supplement the available data, the interview method has been employed to obtain information not available otherwise.

BACKGROUND OF THE STUDY

Before we go into the detailed discussion on labour management relations in textile industry of the State, it may not be considered out of place to give a brief description of the background under which the study is undertaken, i.e., the setting of State economy, the scope and size of industrial sector and labour force employed therein, the environmental background of the sample units, which have a strong bearing upon the nature and extent of labour-management relations.

The Socio-economic Setting

The State of Jammu and Kashmir, consisting of three regions — Kashmir, Jammu and Ladakh — came into being as a single entity towards the middle of the last century followed by the Amritsar Treaty signed by Maharaja Gulab Singh with the British Government on March 16, 1946. The State is strategically located not only for India, but its almost central location in the heart of Asian continent makes it strategically important for the entire continent. It is bounded clockwise by Pakistan in the west, Afghanistan in the north-west, China in the north-east and Punjab and Himachal Pradesh in the south is the 6th largest State in India, covering an area of 2,22,236 sq. km (including 42,735 sq. km occupied by China and 78,114 sq. km by Pakistan). Strategically constituting the northern-most extremity of India, Jammu and Kashmir State is situated between 32.17° and 36.58° north latitude and 73.26° and 80.30° east longitude.

The population of the State, according to 1981 census, is 59.9 lakhs, which is a little under one per cent of the country's total population. The total working population of the State is of the order of 18.19 lakhs which is 30.37 per cent of the total population of the State but just less than one per cent of the working population of the country. The cultivators and agricultural labourers put together and those engaged in manufacturing and construction constitute 60.40 per cent and 11.24 per cent of the total working population of the State, respectively, as per 1981 Census (Government of Jammu and Kashmir, 1985-86: 1).

The frontier State of Jammu and Kashmir, though endowed with rich grandeur, natural beauty and rich natural resources, has been one of the most economically backward States of the country due to various socio-economic, political and geographical factors. Agriculture, which is the main stay of nearly 80 per cent of the population, has remained under-developed due to many inhibitions. The most important natural resources of land, water, forests, minerals, etc., existing in the State have remained unexplored and untapped.

The State is particularly deficient in the field of industrialisation. Though some organised industries, such as, sericulture, woollen, drugs, rosin and turpentine, fur tanning, fruit canning, etc., were established in the State after First World War, these did not bring any effective change in the Industrial scenario because these were established mainly to serve the British interests. The partition of the Indian sub-continent in 1947 and subsequent wars in Kashmir also gave severe blow to the industrial economy of the State.

However, after Independence, particularly since the introduction of economic planning in 1953, the State has been able to register an unprecedented socio-economic development. Looking back at the past three decades of planning, one finds that a transformation has taken place and a firm foundation laid of a developing economy. The net State domestic product valued at current prices has increased from Rs.67.97 crores in 1955-56 to Rs 1,458.76 crores in 1985-86. The per capita income during the same period rose from Rs. 216 to Rs 2,173 (Government of Jammu and Kashmir, 1985-86: 22).

The State Government has made rapid strides in the industrial field. The entire State has been declared industrially backward (category A) and as such it qualifies for the Central and State Governments' special assistance to foster the expansion of industries. All these efforts have paid handsome dividends and there is a humming activity in the industrial front of the State. The number of registered factories has increased from 46 with the employment of 5,809 in 1952 to 720 with the employment of 29,535 in 1985. The number of small-scale units has also gone up from 2,203 in 1973-74 to 18,520 in 1984-85, with the increase in employment from 3,498 to 84,821 during the same period (Government of Jammu and Kashmir, 1985-86: 12). There has also been a considerable headway in the sphere of handicrafts and Khadi and Village Industries.

In the absence of a viable private entrepreneural class and Central Government's lowest participation, the task of industrialisation has largely fallen on the shoulders of State Government. It has stepped in the field in a big way by incepting corporations institutions, industrial boards and estates, of different hues and colours, in all the sectors that go to make a sound industrial base. As against just two public enterprises in the State before Independence, as present there are 19 public sector corporations, with the total employment of about 20,000 persons having a total capital investment of the order of Rs 260.46 crores at the end of 1982-83 (Government of Jammu & Kashmir, 1986: 17). The number of large and medium scale industries in the public sector has gone up from 21 in 1973 to 30 in 1984 with the corresponding increase in employment from 5,515 to 6,468 and value of production from Rs 581.78 to 1,471.85 lakhs during the same period (Govt. of the Jammu & Kashmir, 1983-84: 140-142).

However, in spite of the pragmatic efforts, the level of development in the State is still much below the national average and lags behind many neighbouring States. Manufacturing and mining sectors still contribute only six per cent of the net domestic product against 13 per cent in Punjab, 26 per cent in Maharashtra and 16 per cent at all-India level. Even in this sector, the contribution of organised manufacturing sector is marginal and to the extent of about two per cent (Govt. of Jammu & Kashmir, 1986: 17). Obviously, to take the State economy out of the morass of poverty, a major break-through towards the transformation of the economy would have to come through the establishment of industries in all the prospective and viable sectors, based on a sound and objective industrial policy. But it has to be borne in mind that no policy of industrialisation will work effectively unless it is supported by a sound system of industrial relations. Because research has proved that in ensuring smooth functioning of the economy and sustaining high tempo of industrial growth, very few factors play such a decisive role as harmonious relations between labour and management.

A Profile of the Textile Industry in Jammu & Kashmir

The textile industry in Jammu and Kashmir is the oldest and one of the major manufacturing operations in the State with huge labour force employed in its various sectors. Even in the remote past, the textiles of the State were the living examples of the wonderful skill and dexterity of the artisans. Prof. Barker, in 1933, went to the extent of stating that "the textile industries in Kashmir are so much in advance of those of other parts of India, that Kashmir Textile Industry has more to give than to receive".(1933:6). The industry still occupies a key position in the economy of the State. It consists of three sectors — Silk, Woollen and Cotton. A brief description of the historical development and present position of these sectors is presented below:

The Silk Industry in Jammu and Kashmir is of very ancient origin and occupies a prominent position at the national level. The geographical location, abundance of mulberry trees, socio-economic conditions of the people, the State monopoly, tradition of craftsmanship and congenial climate are favourable factors for the development of silk industry in the State. It came to lime-light during the reign of Zain-ul-Abidin (AD 1420-1470). The industry in its present form was organised in 1897 in Kashmir valley with the cooperation of Sir Thomas Warde, President, Silk Association of Great Britain, who was largely impressed by the immense potential possessed by the State for the silk industry (Kesar, 1980: 14). The efforts were further extended to Jammu province during 1907.

In order to stimulate the inert silk industry of pre-Independence era, it has been re-organised and divided into four units. The working of its three branches (mulberry culture, seed production and silk worm rearing) are being managed by the State Department of Sericulture Development and the fourth one (reeling and manufacture of raw silk and silk weaving) is run by the Jammu and Kashmir Industries Ltd. Silk worm rearing is the biggest Industry of the State as it provides subsidiary occupation to more than 70,000 families in the rural sector and more than 1.25 lakh workers. More than 2,010 villages are engaged in silk worm rearing (Khan, 1981: 15). The reeling, manufacturing and silk weaving provides a whole-time employment to about 5,000 employees and part-time employment to about 30,000 families (Saraf, 1987, II-55).

Jammu and Kashmir has the unique position and distinction among the silk producing areas of the country for producing all the four types of commercially known varieties of natural silk, viz., mulberry, Tasser, eri and muga, which are famous for their softness, tenderness and durability. In India, production of mulberry silk is mainly confined to the State of Jammu and Kashmir which along with Karnataka and West Bengal accounts for about 98 per cent of the country's mulbery silk production (Khullar, 1979: 90). The State has again a special status in view of the fact that 100 per cent of raw silk in the State is filature reeled. For silk reeling, weaving and finishing, various units have been set up in the State sector, as the industry continues to be a State monopoly since 1892.

The woollen textile industry is also one of the ancient and important industries in the State, though its mill sector is comparatively of recent origin. During the Epic Age, the industry is said to have been firmly established in the Kashmir valley and the tradition is: "When Krishna went to the Kurus as a delegate from the Pandavas, the present of Dhritarashtra to him included ten thousand shawls of Kashmir. The fine woollen stuffs given by Janaka in dowry to his daughters are supposed to have been Kashmiri shawls" (Ganju, 1945: 34). From the middle of the 15th century to early 1850s, Kashmir Woollens particularly shawls held almost the same reputation as the muslins of Dacca, brassware and brocade of Banaras and silk of Murshidabad" (Kapoor, 1967: 543).

Being a very cold State, Jammu and Kashmir has always been in need of warm clothing. From the view-point of the geographical environment, the valleys, greenland and fine pastures that it has, the State is bestowed by the nature to be a good wool growing economy. Wool growing and wool manufacturing is the biggest industry of the State which affords subsistence to a large number of people. In the State, the production of wool has increased from 130.89 quintals in 1971-72 to 393.07 quintals in 1983-84 (Government of Jammu and Kashmir, 1983-84: 85).

The woollen industry is spread over both to the organised and unorganised sectors. By turning out a wide variety of products ranging from hand-spun and hand-woven course blankets and *druggs*, carpets, shawls, *pattoos*, tweeds, *namdas*, etc., in the unorganised sector to high quality mill products of woollen and worsted suitings, shirtings and dress materials in the organised sector, the industry earns a lot of foreign exchange, contributes to the State income and provides huge job opportunities.

As compared to either the woollen industry or silk industry, the cotton industry is very small in the State. It is more an industry of the Jammu province than that of Kashmir. It is generally agreed that the climate of the State is unsuitable for cotton cultivation and production of cotton textile goods. But before the cheap mill-made cotton manufacture from other States made inroads in Jammu and Kashmir, the State was almost self-sufficient in this respect. But first quarter of the present century, particularly the post-Independence period, saw the collapse of the cotton industry and since then it has never shown any signs of recovery.

At present very little cotton is grown in the State. A few weavers in different nooks and corners do produce some coarse and middling variety of cloth for local consumption. But, by large, Jammu and Kashmir is not a cotton textile manufacturing State. Some cotton textile factories, mostly in the Jammu province and those too in the private sector, make use of the raw cotton and cotton yarn imported from other States.

On the whole, the textile industry, being the oldest and largest industry in the State, has witnessed a significant growth in the recent past. Not only the number of units has gone up but there has been a diversification of the industrial base. In 1984, 91 registered factories, employing on an average 7,123 workers, were reported working in the State and engaged in the manufacture of cotton textiles, wool, silk and synthetic fabric textiles and other textile products (Govt. of Jammu and Kashmir, 1983-84: 138). The State public sector is playing an increasingly enormous role in the growth and development of the industry. It has established seven large and medium scale industries which produce raw silk, silk fabrics, woollen fabrics, hosiery goods and *raffal* yarn. These factories, in 1984, provided direct employment to 2,183 workers and produced goods valuing at Rs 630.99 lakhs. In the handloom sector of the industry, 16,853 units were reported working in 1978-79 providing employment to 17,569 workers and engaged in the production of *loie, pattoos*, tweeds, blankets, *raffal, pashmina, dusuti*, silk and *khadi* (Govt. of Jammu & Kashmir, 1983-84: 141). Further, taking the figures of 1984, there has been a turnover of carpets, *namdas* and shawls, worth Rs 43.95 crores, which also account for an employment of 1.04 lakh workers (Govt. of Jammu and Kashmir, 1983-84: 121).

In short, the textile industry of Jammu and Kashmir is not only the oldest, but also the largest industry in terms of employment, production investment and its contribution to the State income. Further, the industry has not only been the prime-mover of the labour movement in the State, but also the supreme centre of all labour activities. Much labour trouble has resulted in its silk sector causing the emergence of some of the most effective labour organisations. However, the industry, if manned and managed properly and diligently, can certainly go a long way in arresting the problems of unemployment, under-employment, poverty and poor standard of living of masses of the State.

BRIEF DESCRIPTION OF THE SAMPLE ORGANISATIONS

Organisation I

The Organisation I, situated in Srinagar, is one of the oldest and pioneer silk textile factories in the public sector, established as early as 1939. It is directly under the control of Jammu and Kashmir Industries Ltd. which manages most of the public sector units in the State. The organisation has played a unique role not only in the trade union movement but also in the national movement of the State. The entire machinery of the unit was set on fire during the political upheaval of Quit Kashmir Movement which took the whole valley in its grip in 1945-46. The factory was re-established by installing second had machinery purchased from England and Japan.

The organisation has at present 124 power-looms and is engaged in silk weaving. Its main products include check, crape, champan, *boski*, shefan, chinani, etc. There has been a continuous decreasing trend in the volume of its production overtime. The production which stood at 2,17,000 metres in 1981-82 has gone down to 1,44,612 meters in 1985-86. The main reasons responsible for such a state of affairs have been the obsolete and worn out machinery, labour inefficiency, absence of modern technical know-how, irregular supply of electricity and other inputs, high cost of raw material and poor working conditions.

Besides providing large volume of indirect employment, the organisation directly employes 513 personal out of which 144 belong to management/supervisory cadre. The total work force also includes 41 women employees. The workers are mostly illiterate and unskilled. Majority of them hail from Srinagar and its suburbs. The wage rate of the workers is at par with other public sector employees in the State. About 87 per cent of the workers are unionised. Comparatively there has been no major work stoppage due to industrial disputes during the past 20 years and by and large the industrial relations climate is harmonious. But the organisation has, so far, not taken any worthwhile labour welfare programme and extremely appalling work environment is existing in the organisation.

Organisation II

Raw Silk Manufacture is one of the oldest industries in public sector situated in Jammu. The unit was established by Maharaja Pratap Singh on 6th February, 1907, and is engaged in the manufacture of silk yarn. It started functioning initially with 104 local basins with the employment of 450 workers. In 1937, 48 basins were purchased from Italy and added to the plant, up to 1947, the unit showed improved performance both in quality and quantity of production. During 1939 and 1945, the raw silk produced by the factory was exported in large quantity to Great Britain and for its highest quality of raw silk, the factory was awarded the prestigious gold medal by the British Government. A complete set of 100 basins along with reeling and boiling sets was added to it in 1963.

Up to 1979, the unit continued to employ on an average about 600 employees. But since then, the employment content of the factory has continuously decreased because of its various organisational and financial problems and particularly due to the closing down of one of its filatures. In 1987, it employed 327 workers including 135 women, mostly of post child bearing age. The annual production of the unit during 1986 was of the order of 1800 kg of silk yarn and the wastage of the unit is almost double the production. The organisation is continuously running on loss and showing extremely poor performance on all fronts. The factors which have led to such a state of affairs include among others, the old and worn out machinery, inferior raw material, non-availability of advanced technology of production, political interference, poor conditions of work and psychological work environment which have been responsible for some serious occupational diseases.

The industrial relations climate at the plant is fairly cordial but workers are strongly unionised. Majority of the workers (62%) comes from urban areas, who are adequately skilled but mostly illiterates. However, the working and living conditions of workers are extremely poor and in urgent need of improvement.

Organisation III

As one of the modern public sector enterprises, this organisation has been set up in Srinagar and is spread over 12.25 acres of land. It started in 1970 with the installation and commissioning of a worsted department with 800 spindles and preparatory machines imported from U.K., followed by a woollen department in 1971 with two card lines preparatory machinery and 488 sophisticated woollen spindles imported from Belgium. The finishing plant for the factory was imported from Japan and installed in 1973-74. In 1978-79, 13 looms were imported from U.K. and added to it. Balance preparatory machines for dyeing and finishing departments were purchased from indigenous sources and their installation completed by 1979-80.

The commercial production in the composite mill, utilising capacities of all the departments of worsted, spinning, weaving, dyeing and finishing, commenced from September 1980, and right from that date the factory is engaged in the manufacture of high quality fine worsted suitings, shirtings and dress materials according to the market demands and consumer preferences alongwith the manufacture of woollen and worsted yarns of carpets, crewel, embroidery, tapestry and tweed for meeting the requirements of decentralized sector and the training centres as well as for other sister units.

The machinery installed in the mill, which has been imported from various leading industrial countries of the world, is capable of producing high quality suitings, shirtings and all types of dress materials of various designs and blends which favourably complete with the products of the other modern mills in the country. These, therefore, find consumer accept ability not only in the State but in other parts of the country also. Till date, the mill has produced 50,000 metres of worsted fabrics in all wool blends and other suitable compositions according to the consumer preference suitable for tropical, summer and winter wear.

The organisation in 1987 provided direct employment to 321 employees, including 42 women, and a large number of managerial/supervisory staff. Most of the workers are educated and come from urban areas but fairly is large number is also attracted from outside the States. The unit also generates considerable indirect employment opportunities in various sectors and provided sources for supplementary income of people in urban and rural sectors connected with the consumption, production and sales of the products of the unit.

The organisation provides almost all facilities to its workers, except accommodation and transport. It operates on profit and as such pays annual bonus to its employees. Since 1980, three registered trade unions are functioning in the unit. Comparatively, the industrial relations climate in this organisation has been a bit disturbing as various industrial disputes have taken place on almost every conceivable issue.

Organisation IV

This organisation was established at Srinagar in 1934 as a composite worsted woollen mill on the recommendation of Prof. Barker of United Kingdom. It was initially set up by a private company under the name of Shri Karan Singh Woollen Mills with installed plant capacities of 1,576 worsted spindles, 2,018 woollen spindles, 18 powerlooms, 50 handlooms and full dyeing and finishing departments. The plant and machinery purchased for the mill were almost all second hand and during the Second World War, the whole plant was working to its full capacity. The capacities created were utilized for the production of various types of woollen and worsted yarns to cater to the needs of the cottage industry in the State engaged in the manufacture of carpets, woollen fabrics and blankets.

In view of the obsolete and wornout condition of the machinery and in the absence of any modernisation or replacement worth the name, the production efficiency and viability were adversely effected. As a result, the mill was taken over by the State Government in 1950. In October 1963, the management of the mill was transferred to Jammu and Kashmir Industries Ltd., along with other State public sector units. The corporation undertook indepth studies of the working of the unit particularly with reference to plant and machinery conditions and detailed programme of replacement and modernisation was taken up in 1965-66 in a phased manner.

At present the organisation is engaged in the production of shaddy yarn, blankets, woollen tweeds and worsted carpet yarn, spinning, weaving, dyeing, finishing of woollen fabrics. However over the time, the production capacity of the unit has continuously decreased due to its obstacle machinery, traditional production technology, poor quality of raw material, lack of trained workers and professional management, and the indifferent attitude of the government towards this unit.

At present 245 employees are on the rolls of the unit, including 26 managerial/supervisory personal and 20 women workers. Most of the workers come from urban and suburb areas but are mostly illiterate, untrained and above the age of 45 years. The workers are mostly unionised. The industrial relations situation existing in the organisation is peaceful and no serious labour troubles have taken place. But due to various constraints mentioned above, the production efficiency of its machinery continues to be very low, adversely affecting its financial viability, the employment opportunities and the accumulating loss incurred by the organisation.

Organisation V

This organisation, situated in Kathua district of Jammu Division, is one of the largest textile units of the State engaged in the spinning of cotton and synthetic yarn. It was established in 1963 in the private sector by the Birla Group of Industries and an example of Birlas stead fast devotion and service to the cause of industrial growth of the industrially backward State of the country. It has a Board of Directors with a Chairman. The Chairman and most of the Directors operate from the registered office. The Managing Director head of the factory, is also a member of the Board of Directors.

Since 1964, the company started production with 1,576 cotton and 2,018 worsted spindles. Presently (1988) the factory produces on an average 8,000 kg of cotton and 5,000 kg of synthetic yarn per day, which is supplied to the national market. The employment potential of the unit has continuously increased and it continues to be one of the largest employers of industrial labour in the States. There are 2,487 personal on its rolls including 278 supervisory/managerial cadre employees and 608 women employees. It also employs a large number of contract labour. More than 70 per cent of its workers are the State subjects. They are mostly illiterate, unskilled or semi-skilled.

The organisation has been most conflict-prone in the State. Most of the disputes pertain to bonus, cost of living and retrenchment issues. This is the only sample oraganisation presenting a multiple union structure. There are four unions, one representing the clerical and technical staff and three representing operatives and production workers. Only three unions have been recognised by the management. Majority of the workers are unionised and comparatively their involvement in unions is more active and aggressive. Further, the working and living conditions of workers are comparatively satisfactory and it is the only unit under study which provides conveyance and accommodation facilities to its workers.

2

RESEARCH ON INDUSTRIAL RELATIONS IN INDIA: A Critical Review

INTRODUCTION

THE DISCIPLINE of industrial relations has been a fascinating field of research for scholars, particularly during the past two decades. There have been quite a good number of research studies, invariably dealing with different aspects of industrial relations. The studies have been undertaken to meet the needs of individual researchers and the fund providing agencies. Much of the research of the first category has been of the degree-producing nature. Though the quality and coverage of these researches have a wide range, yet these are not always of problem solving nature because, generally, the individual researchers are attracted towards the problems and topics of their choice, taking into consideration the post-research pay-offs, with an eye on the job market. The research of the second type is a sponsored research to meet the needs of sponsoring agencies, including Government agencies and industrial enterprises — both public and private. Government normally sponsors research in response to the requirements of the priority sectors of the economy and industrial relations research has no special priority in public research support policy. By the industry-sponsored research also only the sectional interests are sought to be promoted.

A worthwhile and comprehensive programme of research on industrial relations needs sufficient funds, imparting development and management of research skills effectively, proper identification of the research problems, attracting competent and adequate number of social scientists to conduct research on the priority aspects of the subject, particularly in the comparatively neglected fields, and remain alive to the new problems and emerging trends in view of the changing socio-economic developments. Unfortunately, none of these facilities have, so far, been provided adequately and, as a result, the volume of research material available on the subject is of an uneven quality. Under these circumstances, it becomes imperative to evaluate critically the existing research on the subject, with a view to place in proper perspective the important contribution in the field, identify the gaps, deficiencies and the comparative neglect of the important research areas and, thus, provide an analytical framework for the future studies in the field of industrial relations.

Against the above backdrop, the present review endeavours to assess the development of research in industrial relations and its major sub-fields in terms of its nature, focus, coverage, method, use of material and conclusions identify the research areas and suggest fruitful and revealing areas and methods of future research in India. However, in view of the subject's diversity, wherein substantial variations in methods and conceptualisation exist, it is very difficult to group all the studies in the field under review. Further, some significant research material is either not easily accessible or still lying unpublished. Nevertheless, a brief summary of the major studies, which are particularly relevant to the present study, together with a critical evaluation is presented here.

The review consists of three sections. In the first section some of the major aspects of the problem have been reviewed followed by a review of the methods employed in such studies. The last section is devoted to the critical evaluation of the present state of research and its future prospects.

REVIEW OF THE MAJOR ASPECTS

Industrial Conflicts

Conflict, in some kind and magnitude, is a part and parcel of nearly all aspects of human life and it is unexpected that industrial relations scene would be without it. The industrial conflict in India is one of the most visible phenomena. The most obvious forms, in which it manifests itself, are strikes and lockouts. Usually, two approaches have been adopted in the study of labour-management conflicts. First, major strikes and lockouts have been studied historically, which clarify the causes and consequences of industrial disputes and, second, an analysis of industrial conflicts has been made analytically, thereby showing the relative importance of various issues in industrial relations.

To review few Indian studies in this context, Joshi (1966), De and Srivastava (1967), Kanappan and Saran (1967), Darshan Kour (1963) and Sivaprasad and Murthy (1977) have identified that the factors contributing to strikes/*gheraos* have been the deep frustration of workers with the pattern of industrial relations, the aggressive employers response, their resistance against the rightful claims of the workers and their practice of taking arbitrary decisions, the failure of the State intervention and government control and the greater social awakening against the unending non-human behaviour of the management. While assessing the relevance of various job factors of workers in a strike context, Tripathi (1976) and Karnik (1967) found that an important cause of strikes is the perception on the part of workers that they are in an unequitable relationship with the organisation.

Analysing 23 case studies, Tripathi (1969) showed that the factors mainly responsible for the unsatisfactory condition of labour management relations in 15 units were multiplicity of unions, union rivalries, lack of mutual adjustment, indiscipline among union members, lack of proper personnel management, strained union-management relationship and the functioning of the unions being conditioned by political factors. Kanappan (1959) also brings to light the similar causes of conflicts in Tata Steels. However, Dayal and Sharma (1970) indicate that organisational variables causing dissatisfaction among the workers led to conflicts. Mukhpadhay (1946) finds that intimidation and discrimination in the presentation of grievances through trade unions lead to labour unrest. On the other hand, in his study on the Central Government employees; strike, Punekar (1960) listed the problems as high aspiration of the people, inefficiency of the officials and their desire to perpetuate nepotism and meagre wages of workers.

In addition to the above causes of conflicts, various other socio-economic factors responsible for worsening industrial turmoil in India have been the theme of various Indian studies. Among all these aspects, the area of wages seem to have induced a relatively larger number of studies because most of the other labour problems centre around wages (Ganguli, 1954). Most of the studies relating to wages focus mainly on the historical examination of wages, wage structure and wage policy in specific industries (Ornate, 1955; Singh, 1955; Verma, 1957; Acharya, 1959; Agarwal, 1960; Nigam, 1960; Bhatacharya, 1965; Datar, 1964; Papola, 1972). Devasarayam (1951),

Rao and Achary (1976) and Monga (1984) found that the inadequate pay, bad working conditions and housing might be regarded as the major causes of tension. Punekar (1952) distinguished between the short-term aspects that led to industrial hostility (e.g., wages, prices, working conditions, hours of work and cost of living) and the long-term aspects (e.g., the speed of industrialisation and the transition of values). The studies of Bali (1967), Verma (1978) and Sharma (1978) have also shown several economic and non-economic factors which cause the emergence of industrial disputes and conflicts and have suggested that unless suitable measures for the eradication of these problems are taken, the cordial climate of industrial relations will only be a myth.

Dispute Settlement Machinery

Along with the study of industrial conflicts, the machinery for the maintenance and promotion of industrial peace has widely been studied. Comparative working of the methods of dispute handling, their limiting factors, suitability and the role of various actors in industrial relations system have been evaluated.

The working of collective bargaining has occupied a greater part of attention of most of the researchers. Mehrotra (1966) and Rao (1961) describe the practices and procedures relating to collective bargaining and derive hope from several agreements reached in various companies. In Karnataka, Patil (1977) finds that more employers (75%) than the trade unions (69.8%) are inclined towards direct negotiations. In his other study, Patil (1976) finds that the Textile Labour Association and the Mill Owners Association of Ahmedabad have been negotiating and entering into collective agreements since 1917-18, always keeping up the spirit of Mahatma Gandhi and other national leaders. The Employers Federation of India (1971) in its monograph stated that 70 per cent of the disputes raised were settled through direct negotiations. Examining the collective bargaining experience in Kerala, Nair (1982) observes that the flexibility and broad-minded realism in management approach, the remarkable degree of trade union unity and the constructive role played by the State in employment relationship are unique features of industrial relations in Kerala that have positively contributed to the growth of a variety of collective bargaining situations in the State at the plant and industry levels.

Contrary to the above, the experiences in most of the other situations have not been encouraging. Guha (1959), Philip (1960), Pilai (1962), Sinha (1964), Bose (1967), Chaturvedi (1976), Tandon (1978) bring to light the constraints in the operation of collective bargaining, the chief among them being multiplicity of trade unions, outside leadership, political intervention, problems of selective and representative unions, apathetic attitude of the parties, and emphasis on adjudication as a part of the Government policy. The official policy of aiming at encouraging collective bargaining, on one hand, and not providing with adequate regulation for choosing sole bargaining agents from among the unions, on the other, has come under severe criticism from Papola (1968), Punekar (1966), Rao (1964) and Singh (1968). However, in spite of all these constraints Mukerjee (1981) and Razdan (1982) are optimistic and they uphold that collective bargaining would continue to be the best method of settling disputes between employers and employees in industry, if the constraints on its operation are removed.

Next to collective bargaining, conciliation has been deemed to be the other legitimate forum of dispute settlement. Numerous area level studies have been undertaken in India to understand the dynamics of conciliation machinery. The Indian Law Institute (1962) reported that the conciliation machinery in central sphere was quite effective and on an average 64 per cent of the cases instituted in conciliation proceedings were settled. The National Commission on Labour (1969) also considered the performance of conciliation machinery as satisfactory. However, Patil (1977) and Yajnik (1977) found the functioning of conciliation machinery in Karnataka and Gujarat, respectively, as most unsatisfactory and largely ineffective. The area level studies of Sharoff (1953), Srivastava (1966), Pradeep Kumar (1966), Singh (1968), Nagaraju (1981) Murthy *et al.*, (1986), and Asdhir (1987) have assessed the functioning of conciliation machinery in Bombay, U.P., Rajasthan, Kanpur, Karnataka Orissa and Punjab, respectively. All of them are critical of the working and effectiveness of conciliation machinery on the ground that the percentage of settlements through conciliation declined and that of withdrawal, failure and pending cases increased and have concluded that the machinery, on the whole, has failed to make any contribution in the sphere of industrial relations by lessening the strikes and by providing an adequate machinery for dispute settlement.

On voluntary arbitration, there have been only a few studies, because of its limited use in India. Chatterjee (1966) and De (1977) identified the skill required by an arbitrator and the part he could play in building healthy industrial relations. Like concilliation, arbitration has also been severely criticised for its poor performance. A study conducted by Ministry of Labour, Government of India (1963) revealed that out of 336 failure cases analysed, arbitration was resorted to only in four cases and only in one case it did actually take place. Srivastava (1966) found that voluntary arbitration as a means of settlement of industrial disputes was not very popular in U.P. The National Commission on Labour (1969) has attributed the failure of voluntary arbitration among other factors to dearth of suitable arbitrators, absence of recognised unions and heavy cost to the parties.

The role of labour courts and tribunals for settling disputes has also received greater attention of various scholars. Banerjee (1963) reports. "Adjudication in India is prevalent not because of its inherent soundness or superiority over other methods, but because in our country workers are poor and uneducated and trade unions are uncoherently organised." Thakur (1962) considered labour courts as expensive and concluded that the majority of the cases ended in settlements or withdrawals and whenever decisions had to be given, these were mostly against the workers. Giri (1972) was also opposite to "any court at all" as they retarded the growth of unions and favoured voluntary negotiations. Aggarwal (1968), Chawda (1971) and Mathur (1962) also reported the delay in settlement of disputes through adjudication. Dass (1974) revealed that the parties in adjudication process found the judicial process extremely difficult to operate and judiciary in industrial disputes itself was finding it difficult to adjudicate in the complexities of problems and played a mediator role more than that of an adjudicator.

Statutory provisions governing labour-management relations have a direct bearing on the landscape of industrial relations of a country. In Indian context considerable amount of research has been carried on for the explanation and discussion of different labour laws, assessment of their implementation and the impact of these laws on industrial relations process. Among the available studies, Dawson (1967), Goyal (1969) and Raho (1966) comment on different aspects of labour legislation, suggest the lacuna in the labour legislation to be remedied. Anand (1967) traces the history of industrial relations leading to the enactment of Industrial Disputes Act and maintains that when strikes and lockouts assume huge proportions causing serious loss to the community, the State cannot be a passive observer of such conflicts. Srivastava (1977) analysed the problems of gratuity in their various aspects in Indian industries and examined how the judiciary had responded to various situations in meeting the emerging situation in labour-management relations. Kennedy (1958), Munson and Nanda (1966), Ornate (1955) and Verma (1957) also bring to light the role of legislation in regulating labour-management relations in India.

It is clear from the above review that in spite of a vast amount of research conducted in India in the field of industrial relations there are no comparative studies on the economic costs and consequences of alternative methods of dispute settlement. It is high time that we make a beginning in this direction. The researchers should discuss and work out alternative methods of dispute settlement with emphasis on preventive measures. The role of the tripartite system in resolving the conflicts in industry needs further exploration not only in terms of a general evaluation of the existing schemes and ways to improve them but detailed case studies on historical basis, on one hand, and analytical cross-section studies, on the other, in order to identify the factors and mechanism making for harmonious industrial relations and their role in the development of industry.

Job Satisfaction and Work Motivation of Workers

The morale of industrial workers, the work climate, the nature of job satisfaction and the factors related to it, influencing the scenario of industrial relations, have been investigated by many behavioural scientists. Two extensive researches carried on by Brayfield and Corckett (1955) and Herzberg *et al.* (1959) have made it possible to see what the Western workers want from their jobs. But no such extensive compilation of Indian studies is available. However, research available on the subject, of whatever nature and magnitude, corroborates the fact that the job satisfaction is very significant for work motivation and performance of employees.

Job satisfaction is influenced by various factors including job situation, personal attributes and demographic characteristics of employees which can never be completely isolated from one another. The recent research findings tend to suggest that there is a "general factor" of job satisfaction, which is correlated to satisfaction with such other factors as compensation, working conditions, job security, group structure, supervision, interest in job, aspirations, personal attributes, etc. This is found to be true in the case of different samples taken from various populations, such as, handicapped and normal, manual and clerical, skilled and unskilled, blue and white collar workers.

Most of the Indian studies indicate that average worker's most persistent desire is for adequate financial return from his job. While summarising various studies, Ganguli (1961) concludes:

> "In India studies in private industries as well as governmental organisations of workers as well as supervisors have brought out the very first place given to remuneration."

The individual studies of Mukerjee (1985), Kathiresan (1987) and Mehta (1978) left no doubt about the fact that poverty-striken workers are more concerned with immediate and personal economic gains and their economic conditions appear to be a central source of life satisfaction. Singh (1971), Tripathi (1974), Narchal *et al.*, (1984), Srivastava and Srivastava (1983) found wage pattern, working conditions and job permanency as the most important factors in workers' job satisfaction. Comparing the important studies, Desai (1968) and Ganguli (1964) also observed some agreement about the importance of security and opportunities for advancement. Sharma *et al.* (1964) and Srivastava (1985) also confirm these findings on the basis of their research. Srivastava (1979) and Dubey *et al.* (1983) reveal that money and status were the most significant determinants of job satisfaction, whereas family life, peace of mind, good environment followed them in that order of importance.

Contrary to these findings, some researchers consider the pay of less significance than security and advancement and that insecurity in job even when accompanied by good objective conditions adversely affects job satisfaction. Workers' consider their jobs as a means through which they can satisfy basic and security needs and that they look favourable to management so long as these needs are to threatened (Dutta, 1959). Further, job satisfaction is related to human needs and their fulfilment through work. In fact, job satisfaction is generated by individual's perception of how-well his job on the whole is satisfying his various needs (Sinha, 1972). Various studies, conducted in Indian context, report that satisfaction and dissatisfaction are not opposite poles of the same continuum. Persons who perceive certain factors of work life as source of job satisfaction may not perceive the absence of the same factors as source of dissatisfaction

(Rao, 1971; 1972; Rao and ganguli 1972; Lahri and Srivastava, 1967).

Job satisfaction is certainly correlated with certain personal attributes and background variables, such as age, educational level, number of dependents, occupational level, marital status (Sinha and Sharma, 1962; Rao and Ganguli 1971; Chattopadhyaya and Venkateshwara, 1972). Sinha and Aggarwal (1970), on the other hand, find job satisfaction inversely related to education level and positively with the income level. Basu and Pestonjee (1974) observed U-shaped relationship between age and job satisfaction. Many researchers find job satisfaction positively associated with organisational climate (Srivastava, 1984), interest in work (Ary, 1982) union involvement and politics (Sharma, 1980), opportunities for promotion (Desai, 1968; Balaji, 1988; Akhter and Pestonjee, 1969). Concluded very beautifully by Sinha and Nair (1965),"a satisfied worker is usually more skilled, is either fresh to the organisation or has put in many years in it and has a few dependents to support. He is very regular in his attendance and is perceived to be more productive and generally adjusted with his supervisor. The impact of the worker's satisfaction on his behaviour is undeniable."

The relationship between supervisory practice and workers' satisfaction shows a definite pattern in many studies (Bose, 1956; Krishan and Hafeez, 1964; Monga, 1978; Desai, 1969 and Zecharia, 1983). De (1975) indicates that job tension correlates negatively with superior-subordinate relations. Chatterjee and James (1965) are confident that an effective supervisor had concern for production as well as the welfare of the workers. Kananidhi (1972) found that women workers were more sensitive to supervision than men. Ganguli (1956) interestingly reported that the members of Communist unions showed greater dissatisfaction in their relation with supervisors than the rank and file of other recognised unions.

An overview of the above review indicates that though job satisfaction and employee motivation to work have attracted considerable attention of scholars, but we are still far from having a valid theory of work motivation. The validity of two popular conceptual frameworks of Maslow and Herzberg is yet to be established insofar as the motivation of Indian workers is concerned. There is, therefore, an urgent need to arrive, through comprehensive research, at some definite conclusion about the employee motivation to work. Unfortunately, in most of the studies on job satisfaction, one often finds generalisation being made about organisations on the basis of a sample of workers from a single firm, instead of organisation as a unit of analysis. Moreover, very few researchers go beyond establishing associations and correlation among variables and it is not possible on the basis of such research to identify intrinsic relationship among variables. Therefore, efforts are over due not only to identify relationships that are genuine but also to determine the relative contribution of each determinant to variation in job satisfaction. Comparative research on job satisfaction is pioneering field and much further research is required before definite conclusion can be drawn.

Workers' Participation in Management

In today's labour relations, workers' participation is one of the most widely and forcefully debated issues. Ever since the findings of Mayo experiments, social scientists have conducted numerous field studies, experiments, case studies and surveys in the organisational setting to understand the dynamics of participative management. Underlying all these studies is the assumption that workers have a desire to participate in management decision-making and by satisfying that desire organisational objectives, such as commitment and productivity, can be achieved to a varying extent (Batnagar, 1977).

Intensive research has been carried out in the past to examine the impact of participation on productivity, performance, job satisfaction, moral of workers, industrial peace and organisational effectiveness. Research conducted in the past few decades has shown that participation of workers in various work and decision-making processes increases their job satisfaction and decreases their work apathy (De, 1984; Saini, 1983), reduces industrial tensions and conflicts (Bhist, 1986; Chaudhuri, 1981; Batnagar, 1977; Ganguly, 1958; Indera and Harigopal, 1985; Narain, 1986; Singh, 1977; Thakur and Sethi, 1972) and works as a positive instrument for the promotion of productivity and creatively (Bhist, 1986; Saini, 1983; Singh, 1977).

Research in workers' desire to participate has pointed out that the majority of the workers favour the idea of giving them a right to influence the process of management, particularly in those areas where their interests are involved (Alexander, 1972; Kane and Singh, 1967; Mannon, 1983, 1984; Monga, 1979; Sahu, 1981, 1983; Saxena, 1955; Tanic, 1969). Some studies have brought to light the relationship between the workers' desire for participation and their background variables, such as education, skill, length of service, interest in job and aspiration, etc. (Arya, 1982; Alexander, 1972; Gupta, 1981; Mehta, 1976; Sinha and Sinha, 1974).

Very few studies have so far focused on the attitude of management personnel towards the workers participation, though some researchers have tried to elicit the thinking and belief of the managers about participation. Mehtras (1966) and Seth (1972) found management hesitant to share with workers their right to manage and that the attitude and outlook of the concerned parties, lack of clear cut distinction from other consultative bodies endangered the effectiveness of Joint Management Councils. But contrrary to these findings, Alexander (1972), Indira and Harigopal (1985) and Mehta (1977) found that the management in general displayed positive attitude towards various dimensions of participative pre-disposition, indicating thereby their strong faith in the scheme. Arya (1980) is confident that "workers" involvement in participation is higher where the workers representatives to participative forums are elected than where they are nominated by unions. Further, higher the acceptance of workers participation in management by management, the higher is the actual participation". Recent studies which have assessed the attitude of managers towards workers participation include those of Arya (1982), Gupta (1981), Gupta (1984), Mannon (1985) and Sahu (1985). But these studies are not sufficient to throw adequate light on the question: What do the managers think about the level of workers participation and how much influence of workers they desire in participation?

Almost all the studies in India have investigated the working of various participative forums. Some empirical findings, in the Indian context, have revealed that the experiences in this direction are to a great extent encouraging as most of the schemes of workers participation have functioned successfully (Lall, 1984; Liberman and Liberman, 1978; Seth, 1972; Warrior, 1978).

Contrary to these views, according to most of the social scientists, workers' participation in management is not functioning effectively in our country in spite of the existence of formal, legal and infrastructural facilities and spoon-feeding. The First (1958) and Second (1960) Commissions on Labour-Management Co-operation agreed that the progress of joint consultation was disappointing because of the unweildy size of the councils, lack of communication, rival unionism and also discouraging response of the management to workers' suggestions. Bhatia (1971), Das (1964), Dayal (1976), De (1984), Gopal and Murthy (1975), Ghosh (1976), Joseph (1987), Kakar (1974),

Sahu (1985), Sinha and Sinha (1974), Tanic (1969), Thakur and Seth (1972) and Warrior (1976) have concluded that participative management has failed to make any significant headway in India and have held the lack of commitment to participation, dependence proneness of Indian personality, lack of participative environment, advisory nature of recommendations of committees, non-implementation of unanimous recommendations, vagueness regarding their extent, scope and functions, inter-union rivalries, union antipathy and the attitude of workers and management, responsible for ineffective working of various schemes of participative management.

However, it is encouraging to observe that various researchers are optimistic about the success of participative management in India in future, provided necessary infrastructure is available. Mehta (1980), Sahu (1983), Sharma (1987), Srivastava (1984) and Warrior (1978) are confident that the future of participative management is not bleak but considerable amount of groundwork is necessary and there is the need for re-thinking about certain structural management practices, if we really want to promote participation. On the other hand, Alexander (1972), Mukerjee (1984), Seth (1972), Sharma (1987), Subramanian (1967), Tanic (1969), Virmani (1978) and various other scholars suggest that participative forums and practices to be effective need favourable attitude among the parties, sincerity of the purpose, seriousness to work with related forums, sound and strong trade unionism and conducive industrial relations climate.

Workers' participation in management, though intensively researched by scholars belonging to wide and varied disciplines, has still many vital aspects which have not been explored completely. In spite of the greater strides, this much-talked of concept has not witnessed any substantial success. Therefore, greater thought and efforts are required to give this movement a definite programme and direction. The issues that need to be studied on priority basis include the attitude and approach of workers and management towards participation, workers' commitment to participate, levels of participation desired and the impact of socio-economic factors on participation. Importance of participative management for increasing organisational effectiveness and providing job satisfaction to employees, on one hand, and the Government's desire for introduction of appropriate participative schemes in Indian industries, in spite of the limited success of the earlier schemes, on the other hand, have created the need for indepth research in this area.

Trade Unionism

Of all the issues discussed in the literature on industrial relations, trade unionism has been a popular field of research, presumably because of the fact that the conflict and co-operation between workers and management are greatly influenced by the nature of workers' organisations and the processes that induce their structures. There have been a good number of research studies on different aspects of trade unions such as their growth and development, organisation and structure, leadership, politics, union involvement and participation in union activities, etc. These include historical studies, area and industry level studies, including the studies on white collar unionism.

To cite, a few historical studies, Karnik (1960), Mathur and Mathur (1962), Padmanabhan (1980) and Singh (1965), traced the history of trade union movement in India, brought out its salient features and made suggestions for its improvement. The other prominent studies of the historical nature include those of Aggarwal (1984), Brown (1949), Dufty (1964), Ghosh (1960), Johri (1967), Nigam (1984), Ornate (1954), Rao (1984), Ratnam (1984) and Sharma (1963), who have raised some issues of considerable importance, such as the process of unionism and its role in the context of economic development, the role and policy of the Government in promoting unionism, labour-management co-operation and conflict and various other issues regarding trade union movement. However, the most distinctive feature of these historical studies is that most of them are macro-studies which have not used behavioural data. These have been of the nature of narration of events and presentation of broad facts rather than an incisive and analytical interpretation of the movement.

A critical gap exists with regard to area, industry and enterprise level studies, for enquiries of this type are very limited in India. Among the available studies in this field, Kulkarni (1946), Kennedy (1954), Singh (1968) and Gaur (1986) have studied the textile trade unionism in Bombay, Ahmedabad, Kanpur and Rajasthan, respectively, mainly relying on historical approach. Mast (1969) and BogrATe (1968) have provided Information about the growth and development of the trade unionism in Indian Railways and Calcutta Docks, respectively, whereas Panday and Vikram (1969) discussed trade unionism in Delhi's Building Industry and studied the influence of technology on unionism.

Various scholars have also studied trade unionism in some selected industries (Akhaure, 1966; Bograte, 1970; Dawson, 1971; Ridgel, 1956; Shukla, 1962; Sinha, 1966) and in some selected areas (Arya, 1980; Monga, 1978; Munson, 1967-68; Panday, 1968; Pande, 1960; Punekar, 1958; Ramaswamy, 1977; Sahoo, 1971; Rao, 1985; Shukla, 1960; Sivayya, 1966; Vaid, 1962). These studies convey useful facts relating to problems of local unionism and the influence of environmental factors and conclude that at the plant level the characteristics of trade unions are not very different from those at the national level.

A significant development in terms of the coverage of studies has recently taken place and some attempts, though very limited, have been made to analyse trade unionism in public services and white collar employment sectors. Goel (1968), James and Rao (1972), Mitra (1968) and Panday (1969) report on the unions of Government employees, whereas Mathur and Papola (1969), Ratnam (1977) and Sinha (1965) explore the growth and practice of the unionism in L.I.C., Indian Ports and Posts and Telegraphs, respectively. Most of these studies aim at studying the organisation and strategies of unions on the basis of some prevalent hypotheses on the white collar unions as distinct from the unions of factory workers. However, this field is rich enough for further research and exploration.

For healthy growth, strength and effectiveness of any organisation, leadership is a vital factor. But there are not many qualitative studies on the character and quality of leadership; though union leadership has been a major area of controversy in India. The studies of Dass (1967), Mathur and Raman (1962), Mathur (1965), Punekar (1958), Punekar and Madhuri (1967), Rao (1984), Seth and Jain (1968), Thakur and Munsons (1969) and Vaid (1967) report on the leadership efficiency, influence of legal aspects on union leaders, background, role, status and styles of local trade union leaders, insider-outsider controversy, their political affiliation and its consequences, historical background of their emergence, etc. The more recent studies conducted by Acharji (1980), Dayal and Sharma (1976), Singh (1980), Ramaswamy (1977), Rao (1986), Reindrop (1971) and Singh (1980) also concentrated on the management of unions by leaders — both insiders and outsiders.

Trade unions provide the grassroot base for the prospective political leaders. In fact, a spell of trade union leadership career tends to have a pay off in the political field. Unions all over the developing world have acquired some political character and India is no exception to it. Halder (1985) feels that the Indian unions are very sensitive politically and multi-unionism has become a fact of life in most of our industries and the intensity, with which we are affected with the byproducts of multi-unionism, has landed us in a peculiar situation. Patil (1976) and Reddy (1972) observed that there is a widespread belief that unions desire association with political parties to secure better leadership and eventually better bargaining power and political parties desire association with trade unions to secure the support of workers. Ashraf (1974), Aziz (1974), Baveskar (1974), Cruch (1966), James (1958), Pattabhi and Ramana (1967), Ramanujum (1967) and Ramaswamy (1973) also noted the relationship between union politics and management politics, relationship between political dependence and union weakness, political manipulations, transfer of union funds for political activities and *vice-versa*, consequences of outside influence, politicalisation of workers and their commitment to unions. There is near unanimity among the scholars that the political parties in union affairs have led to many undesirable consequences. It has had dampening effect on the healthy development of trade unions, has created inter-union as well as intra-union rivalries due to inter-personal and inter-group conflicts among the political leaders and has in particular retarded the development of internal leadership.

The motivation for unionisation and involvement in union activities do not seem to be adequately investigated, though this has been the main field of research in the West. In india, the subject has largely been explored and examined by behavioural scientists. Choudhary (1980), Crouch (1966), Dass (1985), Fonseca (1965), Monga (1979), Seth (1969), Sinha and Sharma (1962) and Vaid (1965) studied the attitude of workers towards unions, their perception of union functions, degree of unionisation and the union participation and its socio-economic variables and concluded that the level of participation was low in Indian situation and reported considerable apathy or hostility among workers towards union work. Sharma (1974) in his study of union involvement found that workers showed a relatively high degree of interest in unions and had a favourable attitude towards them. Dayal and Sharma (1970) observed bank employees not interested in unions. Murthy (1978), Panday and Vikram (1969) and Sinha and Pai (1963) observed that economic and protective functions of the unions seem to appeal to the workers and the union is looked more as the guardian of their interest than as an agency for political power. In the study of Monga and Monga (1981) high level commitment to unionism was found to be associated with the factors, such as job liking, experience and association outside the plant. Sharma (1971) found union participation to be significantly and positively related to four factors: Mental status, occupational status, wages and seniority. The empirical investigations of Ganguli (1954), Mukherjee (1985) and Sinha (1984) assess union membership in relation to job satisfaction.

From the above review it can thus be concluded that though considerable efforts have been made to study some vital aspects of trade unionism, yet some other wider questions have been left out of analysis. Much remains to be done with regard to the organising strategy, initial difficulties, factors promoting trade union growth, etc., through area, industry and enterprise level studies, mainly to make the whole process of the subject more rewarding and less wasteful. There are not many qualitative leadership studies in the country. A closer and systematic analysis of the contribution of outside leaders to the growth of movement and in directing industrial disputes, within the perspective of national concern, still continues to be unexplored. The problem, therefore, needs to be investigated in the light of effectiveness of a category of leaders to fulfil the union objectives keeping in view the wider national objectives.

REVIEW OF THE NATURE OF STUDIES

General/Historical Studies

Many researchers in the country have concentrated on the study of industrial relations at the national level on the basis of aggregate data. The phenomenon of trade unionism, strikes, pattern of industrial relations, genesis of industrial strife in the Indian business environment, historical and institutional framework of labour policy, dispute handling machinery, collective bargaining, participative management and other related aspects have figured in most of the studies having "total industrial relations" as the main theme (Myers and Kanapan, 1970; Subramanian, 1967; Nath, 1970; Dass, 1974; Krishnamurthy, 1970; Rao, 1974; Kennedy, 1966; Reddy, 1979).

Public sector has been the main focus of attention in most of the general and historical studies. Among these, in particular, reference may be made of Dayal (1969), Meher (1969), Gupta and Sexena (1976), Daleda (1976), Kumar (1977), Karim (1972), Mattoo (1976) and Chatterjee (1983) who have given lucid analysis of the issues of industrial relations in public sector and have recommended various direct and indirect measures to bring about harmonious relations between the labour and management.

Comparative analysis of the state of industrial relations in India's private sector *vis-a-vis* public sector industry has both theoretical and practical utilities. But apparently no substantial qualitative studies have been undertaken in this direction. Among the available studies, Pais (1985) has made an attempt to study the comparative position of industrial relations in the private and public sectors Engineering Industry and brought out in detail considerable differences in the working conditions and industrial relations between the two sectors due to the differences in basic management philosophy of public versus private ownership. Khurana (1972), on the other hand, revealed that although industrial relations in both the sectors of Indian industry have progressively deteriorated, the rate of deterioration has been relatively greater in the public sector. Industrial relations in the private sector appear to have reached a level of stability whereas the public sector is still in the process of stabilisation.

Some of the comparative studies on the subject have accounted for the industrial relations situation in India comparing it with what obtains in other countries particularly in Asia and South-East Asia. These studies have discussed at length the pattern of industrial conflict and its determinants, the philosophy of union-management relations, the State intervention, union development and functions and have made possible an appraisal of various types of institutional and organisational structures and their comparative behaviour and performance (Ghosh, 1960; Daya, 1955; Datar, 1968; Verma, 1972).

Area/Regional Studies

In India, fundamental regional variations exist in different parts of the country in terms of the rate of growth, degree of industrialisation, type of technology, socio-economic characteristics of labour and management, organisational problems, leadership pattern, etc. Under these circumstances, one can hardly expect to have a uniform pattern of industrial relations system and structure in all the regions and at all the levels. Recently, need has been felt to understand and interpret the problems of industrial relations in different environments and as a result various regional/area studies have been undertaken. These studies enable to perceive the inter-area and inter-regional differences in terms of the unique features of their environment. Almost all the industrially important regions and areas have so far been brought under such studies.

To review some of these research works, Singh (1983) in his study on Maharashtra concludes:

> "The phenomenon that rich are becoming richer and poor are becoming poorer is at work in the industrial society."

Industrial relations can change for a better only if there is a convincing change in the attitude of employers and employees and if they take responsible and realistic interest in their mutual goals and requirements. Nair (1973) presented a comprehensive picture of all the significant aspects and changing character of industrial relations in Kerala. Deodhar (1978) analysed the field of industrial relations in some selected industrial units in Bombay with an emphasis on the role of management. Batnagar and Sharma (1984) reporting on the industrial relations pattern in Chandigarh found that 40 per cent of the labour welfare officers had, so many times, been victimised for honest performance of their duties in the sense that whenever they mustered the courage to bring to the notice of their employers some of the lapses on their part, they were asked to pack and go.

Some other prominent area level studies include Nagaraju's (1981) analysis of regional level industrial relations system in Karnataka Pilai's (1968) study of industrial relations in West Bengal; Zechariah's (1954) survey of the factors affecting industrial relations in Bombay; Kanwar Lal's (1971) and Agarwal's (1971) separate studies on the deteriorating industrial relations' situation in Madhya Pradesh. The studies of Budani (1971), Kumar (1972), Nair (1973) and Ghoshal (1972) are the other key works conducted in the areas of Rajasthan, Andhra Pradesh, Goa and West Bengal, respectively.

Industry-cum-Region studies

In recent years there has been a tendency to study the problems of industrial relations at the industry-cum-region level. The striking feature of these studies has been the emphasis on empirical methods. Prominent among these are the diagnostic studies of industrial relations and its related aspects in Visakhapatnam Ports Ship-Building Industry (Sivayya, 1967, 1968), Printing Industry in Delhi (Thakur and Munson,

1969), Sugar Industry of Western U.P. (Dass, 1971), Indian Railways (Saran, 1955; Rao, 1970) and the individual studies in Paper Industry (Ganju, 1978), Sugar Industry (Sivyya, 1971) and Engineering Industry (Ayyar, 1967) of Andhra Pradesh.

Textile Industry being one of the oldest industries in India has received part of the attention of researchers particularly in Bombay, Ahmedabad and Kanpur, which are leading centres of textile manufacture and which have witnessed some of the earliest industrial conflicts. The studies in the field include, among others, Majumdar's (1973) systematic study of industrial relations in Ahmedabad Textile Mills; Singh's (1968) and Shrimali's (1970) socio-economic studies of industrial climate in Kanpur Textile Industry; Agarwal's (1971) analytical analysis of industrial disputes in Cotton Textile Industry of Madhya Pradesh and the studies on work regulation, discipline, union involvement and dispute settlement machinery in Cotton Textile Industry of Bombay separately by Morris (1965), Thakur (1962) and Ridgel (1956). Among the recent studies, Mammoria (1978) assessed the problem of industrial relations in selected textile units in Rajasthan against the socio-economic background of workers, the policies of the employers, the management philosophy and the statutory provisions. Laldas (1980), in his study in Textile Industry of Indore, finds that the industrial relations is more a human problem depending for its solution on mutual trust and confidence between the parties. Asdhir (1987) assessed the effectiveness of industrial dispute settlement machinery in Textile Industry of Punjab.

Attempts have also been made to study the industrial relations situation in the areas of public services and white-collar situations. To cite a few important studies in this context, Panday (1967) studied Government-employee relations in U.P., Punekar and Savur (1970) studied the white-collar relations in Bombay; Singh (1977) explained the pattern of staff relations in the Indian Civil Services; Kohli (1983) proved the hypothesis in Indian Airlines that better the labour-management relations, greater will be the productivity and efficiency in the operation of services. On the similar pattern, Malhotra (1980) and Nanda (1980) reviewed critically the leading events and experiences in the field of industrial relations in, 1980s in Banking and Airlines sectors.

Several attempts have been made to study the industrial relations at the unit level where some assessed the nature of industrial relations at the plant level, others had a more specific objective of identifying the factors which contribute to conflicts in industrial relations. Some important studies of this type have been conducted in selected industrial units in Bombay, Calcutta, Meerut and Delhi by Kamath and Associates (1962), Shukla (1968), Sexena (1970) and Dinghra and Chellapa (1971), respectively. Similarly, Mahapatra (1977) and Reeta Mathur (1986) have analysed the worsening situation of industrial relations in Durgapur Steel Plant and Steel Authority of India Ltd., respectively.

Though, case studies may not yield much evidence for generalisation in view of the nature of methodology adopted, yet a large number of case studies, made on a uniform basis, would certainly prove useful once their results are analysed and integrated. It is because, industrial relations present a complex problem and involve an inter-play of various types of factor and as such an intensive study often yields more prominent results and gives a better understanding of the forces acting upon the situation.

THE PRESENT STATE OF RESEARCH AND FUTURE PROSPECTS

The above review highlights some important reports available in literature on industrial relations in India and brings to light the gaps and deficiencies in this popular field of study. It conveys that a good deal of effort has already been made to study a large number of problems in detail, while many other issues have either not been comprehensively studied or not touched at all. Most of the existing studies are, by their nature, general and descriptive and, by and large, impressionistic and devoid of empirical basis. The malady seems to consist in the inability of the subject to attract adequate number of competent researchers, apathy of the employers and Government towards it, inadequate internal and external financial resources to sustain a research programme, some institutional impediments and non-availability of important and standard statistics. With a view to study the industrial relations problems, with an objective and analytical approach, all these problems, inhibiting the growth of research in the field, will have first to be looked into.

Industrial relations is an inter-disciplinary area and as such any study on the subject cannot be considered complete unless due consideration is given to all the socio-economic factors, psychological consideration, emotional reactions, political, legal and administrative aspects which have an important bearing on mutual relationship among the actors in industry. But the focus of research has so far been mainly on the economic and managerial issues whereas the other vital determinants do not appear to have received due recognition. Therefore, the studies on the subject, as rightly suggested by seth (1966), "should be entrusted to the study teams composed not only of economists but also of psychologists and sociologists and that they should combine their findings and try to reach an agreed interpretation of the situation."

The pattern of industrial relations cannot be understood without due reference to the ideology underlying it. Gandhian, Giri's and Marxian philosophies are the three ideological bias underlying Indian studies on industrial relations. The approaches of Gandhi and Giri have attracted greater attention of most of the scholars who have discussed the principles underlying these philosophies and their impact on industrial organisations and industrial relations. Though some mention has also been made of Marx and his influence on industrial relations but so far no detailed study on this leftist ideology has been carried out. There is, therefore, greater need for indepth research in this vital area.

Analysis of the industrial relations in the context of the level and growth of economic activity and the role of industrial relations system in the development of an economy has a vital significance, but, in India, unfortunately, it seems to have been virtually left out of analysis as with the exception of Verma (1979) hardly any scholar appears to have studied this vital issue. Systematic effort to empirically validate and comparatively analyse the performance of public and private sectors of the Indian economy in the field of industrial relations are lacking. These are, therefore, the important tasks awaiting further study and research.

The labour market structure of the country and its impact on the relative bargaining power of the employers and employees' organisations do not seem to have been fully appreciated by researchers. While the nature and development of trade unions have claimed a larger share of attention of most of the scholars, the employers organisation, attitudes and institutional factors having a bearing upon the operations of the labour market have been comparatively neglected and should, therefore, be the leading issues of enquiry in future.

It is disappointing to note that even in such a long time, very little efforts have been made to assess and develop the concepts, research methods and procedures used in the research on industrial relations. The present method of assessing the industrial relations situation, purely by the data of man days lost, is unsatisfactory and calls for a composite type of index to be developed which would be relevant for use at the national, State and industry levels. Further, well-organised research and documentation facilities are indispensable for the growth of industrial relations research because

> "research and documentation services can play an important role not only in strengthening of the labour movement, but also in the acceleration of social and economic development in directions beneficial to workers and their organisations" (I.L.O., 1968).

In conclusion, with a view to strengthen the analytical framework for studies on industrial relations, it is desirable to concentrate the research efforts in the areas put forth in the preceding sections of this chapter. In addition to these significant areas of research, the following form the other fruitful and revealing areas of research and time is overdue to focus attention on them:

1. Modernisation, mechanisation and orderly absorption of technology change without effecting the landscape of employment relationship.
2. Attainment of higher levels of labour efficiency and output.
3. Possible ways of limiting the right to strike or lockout without endangering the democratic values.
4. The social and economic cost of union action to the community, employers and workers.
5. Probing more deeply into the "strategic factors" at the industry level.
6. Relationship between productivity, quality, cost reduction, industrial sickness, overall economic development and industrial relations.
7. Evolving a system of industrial relations based on the trust, openness of communication, authentic relationship and participative involvement of parties.

3

INDUSTRIAL CONFLICT AND CONFLICT RESOLUTION

INTRODUCTION

CONFLICT IS inherent in industrial settings. The industrial relations situation dominated by conflicts, strikes and disharmony has obviously evoked much concern, since conflicts if not resolved in time ultimately lead to work stoppages in the shape of strikes and lockouts resulting in many evil consequences affecting all the sections of the industrial community the workers, the employers and, in general, the public. An understanding of the trends of industrial conflicts over a period of time is imperative for many reasons. As Verma (1979: 129) rightly puts it:

> "First, it clearly indicates the magnitude and direction of conflicts over time. Secondly, it helps to identify certain industries and regions in respect of their high or low propensity towards conflicts. Thirdly, it pinpoints certain issues that need special attention in terms of their effectiveness to generate conflicts. Finally, the trend can be regarded as a point of departure for developing certain feasible measures to attain responsible industrial peace and harmony."

Against this backdrop, the present chapter has been designed to study the nature and extend of conflicts in textile industry of Jammu and Kashmir State, after making a brief sketch of the trend in industrial conflicts in the State as a whole, their break-down rate, measures of intensity of conflicts and workers participation in these conflicts. This is followed by an assessment of the working and effectiveness of various dispute handling measures. With a view to understand the dynamics of labour-management relations in the industry, an attempt has also been made to analyse the attitudes and opinions of workers and management personal towards some vital issues in labour-management relations.

TRENDS IN INDUSTRIAL DISPUTES AND CONFLICTS

Before making an introspection of the intensity of industrial disputes in the State, it will be in the fitness of things to study first the trend in the break-down rate:

The Break-down Rate

Break-down rate, referred to as the percentage of industrial conflicts leading to work stoppages to the total number of cases referred to the State Industrial Relations Machinery for settlements, indicates the working of the State Industrial Relational Machinery. The situation as it existed in the State during the period 1976-86, for which the data are available, has been presented in Table 3.1.

TABLE 3.1: Break-down Rate percentage of Disputes Leading to Work Stoppages) 1976-86

Years	No. of cases referred to industrial relations machinery	Number of disputes	Break-down rate 3/2(in percentage)
1	2	3	4
1976	88	1	1.14
1977	78	2	2.56
1978	66	4	6.06
1979	31	1	3.22
1980	64	8	12.50
1981	42	4	9.52
1982	42	9	21.43
1983	92	4	4.35
1984	49	3	6.12
1985	53	3	5.66
1986	67	3	4.48
Average for 1976-86	61.09	3.82	7.00

Source: Jammu and Kashmir Handbook of Labour Statistics, Department of Labour, Govt of Jammu and Kashmir, Srinagar, 1988, pp. 71-72.

An analysis of the above statistics reveals that on an average about

61 industrial conflicts were reported and referred to Industrial Relations Machinery in the State per year during past 11 years (1976 to 1986), but out of these only a marginal number of about four cases on an average per year have taken the form of strikes, which works out on an average to seven per cent of the total cases. The break-down rate has ranged between one per cent and 21 per cent approximately. The year-wise analysis shows a non-linear trend with respect to both conflicts and number of work stoppages. Whereas, the largest number of 92 cases were referred to industrial relations machinery in 1983, the largest number of nine work stoppages occurred in 1982, which records the highest break-down rate of 21.43 per cent followed by 12.50 per cent in 1980. The lowest figure of break-down rate, i.e.,1.14 per cent was reported in 1976.

Considering the overall magnitude of the industrial conflicts referred to and handled by the State Industrial Relations Machinery, the break-down rate has not been abnormally high, excepting 1980 and 1982. In fact, a declining trend is witnessed since 1984.

The lower and diminishing tendency in the break-down rate should however, not be taken as the operational efficiency of the State Industrial Relations Machinery. But the facts remains that due to weak trade unionism, lack of proper leadership and excessive government interference, the workers are unable to resort to direct actions, such as, strikes. The low-break down rate in the State may also be partly due to the withdrawal of quite a substantial number of cases by the disputants. However, if the break-down rate shows a writing trend, it can involve hardship to both labour and management and would call for an immediate investigation and a possible change in Industrial Relations Policy of the State.The break-down rate figures for 1980 and 1982 are indeed pointers to such a possibility.

MEASURES OF THE INTENSITY OF INDUSTRIAL DISPUTES

The intensity of industrial disputes is generally measured by three variables, such as the number of industrial disputes, the number of workers involved and the number of man-days lost. "Industrial disputes are indicative of the incidence of strikes and lockouts, while as the workers involved are suggestive of the impact they have made on workers. The effect upon the economy can be measured by the figures of man-days lost (Johri, 1967: 140).

The data on industrial disputes and the related matters pertaining to

State after proper analysis are given in Table 3.2, which enables to trace the trends in the intensity of industrial conflicts.

TABLE 3.2: Trends in Intensity of Industrial Disputes, 1970-1986

Years	No. of disputes (D)	No. of workers involved (W)	No. of man-days lost (L)	Index of no. of disputes (Base 1973=100)	Index of workers involved (Base 1973=100)	Index of man-days lost (Base 1973=100)
1970	4	9,112	2,816	100.0	33,74.8	1,324.6
1971	9	260	507	225.0	96.3	23.8
1972	6	140	346	150.0	51.8	16.2
1973	4	270	2,126	100.0	100.0	100.0
1974	7	402	2,988	175.0	148.9	140.5
1975	1	30	570	25.0	11.1	26.8
1976	1	71	320	25.0	26.3	15.1
1977	2	1,282	5,539	50.0	474.9	260.5
1978	4	356	4,768	100.0	131.9	224.3
1979	1	59	946	25.0	21.9	44.5
1980	8	7,289	43,763	200.0	2,699.6	2058.5
1981	4	2,334	5,529	100.0	864.4	260.1
1982	9	7,194	33,786	225.0	2,664.4	1,589.2
1983	4	3,414	16,659	100.0	1,264.4	783..6
1984	3	3,437	10,698	75.0	1,272.9	503.2
1985	3	3,901	13,184	75.0	1,444.8	620.1
1986	3	438	11,011	75.0	162.2	517.9
Period average (1970-86)	4.29	2352.29	10,641.23	107.3	871.2	500.5

Source: Jammu and Kashmir Handbook of Labour Statistics, Department of Labour, Govt of Jammu and Kashmir, Srinagar, 1986, p.71.

Summing-up the above data, it can be stated that during the past 17 years (1970-1986), there have been on an average about four industrial disputes involving around 2,352 workers and resulting in a loss of more than 10,641 man-days. The year-wise study reveals that the year 1980 has the most disturbed year with the large number of eight disputes affecting 7,289 workers and causing a maximum loss of 43,763 man-days, while 1976 appears to have been the least disturbed year with a minimum of one dispute involving 71 workers and registering a lowest loss of 320 man-days.

Table 3.2 makes an interesting and important revelation. Looking at the last three columns of Table 3.2, it is clear that due to the erratic nature of all the indicators of intensity of industrial conflicts, no uniform and regular upward and downward trend is discernible. During the period under study, the index of the number of industrial disputes has varied from 25 to 225 with 1973 as the base year, while that of workers involved from 11 to 3,375. The index of man-days lost also ranged interestingly between 15 and 2,058 approximately. Another important feature of the industrial relation in the State revealed by the data is that no correlation existed between the figures relating to the number of disputes, workers involved and man-days lost due to these disputes.

With a view to study the pattern of industrial disputes in the State, it become imperative to probe into the causative factors of these disputes. But non-availability of the relevant data on the subject is the hurdle in the way of such a vital analysis. However, in the basis of detailed discussions with the trade union leaders, management personnel and the concerned government officials some generalisation can be made regarding the issue. The commonest causes of industrial strife in the State have been the "bread and butter" issues. The question of wages, allowances and bonus which relates to the earnings and levels of living of the workers account on an average for almost one-third of the total number of disputes in the State.[1] The emergence of wages and allowances as the key issues giving rise to the maximum number of conflicts suggests that the economic environment existing in the State adversely affects industrial relations. This is true in a developing economy, such as Jammu and Kashmir, which suffers from low level of economic development and as a result from low wages and low standard of living. The others causes pertaining to personnel and retrenchment, working conditions and welfare measures, leaves and hours of work have been relatively of lesser importance in the State. Thus, the hypothesis that in a developing economy, like, ours, the economic factors tend to dominate the non-economic factors in causing industrial disputes is verified and established as valid in case of Jammu and Kashmir.

CROSS-SECTION ANALYSIS

For the further and proper investigation of the magnitude of the problem, the State-wise, district-wise and industry-wise analyses of industrial conflicts are useful. But, unfortunately, these analyses are not possible in detail because of the non-availablity of such analytical data. However, within the limitation of data, some general idea of the issue is possible.

Compared with all other States and Union Territories of the Indian Union, Jammu and Kashmir takes the 4th lowest rank in terms of conflict proneness. Manipur appears to be the least conflict prone followed by Chandigarh, Andaman and Nicobar, Jammu and Kashmir, Himachal Pradesh and Tripura. However, among the low conflict prone States a trend towards periodic shift from low to high conflict proneness and *vice versa* is noticed. The highest conflict prone States appears to be West Bengal, followed by Maharashtra, Kerala, Tamil Nadu, Bihar and Uttar Pradesh in order of the ranks (Verma, 1979: 145).

The lowest conflict prone situated in Jammu and Kashmir is because of four main factors. First, there is lowest level of industrialisation. It is an admitted fact that the extent of industrialisation has a perfect positive correlation with the extent of industrial unrest. Secondly, the degree of unionisation, which is also directly correlated with the degree of industrial unrest, is very low in the State. Thirdly, with a view to avoid industrial turmoil at the costs, industrial peace has been brought by concession. The Government intervenes in all cases of strikes and lockouts and a large number of cases are disposed of by government intervention. Lastly, there is a very deep rooted feeling in the community of the State that there should be no strike under any circumstances. This "no strike at all costs" attitude, according to Karim (1972: 270) is the basic formula governing the relationship between the labour and management in Jammu and Kashmir. . . ."

Making an inter-district comparison of the magnitude of industrial conflict within the States, Jammu district happens to be more conflict prone among all the districts of the State, accounting for about 32 per cent of the total work stoppages.[2] It is interesting to note that district Srinagar falls next to Jammu district in order of the incidence of work stoppages, in spite of the fact that this (district Srinagar) accounts for a large number of industrial units and employment and has the highest concentration of trade unions, i.e., about 51 per cent of the total unions registered in the State. The other conflict prone districts include Kathua and Baramulla which are also industrial important. In other districts, however, there is almost an absence of any industrial unrest. This leads to the vital conclusion that industrial conflict in the State appears to be very heavily concentrated in a few districts.

Industry-wise, the highest incidence of disputes has been reported in the "Miscellaneous Industry Group" consisting of bricks and tiles, milk, handicrafts, shops and commercial establishments. This is because of the largest coverage of this group. However, in the manufacturing sector, textile industry is identified as most conflict prone industry in the State which accounts on an average for about 15 per cent of the disputes.[3]

WORKERS PARTICIPATION IN CONFLICTS

After studying the trends in the industrial conflicts, it is important to assess the extent of workers' participation and involvement in these conflicts to describe in right perspective the scenario of industrial relations in the State on the criterion of industrial conflicts. For this purpose in view, four criterion measures have been developed, namely:

(a) Dispute Duration Ratio (DDR),
(b) Dispute Coverage Ratio (DCR),
(c) Time Loss Ratio (TLR), and
(d) Membership Involvement Ratio (MIR).

This pattern of analysis has been adopted from Ross and Hartman (1980). Table 3.3 given below summarises the data on these measures.

Dispute Duration Ratio

Dispute Duration Ratio is the ratio of the number of man-days lost to the numbers of workers involved per conflict, which measures the trend in average-duration of conflicts. Table 3.3 shows that an employee involved in industrial dispute, generally speaking, remained off the job for relatively shorter duration, averaging 7.63 days per year, during the period under study. However, the data indicate an unsystematic behaviour. The average duration of the dispute in the State varies from a low 1.9 days to high of 25.14 days. The situation is by and large similar to that of Kerala, where the Dispute Duration Ratio ranges from a low of 1.53 to a high of 20.65 days (Nair, 1973), Karnataka, where the DDR ranges from 2.6 to 18.3 days (Nagaraju, 1981: 170) and Punjab where it varies from 3.9 to 26.9 days (Asdhir, 1987: 118). But the findings are contrary to the ratio of Rajasthan, where it varies from 5.14 to 11.43 days (Gupta, 1987: 20) and the average for India, as a whole, where the ratio has ranged from about four to 13 days during 1962-68 (Khurana, 1972: 428). This main reason for low Dispute Duration Ratio in the State, which is also supported by Ross and Hartman (1960) and Nair (1973), is the low sustaining power of the concerned trade unions to withstand the pangs of strikes and lockouts arising out of the loss of their earnings during the periods of strike activity.

TABLE 3.3: Measures of Worker's Participation in Conflicts,1970-1986

Year	Dispute Duration Ratio (L/W)	Dispute Coverage Ratio (W/D)	Time Loss Ratio (L/D)	Membership Involvement Ratio (in Percentage) (W/M)
1970	3.09	2,278.00	7,040.25	27.78
1971	1.95	28.88	56.33	0.78
1972	2.47	23.33	57.67	0.39
1973	7.87	67.50	531.50	0.71
1974	7.43	57.43	426.86	0.96
1975	19.00	30.00	570.00	0.06
1976	4.51	71.00	320.00	0.15
1977	4.32	641.00	2,769.50	2.74
1978	13.39	89.00	1,192.00	0.74
1979	16.03	59.00	946.00	0.12
1980	6.00	911.12	547.37	13.94
1981	2.37	583.50	1,382.25	4.33
1982	4.70	799.33	3,754.00	13.17
1983	4.88	853.50	4,164.75	6.13
1984	3.11	1,145.67	3,566.00	6.00
1985	3.38	1,300.33	4,394.67	6.62
1986	25.14	146.00	3,670.33	0.73
Period average (1970-1986)	7.63	534.39	2,371.32	5.02

Source: Compiled from Table 3.2 and Table 3.1.

Dispute Coverage Ratio

Dispute Coverage Ratio is the ratio of the number of workers involved in conflicts to total number of conflicts. Table 3.3 depicts that a greater degree of erratic trend is registered in the Dispute Coverage Ratio. Taking the period of 17 years as the whole, about 534 workers have been involved per conflict per year. The year-wise performance shows that the ratio has varied from a low of 23.33 to a high of 2,278 days. The finding is contrary to those of Khurana (1972: 429), Johri (1967: 143), Nagaraju (1981: 170), Nair (1973) and Gupta (1987: 27). The ratio has more or less declined up to 1980 but has since then tended to increase up to 1985. The general upswing in the ratio is the problem result of two causes. First, there has been a rapid growth in the number of relatively large size firms involving large number of workers and the disputes have occured mainly in big firms which are more conflicts prone. Second, there has been considerable increase in the number of trade unions accompanied by a higher union participation of workers.

Time Loss Ratio

The Time Loss Ratio, i.e., the number of man-days lost per industrial dispute, is an important criterion of measuring the extent of industrial unrest in an economy. A reference to column four of Table 3.3, suggests that though on an average about 2,371 man-days have been lost per dispute during 1970-1986, but no regular trend is witnessed. The ratio ranges from as low as 56.33 disputes in 1971 to as high as 7,040.25 disputes reported in 1970. However, on the whole, the Time Loss Ratio in the State has been much less than the all-India average, which varied from 2,210 to 6,390 during 1962-68 (Khurana, 1972: 429) and also that in Rajasthan (Gupta, 1987: 29), indicating thereby a lower degree of industrial unrest in the State.

Membership Involvement Ratio

It is ratio of workers involved in industrial conflicts to total union membership expressed as a percentage. The given data reveal that during 1970-86 around five per cent of the workers involved in industrial conflicts on an average have been union members. Since there have been wide variations in the ratio over the period, no definite conclusions regarding the union members behaviours' towards industrial conflicts is discernible. The Membership Involvement Ratio which stood at the highest of 27.78 per cent in 1970 has been just 0.06 per cent in 1975. However, a comparatively analysis of the ratio during 1970-79 and 1980-86 shows that the ratio on an average has been much more in the latter period than the former one.

INDUSTRIAL CONFLICTS IN THE TEXTILE INDUSTRY

As reported earlier in this chapter, the textile industry has been and continues to be the most conflict prone industry in the State. The high conflict proneness of the industry is attributed to the fact that it has been the oldest and the largest industry in the State in terms of employment and is still developing enormously on large scale. Further, it is the most unionised industry, where the labour movement got birth and has retained its strong-hold in various centres particularly in and around Srinagar, Jammu and Kathua districts.

The first ever labour insurrection in the history of industrial relations of Jammu and Kashmir took place in 1865 in its textile industry. The main cause of the uprising was miserable economic conditions of the weavers of the *shawl* industry of Kashmir, which occurred due to the oppressive an hostile measures adopted by the then head of the Dagshali Pandit Rajkak Dhar – who was supposed to recover and pay to the State Rs. 12,00,000. According to the taxation policy of the State each weaver has to pay five rupees as tax out of his monthly income, which ranged from seven to eight rupees, which in no way was tolerable (Bamzi,1973: 668). However, the uprising was ruthlessly curbed down.

The notable strike by the workers of the government-owned Silk Factory in Kashmir in July 1924, in their struggle against socio-economic grievances and oppressive behaviours of the officials, was another major industrial dispute reported in textile industry (Khan,1980: 37). The strike though failed due to the lack of the proper leadership, organisation structure, cohesion and solidarity among the working class, but it performed a pioneering task in creating the base for the industrial relations system in the State.

After 1937, under the organised strength of Mazdoor Sabha, a number of strikes were witnessed in the textile industry of the State, particularly in its silk sector. One-day strike on 19th August, 1937, in Kashmir Silk Factory and on 13th September, 1937, the industry wide strike were some major disputes which took place in the industry under the leadership of Mazdoor Sabha (Qazi,1986: 46). Due to continues industrial unrest, the government, on 26th January, 1938, had to restore the cuts in wages of textile workers and as a result an amount of Rs. 1,47,371 was paid of the affected textile workers (Khan 1980: 372).

With the creation of Kashmir Mazdoor Union in 1944

re-organisation of the State Central Labour Union in 1953 and introduction of Jammu and Kashmir Trade Unions Act, 2006 (Svt) in 1953, the labour movement entered into a new phase and the workers started expressing their grievances more freely than before. With the result, a number of disputes took place in the State in general and in the textile industry in particular.

In the organisations under study, industrial disputes were reported to have occurred in four out of five units during 1970-1986. Though, on one hand, in organisation IV, industrial relations were cordial as there was no strike during the period under study and in organisation I, organisation II, organisation III, the frequency of strikes and other forms of agitation were comparatively low but, on the other hand, organisation V has proved to be the highest strike prone not only in the textile sector but also in the entire State manufacturing sector. A brief account of the industrial conflicts in sample organisations is presented below.[4]

After 1970, the first strike in organisation I took place in May 1973, when the plant level union urged the workers to launch a one-day token strike in supports of their demands. Though the strike ended harmlessly after one day, but an atmosphere of conflict continued in the factory. The second strike took place in November 1978, and lasted for two days involving all the operative workers of the factory. The third major strike in the organisation occurred in early 1980 which was supported by the workers of almost all the textile units in public sectors and continued for three days. The most important reasons for the strike were wage revision, bonus issues, dearness allowances at Central rates and improvement in service condition of workers. The strike was withdrawn after the appointment of Rajan Wage Review Committee in 1980.

During 1970-86, again three industrial disputes resulted in organisation II. The first strike which lasted for two days took place in 1971, but only about 50 per cent of workers were involved in this strike, which virtually proved a failure. The three-day strike in 1980 was a part of the State-wide public sectors workers' strike. The other major strike in the plant was reported in June 1982, which continued for two days and involved all the workers of the unit accounting for a loss of 652 man-days. The reported causes of these disputes have been the demand for increased cost of living allowances, removal of wages differentials, leave facilities similar to officers and provision of minimum statutory bonus. All these disputes were settled at the conciliation level.

In organisation III, the first strike took place in the year of its inception as a mark of protest by the workers against the hasty decision of the organisation's split from its parent concern (which is organisation IV in our study), undesirable plant location, heavy wage differentials and the lack of residential accommodation. The second strike in the organisation was launched in 1980, in solidarity with the public workers of the State, which involved all the workers of the factory.

As started earlier, in comparison strikes have been the common feature in organisation V which as continued to be most strike ridden industry right from its inception in 1963. The important details of the genesis, nature and settlements of disputes, which occurred in the Organisation up to 1981, are not available. However, an analysis of eight major industrial disputes, which took place in the factory after 1981 for which the details are available is presented below.[5]

During 1981 there were two separate strikes which lasted for six days for the reasons of retrenchment and wages. Both the strikes were called off as a result of the agreements reached between the management and union representatives. In 1982, again two major strikes took place in the plant in June and July for nine and 13 days, respectively, involving in all 2,920 workers and resulting in a loss of 21,360 man-days. The strikes were called off as a result of agreements between the disputant parties. The plant witnessed another strike on the 27th January 1983 which was supported by all the 2,037 workers. In 1984, two disputes took place in the organisation. The first strike occurred on 20th of October and continued for four days, involving all the 2,487 workers employed in it and resulting in a loss of 9,747 man-days. The another short-lived strike took place on 18th of December, 1984. The longest ever strike in the history of the plant was witnessed in 1985, which began on 1st September, 1985, and continued till 19th September, 1985, involving 2,334 workers and resulting in a loss of 11,298 man-days.

From the above analysis, it follows that though the number of disputes is apparently very small, but if we analyse the number of workers involved and man-days lost due to these strikes, given the low level of industrialisation in the State, it becomes crystal clear that these strikes are and would continue to be great impediments in the industrial development of the States, if appropriate steps for their proper handling are not taken in time.

MAIN CAUSES OF DISPUTES AS PERCEIVED BY WORKERS AND MANAGEMENT PERSONNEL

In the scheduled questionnaire, the respondents were required to identified seven main causes of disputes rank-wise, which they feel strain their relationship with each other. Table 3.4 summarises the first seven causes of disputes as perceived by workers and managements personnel.

The analyses of the response reveal that:

1. "Inadequate wages, bonus issues, workers' demand for higher cost of living allowances" and the charges of "Ignorance of seniority, lack of promotion policy", accounting for the highest percentage of maximum possible scores, are the first two main causes of conflicts as expressed both by management and workers of all the organisations.
2. In order of importance poor working conditions, inadequate welfare facilities both voluntary and statutory, large scale suspension, dismissals delay in confirmation, aggressive and irresponsible management/supervisory behaviour, discriminatory policy of management, working hours and shift timings, non-implementation of labour laws, non-redressal of grievances in time and unsatisfactory working of works committees are the causes of disputes enlisted by the workers.
3. Though management also admits that working conditions, welfare facilities, generally account for the industrial discontents, but at the same time argue that the inadequacy is due to a number of limitations on the part of management both financial and otherwise. It is significant to note that management feels that the industrial unrest is also due to the irresponsible and militant approach of the unions, which do not consider the financial constraints of the concern while pressing for their demands. Conflicts also arise due to the strained relationship between management and some union leaders, workers' and union leaders' challenging and reacting to the genuine dismissals, discharges and lay offs.
4. It is interesting to note that, according to management, conflicts have also occurred because of the political considerations, government instability in the State and sympathy calls given by various political and social organisations. But this does not seem

to have an important bearing on industrial unrest so far as workers' perception is concerned.

TABLE 3.4: Main causes of disputes as perceived by workers and management personnel

[Workers (N = 250); Management Personnel (N=60)]

First Seven Ranks	Causes of Disputes	Percentage of max. possible scores obtained	Causes of Disputes	% of max. possible scores obtained
I	Wages not reasonable bonus discriminatory, claim for Central cost of living allowances.	76.23 (1,334)	Wages, bonus, cost of living issues.	69.08 (290)
II	Lack of promotion, seniority ignored, no policy regarding promotion.	61.88 (1,083)	Promotion, seniority claims, promotion policy challenged.	50.00 (210)
III	Poor working conditions and welfare amenities, no uniform medical facilities inadequate.	54.74 (958)	Irresponsible and rude behaviour of unions, financial constraints not considered.	45.00 (189)
IV	Suspension, dismissals, lay off, etc., nonconfirmation.	47.60 (833)	Strained relation between union leaders and management.	42.86 (180)
V	Rude, aggressive and irresponsible management' supervisory behaviour	45.26 (792)	Dismissal retrenchment, bogus sick leaves lay-off and disciplinary action challenged.	37.85 (159)
VI	Discriminatory policies regarding quarter allotment, study tours, working hours, shifts.	38.11 (667)	Working condition, welfare facilities, limitation of management in this regard not realised.	28.57 (120)
VII	Non-implementation of laws grievances not settled, works committees disfunctional.	33.33 (583)	Political consideration, sympathy calls	25.95 (109)

Notes:
1. Results presented here represent all the sample organisations.
2. Overall ranking is done on the basis of the percentage of maximum possible scores.
3. Maximum possible scores = N × 7
4. The following scale of scoring is adopted
   1st rank = 7, 2nd = 6, 3rd = 5, 4th = 4, 5th = 3, 6th = 2, 7th = 1.

The information contained in Table 3.4 on the whole, draws attention to the fact that wage discontent, poor working and living conditions, job insecurity, aggressive response of the parties, working of trade unions, improper functioning of the State Industrial Relations Machinery continue to be major considerations in industrial conflicts and unless these basic causes are removed, no amount of other improvements will help in establishing harmonious labour-management relations. The findings of the study are also supported by Katz (1954: 32), Semelser (1968: 57), Mukherjee (1968: 184), Devasaym (1951: 297), Punekar (1952: 52), Gaur (1986: 124), Singh (1983: 26), Gopalji (1985: 298) and Gupta (1987: 29).

DISPUTE HANDLING

Having analysed the trends in industrial conflicts and the causes underlying them, it would now be worthwhile to cast a glance over the existing mechanism of management of industrial conflicts. In Jammu and Kashmir, Industrial Relations Machinery consisting of both the machinery for direct and third party settlements, is modelled by and large on the prevailing machinery in the country as a whole. The various methods adopted for dealing with industrial conflicts mainly consist of

(1) Grievance procedure,
(2) Works Committee,
(3) Standing Orders,
(4) Direct Bipartite Negotiations through Collective Bargaining,
(5) Conciliation and
(6) Adjudication.

The present section of the chapter deals with the discussion on the working of these methods excepting works committees which will be taken up for study in Chapter vi. However, it appears appropriate to review first, the State policy of Industrial Relations, which guides these methods of dispute handling.

INDUSTRIAL RELATIONS POLICY OF JAMMU AND KASHMIR

The emergence of the Industrial Relations Policy in Jammu and Kashmir States dates back to the era of Independence and before that period it virtually had no set policy on labour. The State had left matters of industrial relations to administrative or voluntary settlement by the parties concerned. However, the evolution of Industrial Relations Policy in the State can be studied under two different periods viz., (a) period, before 1970 and (b) period from 1970 onwards.

Industrial Relations Policy Before 1970

Before Independence, the State of Jammu and Kashmir was ruled by different autocratic rulers, and the industrial relations were conditioned on politico-economic necessities rather than on sound traditions. The only labour laws enacted, as a State policy during the Maharaja's Regime were:

(1) Jammu and Kashmir Factories Act, 1999 (Svt),
(2) Children's Pledging Act, 2002 (Svt.),
(3) Employers Liability Act, 2002 (Svt.),
(4) Shops and Commercial Establishments Act, 2002 (Svt.),
(5) Workman Compensation Act, 2002 and
(6) Trade Employee Act, 2002 (Svt.) (Matto, 1976: 46).

However, despite the passing of these acts these were not implemented in the absence of rules framed under them and there is no evidence on record that could reflect the Government's concern to redress the workers' grievances and built up healthy labour-management relations.

After Independence because of the continued struggle of the Kashmir Mazdoor Union, Jammu and Kashmir Industrial Disputes Act, 2006 (Svt.) and Jammu and Kashmir Trade Union Act, 2006 (Svt.) were passed in 1950-51 on the pattern of Central Acts. But up to 1953, no rules were framed under the laws and no further laws were enacted due to hostile policy of the State Government towards labour, which is clearly reflected by the then Labour Minister's statement.

> "I have no faith in the labour laws and State has no such problem as would warrant implementation".[6]

The first and second labour conventions, held in Kashmir in 1953 and 1955, respectively, criticised the Government's reactionary bureaucratic policy towards the labour. The presentation of their grievances in the form of such submissive and touching titles, such as

'Pukar', 'Lalkar' and 'Mudad', speak of the plight of labour force during this period. As a result of these strides some more enactments, such as Jammu and Kashmir Industrial Employment Standing Order's Act 1960, Jammu and Kashmir Provident Fund Scheme, 1961, and Jammu and Kashmir Payment of Wages Act, 1966, were brought forth.

With the spreading spectrum of industrialisation and growing labour movement in the State, the Government started realising its responsibility in maintaining harmonious industrial relations. As a result, State started intervening in industrial relations by establishing the Labour Department in the State in 1958 and accordingly Labour Welfare Officers and Labour Inspectors were employed for the first time in the history of labour-management relations of the State. Measures, such as works committees, conciliation officers/boards, arbitration and adjudication, became features of the State Industrial Relation Policy.

Industrial Relations Policy After 1970

The period from 1970 onwards witnessed a complete shift in State Industrial Relations Policy. During this period, the pace of industrialisation went up considerably and comparatively an organised labour force emerged. As the matters turned out, the Government took upon itself the key-role of an active third party in industrial relations system and intervened in the interest of industrial peace. With a view to widen the scope of the legal rights provided to the work force under the State laws and make them available, the rights and facilities availed of by their counterparts in other States, a number of Central laws were extended to the State. Viewed in this context, September 1, 1971, is considered to be the "red letter day" in the history of labour relations of Jammu and Kashmir, when by extending the Entry 24 of the Concurrent List of the Constitution to the State, the way was paved for the introduction of as many as 13 Central labour laws.[7] At present about 22 Central and three local labour laws are in force in the State.[8] With the passing of these laws, the Government intervention in the regulation of labour-management relations has assumed much significance.

Making an inter-State comparison of Industrial Relations Policies, an altogether different pattern is witnessed in Jammu and Kashmir. The method of operation of industrial relations in the State is that the unions come up with the demands and send copies of the demands to everybody that counts in the State. This is followed by sending telegrams justifying the demands. Through this method a kind of moral and psychological pressure is built up. Because of the pressure, the Chief Minister or some other authority announces, at a public meeting, the grant of additional dearness allowance or rise in basic pay or grant of the bonus or any other matter that may be the subject of dispute between labour and management (Karim, 1972: 270). If this process is unable to avoid the occurrence of a dispute, then the policy of the government is to intervene and refer it to the State Industrial Relations Machinery with the main purpose to declare the strikes/lockouts concerned as illegal pending the settlement by the concerned bodies. It is for this reason that the industrial disputes in the State have not been more prolonged causing heavier losses.

Thus, from the preceding analysis it clearly follows that due to its defective Industrial Relations Policy, the State, instead of evolving a sound tradition of industrial relations, has bought industrial peace by concessions from time to time to avoid the industrial strife at all costs. Though, it is admitted that the damage done by industrial turmoil would have been far greater than the cost of industrial peace achieved through concessions, but it has hindered the development of a fully matured Industrial Relations System. As such, the System of Industrial Relations is still characterised by excessive but undesirable State intervention and greater dependence on adjudication, which has led to litigation, delay and general feeling of helplessness among both management and workers.

GRIEVANCE PROCEDURE

In any organised industrial unit, howsoever liberal and attractive the terms of service and conditions of work might be, individual employees do have grievances at times. Absence of a machinery for the expeditious handling of individual grievances may give rise to an environment most suitable for breeding tensions, frustration, disloyalty and non-co-operation on the part of workers, which will result in small grievances escalating into collective disputes. However, creation of a formal machinery for the redressal of grievances is not enough if it is devoid of any realisation and commitment by the two parties. "What is important is the procedure — formal or informal — but what is more important is the conscious use of this procedure by the two parties with definite commitment" (Deodhar, 1978: 310).

In Jammu and Kashmir, till the introduction of Industrial

Employment (Standing Orders) Act, 1946, and framing of Industrial Employment (Standing Orders) Jammu and Kashmir Rules, 1972, the redressal of grievances did not receive much attention. But now the procedure for handling grievances has been incorporated in Standing Orders in many enterprises. After the re-organisation of State Labour Department in 1958, various Welfare Officers were posted in big enterprises and were given the task of handling grievances. At present, the Department has 13 labour officers,[9] majority of them in Srinagar and Jammu districts, who are required to maintain liaison between labour and management of the concerned firms to prevent conflicts by timely intervention.

During the course of the survey, it was found that fout our of five Organisations studied had formal grievance procedures, while in Organisation IV an informal grievance procedure existed according to which the workers sought redressal of their grievances through the plant union. Organisation V has evolved a three-tier grievance handling procedure at the levels of immediate supervisor, departmental head and a Bipartite Grievance Committee, with a specific time limit for the resolution process. This procedure is based on an agreement between management and unions of this private sector unit.

In the public sector textile units, almost similar grievance procedure operates. In these units an aggrieved employee can present his grievance to his sectional head who would reply within two days. If the employee is not satisfied, he can approach his departmental head and general manager in that order. If again the grievance remains unsettled, it will be referred to the Managing Director of Jammu and Kashmir Industries Limited, managing these units. If the grievance is not redressed through this process, the worker with the help of his union raises a dispute under Industrial Disputes Act, 1947, and negotiations and conciliation follow to settle the dispute.

In all the cases, most of the grievances related to promotion, allotment of accommodation, house rent, pay fixation, working hours, transfers, work assignments, disciplinary action and production problems, such as inferior quality of yarn and inputs of finishing and dyeing. There were also complaints that a large number of grievances were not pursued by the workers because they feared harassment at the hands of the officials against whom these grievances lay.

With a view to assess what workers felt about the attitude of management towards their grievances, results of the survey are reflected in Table 3.5.

TABLE 3.5: Workers Perception of Management Attitude Towards Grievances

Organisation	Attitude Scale			
	Sympathetic	Unsympathetic	Indifferent	Total
I	31 (55)	9 (16)	16 (29)	56 (100)
II	18 (50)	8 (22)	10 (28)	36 (100)
III	13 (37)	11 (31)	11 (32)	35 (100)
IV	6 (24)	12 (48)	7 (28)	25 (100)
V	52 (53)	34 (35)	12 (12)	98 (100)
Total	120 (48)	74 (30)	56 (22)	250 (100)

Note: Results within parentheses represent percentages to total responses.

An analysis of the data suggests that, on the whole, a majority of 48 per cent respondents feel that the management has a soft and sympathetic attitude towards the grievances of the workers. But in Organisation IV, a similar percentage of respondents is dissatisfied with the informal grievance procedure existing in the unit. The level of workers' satisfaction was highest (55 per cent in Organisation I followed by Organisation V 53 per cent), where the grievance procedures functioned satisfactorily. The χ^2 values

$$\chi^2 = 21.16, df = 8, P < .01.$$

($P < .01$) also reveals that the attitude of management, on the whole, is soft and sympathetic towards workers' grievanes. It is significant to note that most of the respondents did not favour association of the unions with the grievance procedure saying that if the unions participate in the grievance procedure, every genuine grievance would become a dispute and every dispute would automatically turn into confrontation between the management and the unions.

STANDING ORDERS

Prior to 1957, the State of Jammu and Kashmir had no law regarding Standing Orders in the Statute Books. It was only in 1957, that the Government enacted the Jammu and Kashmir Industrial Employment

Standing Orders Act, on the pattern of the Central Act, as amended in 1956. Though the Act came into force in 1960, the rules under the Act were framed and sanctioned only in 1966. In 1971, the Central Act was introduced in the State along with other 12 acts. The rules under the act were framed in 1972 and are completely based on the provisions of the Central Act of 1946. The main provisions of these rules, known as Industrial Employment (Standing Orders) Jammu and Kashmir Rules, 1972, require that the concerns coming under the purview of the rules should draft their standing orders with the knowledge of their workers and the standing orders so drafted should define the rights and obligations of labour and management in respect of terms and conditions of employment.[11] Once the Standing Orders are jointly evolved they have to be certified by the Labour Commissioner who is the Chief Certifying Officer in the State.

The statistics pertaining to the progress of certification of standing orders in the State for the period 1972-85, for which the data are available, are set forth in Table 3.6.

Table 3.6 clearly depicts that though the number of establishments covered under the Act have shown increasing trend over the years, the number of establishments actually having certified the orders has decreased considerably. During 1972-85, on an average, about 44 establishments per year were covered under the Act. But out of these on an average only about 26 had complied with the law, giving an overall response rate of 61.11 per cent. In spite of an increasing trend of workers having benefited by standing orders, a glance over the declining index of response ratio reveals that the progress of standing orders certification in the State has been far from satisfactory. The performance is deplorable particularly in view of the large number of gigantic industrial units coming up on the industrial map of the State.

In the textile industry up to 1985, 12 public and private sector industrial units with the employment of 5,711 workers were covered under the Act, but, of these, only 10 units with the employment of 5,405 had certified the Standing Orders. One of the units not complying with the law was Organisation IV under present study. Though all other organisations under study had certified the standing orders, but none had displayed these on the notice boards of their respective concerns. Further, it has been observed in most of the cases that the standing orders have remained the "letters of law" and have hardly been observed in spirit.

TABLE 3.6: Standing Orders Certification, 1972-85

Years	No. of establishments covered	No. of establishments having certified Standing orders	Response Ratio (%age)	Index of Response Ratio (Base 1972=100)	Workers benefited (Numbers)	Index of workers benefited (Base 1972 = 100)
1972	32	20	62.50	100	5,165	100
1973	30	20	66.67	107	4,695	91
1974	32	21	65.63	105	4,769	92
1975	32	21	65.63	105	5,412	105
1976	34	21	61.76	99	5,741	111
1977	40	22	55.00	88	8,546	165
1978	40	26	65.00	104	10,479	203
1979	40	27	67.50	108	10,631	206
1980	48	28	58.33	93	10,731	206
1981	55	31	56.34	90	11,400	221
1982	51	28	54.90	88	10,666	207
1983	54	33	61.11	98	11,007	213
1984	65	34	62.96	101	11,175	216
1985	67	35	52.24	84	11,290	219
Period average (1972-85)	44.29	26.21	61.11	97.86	8,693.36	168.21

Source: *Jammu and Kashmir Handbook of Labour Statistics, 1986*, Department of Labour, Govt of Jammu and Kashmir, Srinagar, pp. 69-70.

COLLECTIVE BARGAINING

Collective bargaining, with a very long history at its back, has been shaping the labour-management relationship in the textile industry of Jammu and Kashmir. An agreement was reached between the management of Silk Factory in Kashmir and Kashmir Mazdoor Sabha during the Maharaja Regime in 1924 regarding wages and another agreement was executed on October 26, 1938, between them to restore the wage cuts of the workers (Khan, 1980). In January 1957, there was a verbal collective agreement between All-Kashmir Handloom Workers Union, Srinagar, and the Kashmir Silk Industries Association on the subject of ages of weavers. Three years later, in December 1959, there was another agreement between the parties providing for the payment of D.A. to weavers at the rate of 12.5 per cent of basic wages earned (Government of India, 1964: 32). These agreements marked the beginning of a series of collective agreements which took place between the management and workers in a large number of public and private sectors textile industrial concerns in the State.

During the course of survey, it was found that the practice of collective bargaining is very common in textile industry and, in all the organisations studied, the management and unions had signed collective agreements. During the period of 17 years (1970-1986), a huge number of 115 collective agreements were reached. Out of these, as many as 45 agreements (39%) were signed in Organisation V. Of the remaining, 31 agreements took place in Organisation I, 9 in Organisation II, 18 in Organisation III and 12 in Organisation IV.[12] About 55 per cent of these agreements related to wages, cost of living allowance and bonus issues. While others were made with regard to promotion, transfer, shift timings, revision of work load, working conditions, festival advance, uniforms, etc. Institution and implementation of the award of Chatterjee Wage Commission in 1973 and Rajan Wage Review Committee in 1980 are among some major agreements reached between the management and trade unions in the State sector textile industry.

Some of the agreements have been formal, industry-wide agreements reached through centralised collective bargaining between the trade union federations and the management of these industries, pertaining particularly to wages and service conditions. For the public sector textile units such agreements have been reached between the Jammu and Kashmir State Central Labour Union, which is dominant in all these units, and J&K Industries Ltd., which manages all the textile units in the public sector. While in Organisation V, which is in the private sector and owned by Birla Group of Industries, such agreements have been reached between the three recognised unions of the mill collectively and its management. A large number of agreements arrived at by direct negotiations of the parties concerned are signed in the presence of concerned conciliating officer. These agreements get legal validity and bind all the parties to the agreement, including even those workers who are not the members of the signatory union.

From the above analysis, it emerges that collective bargaining is widely prevalent in the State in general and in textile industry in particular. It has the potential of facing the great challenge as a behavioural-oriented process of conflict resolution and various bipartite and tripartite collective agreements concluded have proved very helpful in avoiding many of the major strikes and in maintaining, as far as possible, peaceful labour-management relations in the industry.

CONCILIATION

The conciliation process began in the State of Jammu & Kashmir with the passing of Jammu and Kashmir Industrial Disputes Act, 2006 (Svt.). With a view to bring it at par with the Central Act, it was amended in 1961. The rules framed under the Act, known as Industrial Disputes (Jammu and Kashmir State) Rules, 1972, provide for the same procedure of conciliation in Jammu and Kashmir as the one provided by the Industrial Disputes Act, 1947, and its subsequent amendments.

The present conciliation machinery in the State is headed by the State Labour Commissioner, who is the Chief Conciliating Officer with a State-wide jurisdiction. To assist him, there is a Field Organisation consisting of three Deputy Labour Commissioners – one at the Central level and one each for the divisions of Kashmir and Jammu – and 14 district level Assistant Labour Commissioners, who have the powers to conciliate between the parties to disputes arising in their divisions and districts, respectively. The Deputy Labour Commissioner (Central) has State-wide jurisdiction along with the Commissioner of Labour.

Unfortunately, the relevant statistics needed for the proper evaluation of the working and effectiveness of the conciliation machinery are not available in the State. However, within the limitations of the data available, an effort has been made to probe into the problem in Table 3.7.

From Table 3.7 no definite trend emerges with respect to various variables. However, it is observed that on the whole, during the period of 11 years (1976 to 1986), on an average about 61 cases per year were received for conciliation and a total of 89 cases were actually taken up for conciliation every year. Out of these, the average number of cases settled through conciliation machinery were 42.73 and the machinery failed in more than 17 cases per year leaving on an average around 31 cases pending at the end of the year.

TABLE 3.7: Working of Conciliation Machinery, 1976-86

Years	No. of disputes received for conciliation	Total No. of cases taken up for conciliation	Cases settled during the year	Cases failed at conciliation level	Cases pending at the end of the year	Percentage of cases settled through conciliation (4/3)	Percentage of cases failed at conciliation level (5/3)	Percentage of cases pending at the end of the year (6/3)
1	2	3	4	5	6	7	8	9
1976	88	104	33	27	44	31.73	25.96	42.31
1977	78	122	83	8	51	68.03	6.56	41.80
1978	66	117	76	14	27	64.96	11.96	23.08
1979	31	58	27	11	20	46.55	18.96	34.48
1980	64	84	38	22	24	45.24	26.19	28.57
1981	42	66	13	15	38	19.67	22.73	57.57
1982	42	80	43	14	23	53.75	17.50	28.75
1983	92	115	74	25	16	64.35	21.74	13.91
1984	49	65	23	18	24	35.38	27.69	36.92
1985	53	77	31	24	22	40.26	31.17	28.57
1986	67	89	29	13	47	32.58	14.60	52.81
Period average (1976-86)	61.09	88.82	42.73	17.36	30.55	45.68	20.46	35.34

Source: Compiled from the official records of the office of the Labour Commissioner of Jammu & Kashmir, Srinagar.

Table 3.7 reveals that, during the period under review, on an average about 46 per cent of the total cases taken up for conciliation, have been settled per year. Though the success rate has marginally increased over the years, it must be noted that the number of cases taken up for conciliation during the period has been increasing correspondingly and that the increase in the number of settled cases through conciliation is not proportionate to the increase in the total number of cases taken up for conciliation. Further, the number of conciliation settlement cases include those cases also which are settled by the disputant parties themselves. Such bipartite settlements are signed in the presence of conciliation officer to make the agreement binding on the parties under section 18 of Industrial Disputes Act, 1947 (Patil, 1976: 48).

A look at the column eight of Table 3.7 reveals that the State Conciliation Machinery has failed to make settlement in more than 20 per cent of the cases. Further, during the period, not only more than 35 per cent of the cases have remained pending per year, but this trend of pending cases has also registered an increase over time. The percentage of the cases failed and those pending with conciliation machinery taken together make up a huge figure of about 55 per cent cases in which the conciliation machinery has either failed to make any agreement at all or has delayed the conciliation proceedings. Making an inter-State comparison of the relevant figures, it is revealed that conciliation failures in Jammu and Kashmir State are much more than in many other States (Patil, 1977; Kumar, 1966; Nagaraju, 1981; Murthy, Giri and Rath, 1987; Gupta, 1987).

In Textile Industry, though in the absence of relevant data, no detailed assessment of the working of Conciliation Machinery is possible, but as per the discussions with the workers and management, the procedure does not seem quite prevalent in the sample organisations and only a limited number of conflicts have been referred for conciliation. Nevertheless, majority of respondents, both from workers and management, have shown their strong favour for conciliation as would be clear later in this chapter.

On the whole, the above facts are sufficient to prove that the working of Conciliation Machinery in the State of Jammu and Kashmir has been far from satisfactory and has not been able to pave the way for establishing cordial relationship between the employers and employees.

DESIRED FORMS OF DISPUTE SETTLEMENT

This section seeks to analyse workers' and management personnels' views and attitudes towards various forms of dispute settlement. In total, six different methods were given and the respondents were asked to rank these according to their preference in order of their importance in effective settlement of disputes. Table 3.8 provides data as regards the respondents favour or disfavour towards these methods.

The method-wise analysis of the results reported in the Table 3.8 reveals that:

1. Both workers and management of all the organisations studied are inclined to favour mutual negotiations, through collective bargaining. One trade unionist in support of his point of view said; "Collective Bargaining helps the disputants to come closer and appreciate each other's viewpoint. Why should a third party without any interest in dispute interfere?" However, it was

alleged that the top management competent to take decisions on spot is not involved in negotiations and bargaining is not held in conducive atmosphere. One manager in Organisation V went to the extent of accusing: "Instead of holding negotiations at the bargaining table, these are held in Minister's chamber". The other management respondent commented that if the management were to take a strong step, the Minister or the concerned M.L.A. would say : "Why have you put me into trouble"? However, both management and workers feel that since the process of solving disputes through collective bargaining is a developing one, it should be encouraged and should get precedence over other methods available for the purpose.

TABLE 3.8: Desired Forms of Dispute Settlement as Perceived by Workers and Management Personnel

Alternative methods	Workers (N=250)			Management personnel (N=60)		
	Scores	Percentage of maximum possible scores obtained	Rank	Scores	Percentage of maximum possible scores obtained	Rank
1. Strikes	458	30.53	V	69	19.17	VI
2. Mutual Negotiations	1,083	72.20	I	279	77.50	I
3. Conciliation	875	58.33	II	180	50.00	III
4. Adjudication	333	22.20	VI	90	25.00	V
5. Voluntary arbitration	667	44.47	III	110	30.55	IV
6. Political/Government Interference	583	38.87	IV	220	61.11	II

Notes: 1. Results presented here represent all the sample organisations.
2. Overall ranking is done on the basis of the percentage of maximum possible scores obtained.
3. Scoring is done as per following scale:
1st Rank = 6, 2nd = 5, 3rd = 4, 4th = 3, 5th – 2 and 6th = 1.
4. Maximum possible score = N X 6
5. $\chi^2 = 56.21$ df – 5 P < .01.

2. Next to collective bargaining, conciliation seems to be the most desired method of dispute settlement among the workers.

Favouring the method, one union leader said: "The Conciliation Officers hold negotiations in proper and effective way and are able to find alternative and better solutions to the problems." By comparison, management feels that if mutual negotiations between labour and management fall, government should intervene to settle the dispute before taking it to conciliation.

3. Both management and workers show almost equal inclination against voluntary arbitration, adjudication and strikes. Both the groups have the feeling that strikes and legal remedy should be availed of as a last resort only. Majority of them felt that the legal decisions only compel the parties to accept the verdict of adjudicators and arbitrators, but do not bring them emotionally closer and create a desire among them to work in close co-operation.
4. It is encouraging to note that on the whole, to a greater extent, both the groups seem to agree on the common methods of resolving their conflicts. The χ^2 value which is statistically significant ($P < .01$) lends support to this observation.

The results revealed above are to a greater extent in agreement with some earlier research findings in Indian context [Arya (1985: 193), Verma (1981: 31), Patil (1977: 200), Choudhuri (1974: 139), Chawda (1971: 77), Kohli (1983: 100)].

WORKERS' AND MANAGEMENTS' SUGGESTED MODES OF CONFLICT RESOLUTION

We now propose to put forth the measures which workers and management personnel suggest for the effective resolution of industrial conflicts. The respondents were asked to identify, in order of important, seven main means of conflict resolution and promotion of industrial peace in their organisations. The rank-wise responses reported in all the organisations studied are summarised in Table 3.9.

Since both labour and management have considered inadequate wages, bonus and C.O.L.A. issues as the first fundamental cause of conflict between labour and management (see Table 3.4), it is revealed by the Table 3.9 that both the groups suggest that peace in industry is not possible unless solution to this grave problem is sought.

TABLE 3.9: Suggested Modes of Conflict Resolution as Perceived by Workers and Management Personnel

First seven Ranks	Workers (N = 250)		Management Personnel (N = 60)	
	Modes of conflict Resolution	Percentage of max. possible scores	Modes of conflict Resolution	Percentage of max. possible scores
I	Adequate wages, bonus, profit sharing schemes	73.83 (1,292)	Adequate wages, bonus, profit sharing schemes	67.38 (283)
II	Job security, job satisfaction, promotion prospects	69.03 (1,208)	Congenial work atmosphere, good working conditions, labour welfare programmes.	61.19 (257)
III	Congenial work atmosphere, good working conditions, labour welfare programmes	59.54 (1,042)	Make workers/unions conscious of the financial position and other limitations of the company	50.95 (214)
IV	Genuine awareness of workers' legitimate grievances, their timely settlement, implementation of standing orders.	47.60 (833)	Proper, conscious and responsible union leadership	40.71 (171)
V	Adopting human relations approach, generous attitude towards labour.	40.46 (708)	No Government/Political interference	36.67 (154)
VI	Improvement in Industrial Relations Machinery, enforcement of labour laws	35.71 (625)	Adopting human relations approach, impartial, generous attitude towards labour.	30.71 (129)
VII	Participative management, labour management co-operation, two-way communication.	26.17 (458)	Proper collective bargaining, convincing change in the attitude of labour.	22.38 (94)

Notes: 1.Overall ranking is done on the basis of the percentage of max. possible scores obtained.

2.Maximum possible scores = N × 7.

3.The scale of scoring: 1st rank = 7, 2nd = 6, 3rd = 5, 4th = 4, 5th = 3, 6th = 2 and 7th = 1.

The other suggestions put forth by labour and management, however, vary in order of importance. Whereas workers feel that to maintain cordial labour-management relations, in addition to reasonable wages,

(1) proper job security and promotion avenues should be available,

(2) there should be congenial work atmosphere, proper working conditions and welfare facilities,
(3) management should have genuine awareness of the workers legitimate grievances and take possible steps for their timely settlement and implementation of standing orders,
(4) management should evolve human relations approach and adopt generous and impartial attitude towards labour,
(5) State Industrial Relations Machinery should be improved and labour laws strictly enforced and
(6) workers should be involved in decision-making and two-way communication between labour and management strengthened.

In comparison, the management, though strongly agrees with most of the above suggestions, but, at the same time, feels that to remove industrial discontent, it is indispensable that the workers and unions should be made conscious of the financial position and other limitations of the concerns. Further, unions should have proper conscience and responsible leadership.

To sum-up, both management and labour unanimously agree that to sustain better employer-employee relation what is needed is the eradication of basic problems underlying conflicts. Industrial relations is never a one-sided game. The positive approach of one party towards the whole issue needs to be favourably responded by the other. If only two sides learn to "co-exist" and mutually accommodate each other's attitudes and responses, the drift in industrial relations can be arrested. Both the parties should take genuine interest in each other's problems and join hands in times of crisis and resort to peaceful and constructive means in order to establish long lasting peace in industry, which is in the interests of both the parties and the economy as a whole.

CONCLUSION

From the foregoing discussion four principal conclusions emerge. First and foremost is that, apparently, a marginal number of industrial conflicts has been reported in the State of Jammu and Kashmir. But as is well known that the strike statistics do not necessarily reflect the total picture of the State of industrial relations, the State Government has no doubt made all efforts to intervene and acquire industrial peace by concessions. Though the frequent State intervention in the industrial affairs has brought temporary peace in the industrial sector, yet it has not been able to bring about industrial harmony, which is essential to create sound labour-management relations with lasting industrial peace.

Secondly, the textile industry, being the oldest, largest and most unionised in the State has been claiming a substantial percentage of industrial conflicts right from the beginning and this propensity of conflicts has increased over time with the growth in the industry and expansion of trade unionism in it. Though, there has been a dispute on every conceivable issue that can emerge in the day-to-day operation of an enterprise, yet most important causes of disputes relate to wages, allowances and bonus. These conflicts invite macro-solutions, since these cannot be settled in a large number of cases at the plant level.

Thirdly, it is encouraging to find that barring a bare minority, by and large, both workers and management have consistently shown favourable attitude towards certain decisive issues in industrial relations, such as the causes of conflicts, grievance handling, mutual negotiations and other ways of conflict resolution, which serves as a concrete evidence of their genuine interest in having harmonious labour-management relations.

Fourthly, the direct measures of dispute handling have, by and large, been able to create a conducive environment for peaceful labour relations. But the State Industrial Relations Machinery in the absence of a sound Industrial Relations Policy has not succeeded in fulfilling its stated legal responsibility. As a result the failure ratio has enormously increased and the cumulative lag between the occurrence of disputes and their settlement has shown an upswing.

An overview of the above facts strongly suggests that the absence of strikes and lockouts should not necessarily be taken as the industrial harmony. Different forms of industrial discontent other than strikes and lockouts are as dangerous as the strikes and lockouts. The manifestation of the lurking danger of industrial discontent, in the form of go-slow, absence of commitment to work due to the lack of job satisfaction, etc., is posing a serious challenge to the management of industrial relations. Realising the importance of the issue, these and related matters have been examined at length in the next chapter.

NOTES

1. Based on Annual Administrative Reports (various issues), Department of Labour, Government of Jammu & Kashmir, Srinagar.

2. Annual Returns under Industrial Disputes Act (various issues), Department of Labour, Government of Jammu & Kashmir, Srinagar.
3. *Ibid.*
4. Based on information obtained from the Personnel Departments of the sample organisations and Annual Administrative Reports of the Department of Labour, Government of Jammu & Kashmir, Srinagar
5. Annual Administrative Reports (various issues), Department of Labour, Government of Jammu & Kashmir, Srinagar.
6. The *Daily Mazdoor*, Srinagar, 10, June, 1966, p. 3 (Courtesy S.C.L.U., Srinagar).
7. Government of Jammu & Kashmir, Department of Information, *Labour in J&K – A new Deal* p.6.
8. For the list of labour laws inforce in Jammu & Kashmir, at present please refer to Appendix III.
9. *Annual Administrative Report, 1984-85*, Department of Labour, Govt. of Jammu & Kashmir, Srinagar, p. 12.
10. Based on the discussion with Labour Commissioner of J&K State.
11. Govt. of Jammu & Kashmir, Department of Labour; *Labour laws in J&K*, III pp. 461-64.
12. Personnel Departments of the Sample Organisations.

4

WORKING AND LIVING CONDITIONS AND JOB SATISFACTION OF WORKERS

INTRODUCTION

IT HAS been observed in the preceding chapter that the State of Jammu and Kashmir presents an example where comparatively no major strikes and lockouts have taken place, yet the relationship between management and labour in industries has not been very cordial. The main reason seems to be that proper wages and physical and psychological work environment have not been made available to the workers. In the words of John Marsh, "If you are to achieve industrial peace it follows that your work people must have fair wages, good conditions of work, reasonable holidays, free from fear, security of employment, etc." (Kudchedkar, 1979: 106).

The absence of such things leads to the workers' dissatisfaction from jobs.

The industrial psychologists have established that the dissatisfaction on the part of workers is the greatest cause of industrial turmoil. Job dissatisfaction is one of the most significant areas of industrial psychology and a major perplexing problem that management is generally faced with in industrial organisations. it affects not only the efficiency of the workers but also such behaviours as slow down, absenteeism, accidents, employee turnover and other disciplinary problems. The results of the existing research corroborate that if the need achievement motives of workers are known, the management would be able to make better utilisation of human resources in the organisation, optimise their overall adjustment at work, design programmes stimulating workers, carry them out in an effective manner and as such obtain the desired level of efficiency.

Keeping the above perspective in view, an attempt has been made in the present chapter to:

1. Analyse various conditions of work under which the textile workers of the State work, such as earnings and levels of living, working conditions and welfare amenities, etc.
2. Examine at the empirical level the extent of worker's job satisfaction from various economic, physical, social and psychological factors in work situation; and
3. Determine the relationship of job satisfaction of workers with their various background factors.

WORKING AND LIVING CONDITIONS

Earnings and Levels of Living

The earnings and levels of living of workers have a strong bearing on industrial discipline. It is obvious from the previous chapter that only the earnings aspect alone (Wages, D.A., Bonus, etc.) account for more than 33 per cent of the industrial disputes in the State. It is logical because the majority of the industrial workers are economically poor. Though the wages have registered a continuous rise yet the rate of increase in real wages is not similar to the increase in money wages. Table 4.1 reveals the movement of money wages and consumer price index in the manufacturing sector of the State.

It is obvious from Table 4.1 that in Jammu and Kashmir State wages and consumer price index increased substantially during the period 1970-1983. The worker's per capita annual earning has increased from Rs. 1,630 in 1970 to Rs. 7,146 in 1983, registering an increase by 338.40 per cent during the period of 14 years (at an average annual rate of 24.17 per cent). In comparison, the national average of per capita earnings has increased from Rs. 2,726 to Rs. 9,436, i.e., by 246.15 per cent during the period under study.[1] But an important revelation of Table 4.1 is that as far as the year-wise per capita annual earnings of factory workers are concerned, the State of Jammu and Kashmir has not only always lagged behind the national average but in 12 out of 14 years under study, its rank has ranged from 1st to 3rd lowest compared to all other States of the country.[2]

In past some years the State economy has witnessed an unprecedented inflationary trend. It is obvious from Table 4.1 that the consumer price index for industrial workers in the State has gone up from 171 in 1970 to 560 in 1983 registering an increase of 227.48 per cent (average yearly rate being 16.25 per cent) which has been the highest compared to national growth rate of 189.13 per cent (average yearly rate being 13.15 per cent) during the same period.[3]

TABLE 4.1: Average Per Capita Earnings and Price Index in Manufacturing Industries of Jammu and Kashmir, 1970-83

Years	Per Capita earnings (Rs.)	Comparative rank (Lowest)	Consumer Price Index (Base 1960=100)
1970	1,630	I	171
1971	1,695	I	177
1972	2,081	I	184
1973	2,151	II	202
1974	2,788	VII	238
1975	2,843	VII	270
1976	2,087	I	290
1977	2,672	III	318
1978	3,400	II	330
1979	3,186	I	347
1980	4,069	I	397
1981	5,082	I	460
1982	6,334	II	511
1983	7,146	II	560

Sources: 1. *Statistical Abstract of India* (various issues).
2. *Indian Labour Year Book* (various issues).

No doubt there has been a substantial improvement in the earnings of workers in the State, but owing to the increase in prices the workers have not benefited from the increase in earnings. The inflation of this nature and magnitude has seriously eroded the workers' purchasing power and majority of the workers are leading a miserable life. According to an earlier study about 44 per cent of the workers working in the State public sector industries are in debt. Their consumption pattern is very simple and is confined mainly to the basic necessities. The food stuffs account for a major portion (58.37%) of their total expenditure and the expenditure on other requirements is almost insignificant (Gani, 1984: 76). As per the well known Law of Engel, this high percentage of expenditure on food stuffs is indicative of the very poor level of living of the industrial working class (Saxena, 1974: 670).

In the textile of the State, the problem of wages has remained an unresolved burning issue. An idea of the miserable life and extremely poor standard of living of the textile workers before Independence can be had from the following statement:

> "The standard of living of workers engaged in the textile industry as a whole is very low. Their food is poor, clothing tattered and houses in the most dilapidated conditions. They cannot afford to take milk and eat mutton, say, even once a week. Their staple food in the Kashmir Province is rice, which they eat with an ordinary kind of cooked vegetable leaves, called '*hak*'. Some of them can't even afford that much. The standard of living in the Jammu province is even poorer than that of Kashmiris. *Ghee* or butter is unknown to them, yet they carry on to add to their family earnings which are very poor" (Ganju, 1945: 109).

Even after Independence the economic condition of the textile workers in the State continued to remain poorer as compared to the workers of other textile centres of the country. It is obvious from the first Occupational Survey Report that, in 1958-59, the average daily minimum and maximum rate of wages of workers in the silk textile industry (for which the data are available) stood at Rs. 1.79 and Rs. 3.00, respectively, and were the lowest in the country where the minimum and maximum wage rates are Rs. 3.28 and Rs. 4.48, respectively, as a whole (Govt. of India, 1958: 220). Even in 1975, the average daily minimum and maximum wage rate of Rs. 6.72 and Rs. 9.83 in the textile industry of the State was the second lowest in the country after Bangalore. The national average varied from Rs. 10.87 to Rs. 13.70 (Govt. of India, 1975: 28).

Due to the paucity of relevant data, it is difficult to make a comparative analysis of the present wage rates in the textile industry of the State as a whole. However, on the basis of the statistics available for the silk textile industry, an idea of wage level existing in different major industrial centres of the country can be had. The relevant information in this regard is exhibited in Table 4.2.

An analysis of Table 4.2 reveals that taking the silk textile industry of the country as a whole, the index of wages has increased from Rs. 268 in 1976 to Rs. 526.2 in 1983, which indicates 196.34 per cent rise in wage rates. Though comparatively Jammu & Kashmir State has registered a higher percentage of increase in the index of wages during the period of eight years — from Rs. 184.2 in 1976 to Rs. 572.2 in 1983 — yet a further probe in the data would make it clear that excepting a sudden increase in wage rates in past two years (the information for which is provisional), in most of the other years the State has not only been amongst the lowest three ranks but also never near the national average. The other centres registering the highest increase in wage index include Bengal (250.37%), Residual Group (228.44%) and Bombay (214.43%), whereas the lowest rise in wage rates was witnessed in Amritsar, Surat and Bhiwandi.

TABLE 4.2: Comparative Index of Wage Rates in Silk Textile Industry, 1976-83

Centres	Years							
	1976	1977	1978	1979	1980	1981	1982	1983
Surat	292.7	309.4	332.0	295.4	415.0	459.6	497.9	564.6
J & K	184.2	203.8	317.4	344.8	351.3	35.3	495.5	572.2
Bhiwandi	272.2	268.1	303.7	294.1	325.7	368.9	490.0	543.7
Amritsar	255.8	300.1	283.8	321.8	330.8	337.5	372.6	435.2
Bangalore	226.3	256.2	275.3	313.8	392.8	441.9	514.8	566.6
Bombay and suburbs	259.9	306.0	315.3	346.2	414.8	456.1	515.0	557.3
Residual	233.1	241.1	301.4	327.5	362.4	425.2	479.5	532.5
All India	268.0	270.5	307.5	331.5	374.5	416.9	480.0	526.2

Source: Indian Labour Year Book, Labour Bureau, Simla (various issues).

During the study, it was found that some of the textile workers had undertaken independent work, such as the sale of vegetables, pulling hand-carts, running evening shops, working as commission agents, etc., to supplement their income for better living. However, such cases were few and the additional income generated was irregular.

An introspection of the trends of the economy and present wage structure, reveals that after every two or three years, there is a need to review and revise the wage structure. In the private sector of the textile industry, the first major agreement regarding wage fixation took place in January 1957, between All-Kashmir Handloom Workers Association and Kashmir Silk Industries Association (Govt. of India, 1964: 31). Then a series of agreements on the subject of wages followed. But, on the whole, the wage fixation has so far remained a rule of thumb in this sector. Presently, as per the agreement between the private textile industries and their respective unions, the workers in these industries are paid wages similar to those of the textile workers of Punjab. With a view to reconstruct the wage structure of the workers in the State Public Sector, the State Government set up two comprehensive wage committees, viz., Chatterji Wage Commission in 1973 and Rajan Wage Review Committee in 1980. In 1983, Government appointed an informal committee of the secretaries of the public sector corporations of the State. The Committee periodically reviews and considers the problems of revision of pay-scales. As per the recommendations of the committee, in all the public sector industries (including the textile ones), the minimum wages have been fixed (with effect from 1-9-1987) at Rs. 18 per day as basic wages plus Rs. 1.75 per day as cost of living allowance. Medical allowance of Rs. 50 per month has been provided. In respect of consolidated and casual employees the basic pay has been increased by 10 per cent.[4]

However, in spite of all these commissions and other measures the economic condition of workers has not improved. Whatever little improvements have taken place in the earnings of workers have been off set by the sharp increase in the prices of goods and services. As such, the workers are highly discontented on account of their inadequate earnings and low levels of living.

WORKING CONDITIONS AND WELFARE FACILITIES

Dust and Fumes

The manufacturing processes such as carding and finishing in woollen and mixing, blowing and carding in cotton textile factories create considerable dust hazards and the processes, such as dyeing and bleaching in the woollen and cotton and reeling and cocoon boiling in silk textiles produce fumes and gases. There is a legal binding on the part of an industry to provide appropriate facilities with a view to protect the workers against the ill-effects of such processes. Almost all the cotton, silk and woollen factories under study were to a great extent defaulters in this respect. In silk textiles, during summer, it is practically difficult to work on boilers, particularly in Jammu region. The juice heating tanks were found uncovered and efflusive steam made the temperature of the surroundings unbearable. The atmosphere kept moist by steam and spray badly affects the worker's efficiency. As reported, this has resulted in occupational diseases (such as *Asthama*) of 20 workers in Organisation II.[5] The storage of cocoon wastes in *Kachha* tanks leads to an unbearable stinking smell.

Nearly 60 per cent of the units studied reported the use of exhaust ventilation and water sprinkling to avoid physical hazards created by dusty processes. But during the survey, the steps taken in this connection were observed to be inadequate and most of the workers were found covering their mouths and noses with pieces of cloth and were unable to even breathe properly.

Lighting and Ventilation

As regards lighting and ventilation, conditions were found to be more or less satisfactory in the newer textile units, such as Bemina Woollen Mills in Kashmir, where factory buildings are to some extent ventilated and lighted and where sanitation and factory layout is comparatively satisfactory. But in older silk and woollen factories, both in Srinagar and Jammu, the provision of these facilities is highly inadequate and intolerable. Old unsuitable structures, proximity to other buildings, dirty window panes, walls and ceilings are the common drawbacks responsible for unsatisfactory natural lighting and ventilation. Some processes are carried on in premises, like, stables and low roofed, dark, ill-ventilated rooms, with uneven floors unsuited for any type of work. Thus, the ventilation and lighting arrangements in these factories are extremely poor and in urgent need of improvement.

Cleanliness and Conservancy

All the factories under study are required by law to be cleaned once in every 14 months and repainted or revarnished at least once in every five years. But the standard in this regard varied considerably. All the factories though cleaned occasionally have rarely been repainted or revarnished, most of them never since their inception in early '40s or '60s. Corroborating this viewpoint, an all-India survey found that the highest percentage of silk textile factories (81%) with unsatisfactory cleanliness, conservancy and sanitary conditions were in Kashmir (Govt. of India, 1964: 56). As per the present study, in 80 per cent of the units studied, there is no proper arrangement for the disposal of trade wastes and effluents and as a result there is large accumulation of dirt on work places. In just 40 per cent of the units, there were water-borne sewers or septic tanks and the rest had only dry type of lavatories with or without panes. Same was the case with urinals. The absence of adequate urinals in many factories compel the workers urinate at the corners and sides of factory buildings which results in very dangerous physical and psychological work environment. Added to this problem is the extreme cold in winter and leaky roofs in the rainy seasons.

Washing and Bathing Facilities

As mentioned earlier, the production process in almost all the units of the textile industry create dust, fume, gas and dirty working environment, which necessitates washing and bathing facilities at work place. Nearly 60 per cent of the woollen and cotton factories studied had made arrangements for washing and bathing purpose. In majority of the cases, taps on stand pipes in the lawns were provided for the purpose. However, in silk factories, much importance is not attached to washing facilities, where the manufacturing process is clean and comparatively no dirty material is involved. In two of the units which employed excessive women labour, there were exclusive washing and bathing facilities for women.

Under law 80 per cent of the textile units under study are required to provide not only drinking water but drinking refrigerated water etc., during the summer months. The majority of the units reported to have provided the facility of drinking water but only 50 per cent of these provided cold water. In this respect the woollen industry has particularly lagged behind.

Working Posture and Seating Arrangement

Despite a clear law in this respect only 20 per cent of the textile units had actually implemented the provisions and provided seats for the workers while on work. Most of the factories were overcrowded. Weaving, spinning, dyeing, finishing and other processing machinery were found installed in the sheds beyond optimum capacity. After that if some space was left, some twisting, dubbing and folding work was carried on, with the result hardly any room was left for free movement of workers.

The main argument, frequently put forward by the management for not providing seats, was that the nature of production processes needed constant movement, provision of the seats would make the workers lazy and slack. In some cases management argued that no body even asked for seats. As a result an overwhelming majority of the textile workers in the State are forced to work in arduous standing posture, most of the time, without adequate facilities for rest in between working periods.

Canteens, Rest Pauses and Recreational Facilities

An assessment of welfare facilities, like, canteens, rest pauses, creches and other recreational facilities, presents an unsatisfactory state of affairs. Under the J & K Factories Rules, 1972, it is obligatory for 80 per cent of the sample textile units to provide canteens. Though 100 per cent reported compliance with the law, but the canteens in general seemed to be in poor condition. Only in Organisations III and V there are Canteen Management Committees while in rest of the Organisations, the canteens are either run by the private contractors or by the employees of the factories concerned. Almost all the canteens provided nothing except tea and snacks and the facility of cold drinks, milk and meals was conspicuous by its absence. The quality of the items supplied was found to be very poor and rates unreasonable, in view of the poverty of workers and quality of goods supplied, a large percentage of workers did not avail the services of canteens. The space, sitting arrangements, lighting, etc., were unsatisfactory. In the absence of rest rooms, the workers used these canteens as rest shelters also.

Some of the manufacturing processes in textile industry seem to attract large number of women labour. Though 60 per cent of the sample units employed women in large numbers and were under legal obligation to provide creches, but none complied with the law.

No facilities or plans existed in any of the units for the education of workers or their wards. In Organisation II, some worker-teachers were found holding the classes under the "Worker-Education Programme" but there were complaints that the management did not encourage such practice. Little attention has been given to the means of recreation in all the industries and the facilities available in this regard are very inadequate, almost insignificant. Visits to the recreational centres revealed that some novels, magazines and newspapers mostly in local languages, radios and some indoor games were available. The workers were seen utilising the facilities during their off-hours, but the participation of workers was limited due to their old age, illiteracy and rural taste and outlook.

Medical Facilities

In the course of the survey it was found that 80 per cent of the textile factories maintained dispensaries, where the ordinary ailments of the workers were being treated. Minor equipments, such as stretchers, blankets and first-aid boxes containing iodine, gauze and dressing, splints, bandages, etc., were available though inadequate in quantity. But in the provision of ambulances and of prompt surgical and medical attention to the workers, the factories are doing really no service to the workers. There are no qualified doctors and nurses and the dispensaries are run under the charge of compounders. This is also stated in the report of the Survey of Labour Conditions in Textile Industry in India (Govt. of India, 1964: 71). In the absence of proper safety measures, numerous accidents have been reported, particularly in Organisation V. Rajan Committee (1980: 36) also observed that adequate safety precautions have not been taken and the standards for hygienic precautions appear to be deficient. When enquired about these appalling conditions, the management in almost all the units expressed their inability to comply with all legal requirements such as medical staff, beds, equipments, ambulances, etc. prescribed under rules, due to their meagre financial resources. The E.S.I. Scheme which came into force in April 1948 in the rest of the country has still to make its beginning in the State. The Chatterji Committee (1973) had recommended that "pending the introduction of E.S.I. Scheme, each worker should be paid the contribution, which the companies would have paid on his behalf to the E.S.I., if the scheme had been in operation." On the basis of this recommendation all the public sector workers, including the textile workers, are paid a monthly medical allowance of Rs. 50. However, majority of the workers, wished the E.S.I. Scheme to be enforced in their units immediately.

Housing

For the improvement of the general living conditions of workers, the provision of adequate housing facilities is indispensable, particularly where the workers have to work during night shifts. Generally, the existing conditions of housing of textile workers are extremely unsatisfactory. Excepting Organisation V, no other factory under study provides any type of accommodation facility to workers. In Organisation V, 644 one-room and two-room tenements with kitchen and bath-room facility were provided to the general production workers and 150 sets consisting of two or more rooms with comparatively better facilities were allotted to managerial, technical and supervisory staff. The conditions in these tenements were on the whole satisfactory. The rent was reasonable and accommodation adequate. The factory maintains a large staff consisting of sanitary inspectors, overseers, conservancy cart drivers, sweepers, etc. An overwhelming majority of workers of the sample units were found living either in their own houses or in rented houses. The conditions in these houses, as perceived by the workers, were very poor. The rent paid was beyond the means of workers. The housing conditions of industrial workers in the State on the whole are deplorable. "The Subsidised Housing Scheme", which came into operation in rest of the country in early '50s, has not been introduced in the State yet.

Shift Work, Working Hours, Leaves and Holidays with Pay

The statutory provisions with regard to these conditions are being observed in the textile industry of the State. Out of the units under study, Organisation V works for three shifts besides a general shift. Organisations I and III run two shifts and the rest two have only one shift. No women was reported to be working in the night shift. There is a system of rotational shift and no special compensation exists for night shift work.

Almost everywhere in the textile industry, the workers work for eight hours a day and 48 hours a week. The hours of work in establishments running three shifts daily in practice amount to 45 per week and on Fridays, in Kashmir, the working hours do not exceed six hours a day. The workers get a rest interval of half an hour during the shift of eight hours and one hour in the general shift. The working hours for women are the same as those for men. But in almost all the factories the timings are not strictly observed.

There is almost a uniform system of leaves and holidays with pay. These include besides, weekly offs, paid eight day national and festival holidays, 15 days sick leave and one day earned leave for every 20 days worked. However, it is alleged that these facilities are selective and given to and enjoyed by largely the white collar employees. Most of the production workers complained that leave and holiday benefits are granted to them not as a matter of right but as one of favour and there are complaints of much discrimination and partial treatment.

In short, the above discussion unfolds a very grim story of the economic, working and living conditions of the textile workers of J&K, which have had a marked influence on their health, efficiency and quality of life. The presence of poor physical and psychological work environment has made a significant difference in the attitudes and the morale of the employees and has consequently led to the greater degree of dissatisfaction of workers from their bobs.

WORKERS JOB SATISFACTION

Job satisfaction comprises those outward and inward manifestations which give an individual a sense of enjoyment or accomplishment in the performance of his work (Narchal, *et al.*, 1984: 367). It is the result of various attitudes an employee holds towards his job. "These attitudes" suggest Blum and Naylar (1968: 364) "are related to the job and are concerned with such specific factors as wages, supervision, steadiness of employment, conditions of work, advancement opportunities, recognisation of ability, fair evaluation of work, social relation on the job, prompt settlement of grievances, fair treatment of employer and other similar terms". Positive attitudes towards jobs are conceptually equivalent to job satisfaction and negative attitudes towards the jobs are equivalent to job dissatisfaction (Vroom, 1964: 99).

Ever since the publication of Hoppock's (1935) monograph on job satisfaction, a substantial amount of research has been conducted on the nature of job satisfaction, the influence of various aspects of work roles on the job satisfaction and its impact on various aspects of efficiency and behaviour of workers.

The results of various research studies in India and abroad have invariably shown positive inter-correlation between workers' job satisfaction and attitude towards the company and its management (Whery, 1954; Dabas, 1958; Roach, 1958; Harrison, 1961; Knowles, 1964; Hullin, 1968; Farris, 1971), promotional opportunities (Stagner, 1950; Harrison, 1961; Kendal, *et al.*, 1963; Vroom, 1964; Desia, 1968), the context of the job (Walker, *et al.*, 1962; Hoppock, 1935; Roach, 1958; Schwalrz, *et al.*, 1963; Sharma, 1973); supervisory behaviour (Herzberg, *et al.*, 1957; Khan, 1960; Harrison 1961; Kendal, *et al.*, 1963; Krishna *et al.*, 1964; Desia, 1969; De, 1975; Arya, 1982), financial rewards (I.L.O., 1951; Ash, 1954; Roach, 1958; Kendal, *et al.*, 1963); working conditions (Wherry, 1954; Dabas, 1958; Harrison, 1961; Seigel, 1962), co-workers (Twery, *et al.*, 1958; Kendal, *et al.*, 1963), job security (Herzberg, *et al.*, 1957; Mukerjee, 1968), job status (Mann, 1953; Gurin, *et al.*, 1960; Rao and Ganguli, 1971), organisational climate (Ganguli, 1964; Inderson, 1973; Dingra and

Pathak, 1973; Sharma, 1975; Kumari, 1978; Pillai, 1978) and wages (Herzberg *et al.*, 1959; Smith and Kendal, 1963; Srivastava, 1979; Srivastava, 1984; Mukerji, 1985).

Further job satisfaction is frequently found to be related to different factors of workers' behaviour and performance. Investigators on the basis of their research suggest that the workers' job satisfaction increases turn over (Web and Hollaner, 1956; Bose, 1958; Srivastava, 1984), reduces absenteeism (Singh and Singh, 1980; Balu, 1971; Wastan, 1981; Srivastava, 1984; Narchal, *et al.*, 1984), decreases the incidence of accidents (Hill and Trist 1953; Pestonjee *et al.*, 1977) and improves job performance (Lawshe and Nagle, 1953; Kartz, *et al.*, 1961; Smith and Kendal, 1963; Edward, *et al.*, 1987).

In spite of the substantial amount of research on the subject, there has been a controversy over the importance of various aspects of job to the workers. Most of the Western studies (American being the dominant) reveal that employees do not rate 'wages' as the most important factor of job satisfaction. Workers in the West are more particular about the type of the work and opportunities for advancement than pay. But, here in India our level of development and cultural values tend to monotize our motives, i.e., money is the key to job satisfaction. Review of research and opinion on the subject in Indian context suggest that the most persistent demand of an Indian worker is adequate financial return from his job, besides desire for job security, better working conditions and opportunities for advancement (Sharma, *et al.*, 1964; Lahri, 1965; Mukherjee, 1968; Akhter, *et al.*, 1969; Shirmali, 1970; Tripathy, 1974; Dolke, 1975; Mehta, 1978; Mukherjee, 1985). This holds true in view of general economic backwardness, ever-increasing unemployment and cost of living accompanied by general rising aspirations prevailing in India.

In view of the vast amount of research available on the subject, "a work role most conducive to job satisfaction appears to be one which provides high pay, substantial promotional opportunities, considerate and participative supervision, an opportunity to interact with one's peers, varied duties and a high degree of control over work methods and work place" (Vroom, 1964: 173).

The Survey Results

In the present study, with a view to measure the level of job satisfaction of textile workers in the States, a scale developed and standardised by Ganguli (1954) has been used with slight modifications. The scale used consists of 30 internally consistent statements with significant correlation between their individual item scores and total scores and measures nine dimensions of job satisfaction. Each item has been scored on Likert's five-point scale of Summated Ratings, thereby yielding a score for each worker ranging from a minimum of 30 to a maximum of 150.

Two separate approaches for studying workers' job satisfaction have been followed. First, the workers' satisfaction from various aspects of job (segmental approach), such as pay, job security, working conditions, welfare facilities, advancement opportunities, company policies, job liking supervisory and interpersonal relations, etc., has been studied followed by an overall assessment of the workers perception of their jobs in totality (Holestic approach).

Workers' Satisfaction from Various Aspects of the Job

The responses of the sample workers with regard to their satisfaction from various aspects of the jobs have been shown in the Table 4.3.

TABLE 4.3: Aspects of Job and the Workers Level of Job Satisfaction

Aspects of job	Level of satisfaction (per cent)		
	High	Medium	Low
1. Wages	22.0	29.6	48.4
2. Job security	32.8	32.4	34.8
3. Welfare conditions	23.2	33.2	43.6
4. Welfare facilities	16.8	36.4	46.8
5. Job interest	27.2	35.2	37.6
6. Supervisory behaviour	28.4	33.2	38.4
7. Relations with co-workers	34.4	36.0	29.6
8. Promotion opportunities	22.4	36.4	41.2
9. Personnel policies of company	20.4	33.2	46.4

As regards wage satisfaction, it is evident from Table 4.3 that a majority (48.4%) of the workers are to a great extent dissatisfied with their wages. In comparison only a less percentage (29.6%) is moderately satisfied and still lesser than that (22%) highly satisfied with the payment aspect of their jobs. The dissatisfaction of the workers is mainly due to their perception of wages being less as compared to the wages of workers in other industries/sectors of the State. The wage dissatisfaction has been the main cause of industrial conflicts in the textile industry, which confirms the earlier finding of this study in this regard (Chapter 3).

Along with wages, the welfare facilities and the physical environment at the work place have a strong bearing on the workers' job satisfaction. Table 4.3 highlights that a majority of the workers express extremely lower degree of satisfaction with various welfare facilities (46.8%), like housing, medical, canteen, transport facilities and other welfare amenities and working conditions (43.6%), like, ill-treatment, ventilation, temperature, cleanliness and other atmospheric conditions.

The feeling of the insecurity of service influencing human work behaviour is the main cause for lower degree of job satisfaction of workers. About 35 per cent of the workers are highly dissatisfied with the security of tenure in the job.

A general liking for and interest in job are potent factors in the overall job satisfaction. The analysis of workers' attitude reveals that a majority of about 38 per cent of the workers is to a very low extent interested in the jobs, which leads to their overall dissatisfaction. In addition to various socio-economic factors, this lower degree of interest in the job is also attributed to other factors, such as monotonous nature of job, work being too tiring, lack of opportunities to use fully their capabilities, ideas and new work methods, which also affect the performance of workers on the job and reduce their efficiency. But the workers continue to stay in the job because of their helplessness in the absence of any other viable alternative employment opportunity.

The inter-personal relationship on the job situation is very important. The present study has revealed that while as workers express comparatively higher (34.4%) and moderate (36%) degree of satisfaction with co-workers, they show a lower level (38.4%) of satisfaction with supervisory behaviour.

Opportunities for promotion constitute an important variable in job satisfaction and work commitment. To the extent a worker perceives favourable chances of advancement, he tends to be satisfied on the job assigned. But in the present study, as is evident from the given data, the present job does not provide much chances of promotion to the workers, which account for a lower level of job satisfaction for an overwhelming majority (41%) of the workers. Further, a perusal of the data indicates that, on the whole, a large number of textile workers (46.4%) in all the sample units is highly dissatisfied with various personnel policies of the companies concerned regarding promotion, wages, transfers, confirmation, dismissal, etc.

The summary of above discussion leads us to the important conclusion that on the whole textile workers are dissatisfied with their jobs due to inadequate wages, job insecurity, poor working conditions and welfare facilities, lower interest in job, apathetic attitude of the supervisors, perception of low chances of promotion, lack of objective personnel policies and their poor implementation, which often result in most severe and violent type of conflicts between labour and management.

Overall Job Satisfaction

Having analysed workers orientation to various aspects of the job, an attempt is made here to present the picture of overall job satisfaction of the workers. For this purpose, the scores of the workers obtained from each Organisation, on all the aspects of job discussed above, are pooled together to compute the overall index of job satisfaction of workers. The index so formulated is described in Table 4.4.

TABLE 4.4: Index of the Degree of Job Satisfaction

Scores	Degree of job satisfaction	No. of workers	Percentage
111-150	High	63	25.20
71-110	Medium	85	34.00
30-70	Low	102	40.80
Total		250	100.00

A perusal of the information contained in Table 4.4 suggests that the scores of job satisfaction are skewed on the negative side, thereby indicating that the textile workers of the State on the whole do not possess favourable attitude towards the job. Majority (40.8%) of the workers shows a lower degree of job satisfaction. In comparison, a less percentage (34%) is moderately satisfied and still lesser percentage (25.2%) is highly satisfied with their jobs. This finding of the study appears to be reasonably valid in view of the deplorable socio-economic conditions of the workers and other factors influencing job satisfaction.

It would be worthwhile to make a comparative analysis of the results of this study with other research evidences on the subject in the Indian context. Table 4.5 summarises the relevant information from major studies on job satisfaction in India.

The statistics contained in Table 4.5 reveal that the individual studies of Srivastava (1974) in Chandigarh, Mukerjee (1985) in West Bengal and Johri (1969) in Delhi, representing different nature samples, largely support the findings of the present study. While as the findings of most of the other studies are contrary to those of the present study, including those of Pestonjee (1974), Ganguli (1964), Srivastava (1985), Dubey, Uppal *et al.*, (1983), Srivastava (1984), Srivastava and Srivastava (1983) and some other studies not referred to above including those of Sinha and Aggarwal (1971), Sinha and Sharma (1962). In majority of these studies it is found that workers are moderately satisfied with their jobs. The general concentration is in the middle and a negligible percentage is concentrated at the extreme ends of the job satisfaction — dissatisfaction continuum (Srivastava & Srivastava, 1983).

DEGREE OF JOB SATISFACTION AND ITS CORRELATES

In the present section of the chapter, the frequency of the respondents falling in the groups of high, medium and low degrees of job satisfaction are studied in relation to various background factors. The χ^2 test of significance has been applied in order to find out the significance of differences.

Age and Experience

It was hypothised that the degree of job satisfaction bears some relation to the worker's age and his total work experience. Young workers with comparatively less experience, who are at the beginning of their career and are filled with high hopes of earnings and a better career, are significantly satisfled with their jobs. As the workers advances in age and experience, the frustration overtakes him due to successive competition and aspirations, and as a result he expresses dissatisfaction. The workers with longer service, who are approaching towards the end of their career and who take the work as a matter of routine are again satisfied with their jobs than those with medium tenure. This observation is reasonably valid insofar as the present study is concerned. The relationship between the degree of job satisfaction and age is described in Table 4.6.

Table 4.6 shows that out of the young and old age group of workers the majority was either highly or moderately satisfied with their jobs. Of the middle age group, a majority (48.08% and 55.56%, respectively) expressed lower degree of job satisfaction. Statistically, age of the worker is found significantly associated ($P < .05$) with the degree of job satisfaction. The findings of this study in this regard are

TABLE 4.5: Job Satisfaction of Workers in View of the Major Studies in India.

Researcher/year of study	Sample/scope and size	Levels of job satisfaction (percentage)			
		Highly satisfied	Moderately satisfied	Moderately dissatisfied	Highly dissatisfied
1. Pestonjee (1974)	Industrial workers, Ahmedabad (N=N.A.)	21	42	37	—
2. Ganguli (1964)	Engineering workers, Calcutta (N=284)	3	63	29	5
3. Srivastava (1974)	Industrial workers, Chandigarh (N=173)	23	36	41	—
4. Dubey, Uppal *et. al.*,(1983)	Bank Officers, India (N=88)	44	42	—	14
5. Srivastava (1974)	Industrial workers, Chandigarh (N=135)	3	51	39	7
6. Srivastava (1984)	Public and private sector textile workers Kanpur (N=856)*	22	52	26	—
7. Mukerjee (1985)	Jute workers Bengal (N=310)	5	10	66 **	19
8. Johri (1969)	Building workers, Delhi (N=713)	35	—	61	4
9. Srivastava (1985)	Industrial workers, H.A.L., Kanpur (N=100)	70	—	20	10

* Scores of public and private sector workers pooled together.

** Scores of "Moderately satisfied" and "Neither satisfied nor dissatisfied" pooled together.

— Represents the level of job satisfaction not covered.

TABLE 4.6: Age and Degree of Job Satisfaction

Age group (in years)	Degree of job satisfaction (Percentage)			
	High	Medium	Low	Total
Below 25	36 (34.29)	31 (29.52)	38 (36.19)	105 (100)
25 - 35	7 (13.46)	20 (38.46)	25 (48.08)	52 (100)
35 - 45	6 (13.33)	14 (31.11)	25 (55.56)	45 (100)
45 and above	14 (29.17)	20 (41.67)	14 (29.10)	48 (100)
Total	63 (25.20)	85 (34.00)	102 (40.80)	250 (100)

$\chi^2 = 14.93$ df = 6 $P < .05$.

in line with those of Super (1939), Friedlender (1964), Sinha and Nair (1965), Davis (1977), Sinha and Agarwal (1971), Prasad (1965), Srivastava (1984), Singh and Singh (1980), Basu and Pestonjee (1974), but contrary to those of Chaterjee (1961), Verma (1981), Rao (1970), Ghosh and Shukla (1967), Natraj and Hafeez (1965), Narchal, *et al.*, (1984), who indicate that the element of age is not at all important in job satisfaction.

The association between the experience and degree of job satisfaction is depicted in Table 4.7.

Table 4.7 reveals that a very high percentage (57.14% and 60.71%) of the workers in the middle experience groups shows a very low degree of job satisfaction as compared with the groups at two extremes of work experience. The experience is also found statistically significant ($P < .05$). This finding is in accordance with the findings of Hull and Kostard (1942), Ganguli (1955), Sinha (1960), Sinha and Agarwal (1971), West (1977), Singh and Singh (1980), Narchal *et al.* (1984), but at variance with the findings of Chatterjee (1961), Natraj and Hafeez (1965), Verma (1981), Rao (1970) and Srivastava (1984).

TABLE 4.7: Length of Service and Degree of Job Satisfaction

Experience (in years)	Degree of job satisfaction (Percentage)			
	High	Medium	Low	Total
Below 10	41 (28.67)	52 (36.36)	50 (34.97)	143 (100)
10 - 20	6 (12.29)	12 (28.57)	24 (57.14)	42 (100)
20 - 30	5 (17.86)	6 (21.43)	17 (60.71)	28 (100)
30 and above	11 (29.73)	15 (40.54)	11 (29.73)	37 (100)
Total	63 (25.20)	85 (34.00)	102 (40.80)	250 (100)

$\chi^2 = 15.05$ df = 6 P < .05.

TABLE 4.8: Skill and Degree of Job Satisfaction

Level of skill	Degree of job satisfaction (Percentage)			
	High	Medium	Low	Total
Skilled	26 (32.50)	31 (38.75)	23 (28.75)	80 (100)
Semi-skilled	30 (26.79)	37 (33.03)	45 (40.18)	112 (100)
Unskilled	7 (12.07)	17 (29.31)	34 (58.62)	58 (100)
Total	63 (25.20)	85 (34.00)	102 (40.80)	250 (100)

$\chi^2 = 15.57$ df = 4 P < .01.

Skill and Education

Skill and education generally bear a positive correlation to each other and both are expected to bear some relation to the degree of job satisfaction of workers. Highly skilled and educated workers have strong attachment to their jobs because such jobs generally carry more prestige and remuneration and, therefore, show higher job satisfaction than those at the other extremes. To what extent the level of skill and education influence the level of job satisfaction is analysed in Table 4.8 and Table 4.9, respectively.

It appears from Table 4.8 that a majority of the skilled workers (weavers, spinners, dyers, maintenance mechanists, etc.) are either highly (32.50%) or moderately (38.75%) satisfied with their jobs. Whereas a lower degree of job satisfaction has been expressed by semi-skilled (40.18%) and unskilled (58.62%) workers. Statistically, the level of skill seems to have a decisive influence on the degree of job satisfaction. As such it is asserted that an individual derives satisfaction from jobs which permit him to use his skill and abilities. The studies of Johri (1969), Rao (1971), Rajbir and Vasudeva (1976) and Verma (1981) have also reported the positive relationship between the skill and the level of job satisfaction.

TABLE 4.9: Education and Degree of Job Satisfaction

Level of education	Degree of job satisfaction (Percentage)			
	High	Medium	Low	Total
Illiterates	33 (25.78)	39 (34.47)	56 (43.75)	128 (100)
Up to 10 years of schooling	26 (23.64)	43 (39.09)	41 (37.27)	110 (100)
More than 10 years of schooling	4 (33.33)	3 (25.00)	5 (41.67)	12 (100)
Total	63 (25.20)	85 (34.00)	102 (40.80)	250 (100)

$\chi^2 = 2.96$ df = 4 Not significant

Table 4.9 clearly reveals that a higher percentage of illiterate workers shows a lower level of job satisfaction (43.75%), higher percentage of moderately educated workers shows moderate level of job satisfaction (39.09%) and that of comparatively highly educated workers, higher degree of job dissatisfaction (41.67%). Statistically education does not appear to influence the degree of job satisfaction. The reason seems that education generates greater expectancy and aspirations with the conditions of work but prospects of an average worker in India are ill-suited to fulfil them (Sinha and Agarwal, 1971). Some earlier studies on the subject also do not find any relationship between the amount of schooling of the workers and their level of job satisfaction. These include Ganguli (1955), Sinha (1960), Sinha and Nair (1965), Sinha and Sharma (1962), Ghosh and Shukla (1967) and Mukerjee (1985). But the observations of Prasad (1965), Sinha and Agarwal (1971), Srivastava (1984), Singh and Singh (1980) and Rao (1971) do not support this viewpoint.

Wages

It is a general hypothesis that income is a very important variable which influences job satisfaction. In other words, higher the pay of workers more is the degree of job satisfaction. The same is true of the textile workers of Jammu and Kashmir. The findings in this context are reported in Table 4.10.

TABLE 4.10: Wage Level and the Degree of Job Satisfaction

Wage group (in Rs.)	Degree of job satisfaction (Percentage)			
	High	Medium	Low	Total
Below 700	5 (11.63)	12 (27.91)	26 (60.46)	43 (100)
700 - 1,000	36 (24.49)	54 (36.73)	57 (38.78)	147 (100)
1,000 and above	22 (36.67)	19 (31.66)	19 (31.67)	60 (100)
Total	63 (25.20)	85 (34.00)	102 (40.80)	250 (100)

$\chi^2 = 13.59$ df = 4 $P < .01$.

It is evident from Table 4.10 that an overwhelming majority of the workers in the lower wage group (below Rs. 700) expresses a lower level of satisfaction with their jobs. Among those highly dissatisfied, the higher percentage (38.78%) also belongs to the middle wage group (Rs. 700-1,000). Comparatively, in the highest job satisfaction category a majority of workers (36.67%) was highly paid (Rs. 1,000 or more). The higher degree of positive association between income level and job satisfaction ($P < .01$) also corroborates the fact that job satisfaction depends to a greater extent on the pay envelope of the workers. Employers may be successful in getting workers at a lower wage level in view of large scale unemployment, but maintaining their motivation at work and enhancing quality and productivity may be the real problems faced by the employers, if they ignore the dissatisfaction level with wages. Herzberg, *et al.* (1959) found salary associated both with job satisfaction and dissatisfaction of employees. Some other studies conducted in various parts of the world such as Thompson (1939), Merriott and Denerley (1955), Terman and Oden (1959) and Smith and Kendal (1963) also provide support for such a relationship. The studies conducted in India particularly those by Verma (1981), Natraj and Hafeez (1965), Srivastava (1984), Sinha and Agarwal (1971), Singh and Singh (1980), Kathiresan (1987), Rajbir and Vasudeva (1976) too have observed the positive relationship between income and job satisfaction.

Marital Status and the Number of Dependents

The marital status and the number of dependents to support influence the workers' socio-economic responsibility towards their families. The higher the responsibilities of a worker, higher may be his anxiety to get more and more from his job. If the job fails to help him in meeting his responsibilities, he tends to be dissatisfied with his job. On this assumption we may expect a lower degree of job satisfaction among workers who are married and those having a large size family to support. Table 4.11 provides relevant information to assess how far the marriage has anything to do with the job satisfaction.

The majority of the textile workers under study were found married who usually bore the bulk of the responsibility of their families. Table 4.11 reveals that a majority of about 40 per cent of the married workers is to a great extent dissatisfied with their jobs. Interestingly, among the unmarried group of workers, a majority (42.53%) shows lower level of job satisfaction. The χ^2 values also suggest that workers being married or unmarried do not bear any significant relationship with the degree of their job satisfaction. This observation is in agreement with those of Sinha and Agarwal (1971), Sinha and Nair (1965) and Guha (1978) but contrary to the observations of Singh and Singh (1980) and Sinha and Sharma (1962) who found that the marriage affects the job satisfaction considerably.

With a view to assess that whether the burden of dependents makes any difference in the degree of job satisfaction of workers or not, the relevant data have been provided in the Table 4.12.

TABLE 4.11: Martial Status and Degree of Job Satisfaction

Marital status	Degree of job satisfaction (Percentage)			
	High	Medium	Low	Total
Married	39 (23.93)	59 (36.20)	65 (39.87)	163 (100)
Unmarried	24 (27.59)	26 (29.88)	37 (42.53)	87 (100)
Total	63 (25.20)	85 (34.00)	102 (40.80)	250 (100)

$\chi^2 = 1.27$ df = 2 Not Significant

TABLE 4.12: Number of Dependents and Degree of Job Satisfaction

No. of dependents	Degree of job satisfaction (Percentage)			
	High	Medium	Low	Total
Below four	35 (32.41)	37 (34.26)	36 (33.33)	108 (100)
Four and more	28 (19.72)	48 (33.80)	66 (46.48)	142 (100)
Total	63 (25.20)	85 (34.00)	102 (40.80)	250 (100)

$\chi^2 = 6.70$ df = 6 $P < .05$.

The hypothesis, that higher the number of dependents, lower is the degree of job satisfaction, holds true in the case of present study as Table 4.12 shows a significant relationship ($P < .05$) between the burden of dependents and the degree of job satisfaction. A further explanation of the data reveals that a higher proportion of workers having four or more dependents to support (46.48%) are highly dissatisfied with their jobs as compared to those with fewer dependents. Morse (1953), Singh and Singh (1980) and Narchal, *et al.* (1984) also support the findings of this study. But Sinha and Agarwal (1971) and Sinha and Nair (1965) find that the burden of dependents hardly makes any difference in the employees' degree of job satisfaction.

CONCLUSION

Summing-up the discussion of the present chapter it may be concluded that the textile workers of Jammu and Kashmir work in appaling working and living conditions. Majority of them earn inadequate wages, work in standing position and are exposed to dust, fumes, gases and steam, etc. They have been deprived of the proper wholesome drinking water, washing and bathing facilities and live under poor housing conditions. The welfare activities undertaken by the State Government, based on its vague and defective Labour Policy, have not been able to bring about any appreciable change in the welfare of the vast working class. The working of various social security measures is far from satisfactory. Management, in most of the cases, rarely do more than what they are forced to do by law and, even where rules are observed, the tendency is to conform only to the letter of the law and break the spirit of it. However, the things are much better in the private sector as compared to the public sector. The main factors which have led to the deterioration in these conditions include the apathetic attitude of management, illiteracy and unawareness of workers and lack of proper inspections by the concerned authorities.

The above state of affairs is responsible for majority of workers' dissatisfaction with their jobs. Comparatively speaking, workers dissatisfied with their jobs are either too old or too young, possess lesser skills, are either illiterates or too highly educated, whose job tenure is neither too short nor too large, who earn relatively low wages and have a large family to support. The adverse impact of the workers' job dissatisfaction on their work behaviour is undeniable. As rightly summarised by Paterson and Capwell (1957: 20):

> "The worker dissatisfied with his job in contrast is often rigid, inflexible, unrealistic in his choice of goals, unable to overcome environmental obstracts, generally unhappy and dissatisfied".

Therefore, the management would have to be particularly vigilant about the motivational requirements of these workers.

NOTES

1. *Statistical Abstract of India 1982*, Central Statistical Organization, Govt. Of India, and *Indian Labour Year Book 1987*, Labour Bureau, Simla.
2. *Ibid.*
3. *Ibid.*
4. Order No. JKI/5, 1988, dated 5.1.88 (Jammu and Kashmir Industries Ltd., Srinagar).
5. Based on the interview with the union president of the Organisation and also confirmed by the Management.

5

WORKERS' EXPECTATIONS

FOR INDUSTRIAL peace, the relationship between employees and employers at the shop-floor level should be as harmonious and cordial as possible. But harmony in the relationship is not possible unless the inter-personal relations between the rank and file, supervisors and management are improved. There is a growing body of evidence that socio-economic and psychological factors influencing the inter-personal relationship between the operative employees and management — both at the supervisory and executive levels — play a significant role in the development of good or bad industrial relations.

Understanding of these factors is essential in any endeavour to provide motivational inputs. Scholars in human relations are on a continuous search to ascertain as to what workers want from their jobs and how to activate them to contribute their best. However, the review of existing research in the field reveals that there is not much empirical evidence to show as to what workers expect from their supervisors and management. In India, particularly, results of empirical studies are sufficiently equivocal to justify an open mind on the issue.

Therefore, now, when our industrial relations are getting more strained, it sounds surely logical to study the expectations of operative employees from their supervisors and management. Such a study should not be considered to be a matter of casual exercise. Rather it should be a regular process to enlighten the higher-ups about the persisting needs of workers. There is a strong conviction that if the amount of employee expectations are known and if the supervisors and management are able to comprehend these expectations, it would certainly yield rewarding results in designing the personnel policies, improving the job performance of employees and in reducing the conflicts in labour-management relations. The supervisors and executives would be able to judiciously devise the improvements necessary in the job contents and make available to the concerned employees appropriate goals in the perspective of needs claiming very high priority. It has been emphasised that such studies should have a strong foundation of facts and information, gathered through attitude surveys of employees, otherwise the very purpose is likely to become meaningless. While analysing employee needs and goals, Davis (1977) has emphatically asserted that the improvement must be viewed by the employees and not as viewed by the management. Employees are the best judges of what improves their job.

With the above backdrop in view, an attempt has been made in this chapter to study the expectations* of workers from management both at the supervisory level and higher levels. The study of employee expectations from supervisors and management separately is based on the assumption that employee expectation vary from level to level with respect to management.

EXPECTATIONS FROM SUPERVISORS

In all the levels of management, the term 'supervisor' is used for people who direct the activities of subordinates. It refers to the person who is primarily in charge of a group of employees in an undertaking and responsible for their work. In common usage, the term tends to be used only in the lower ranks of management hierarchy. In textile industry, which is comparatively labour intensive and not mechanised to a higher degree, the span of supervision or control is bound to be fairly wide. Here the span applies to the horizontal reach of the supervisor and control applies to direct supervisor-worker relationship.

A supervisor described by touchy titles, like, man in the middle, eyes and ears of management, the pusherman, the leading ambulance man, the kingpin and the link pin between the labour and management, has a special role of being the keyman in the centre of industrial relations stage of different organisations. He is a reflection of managements' effectiveness, workers' efficiency and organisational productivity. Standing on the dividing line between management and operatives, the supervisor translates the managements' thinking to the workers and voices the workers' points of view to the management. If both, workers and management, accept and recognise the supervisor as 'Their man', it would facilitate him to play a more constructive role in

* In the present study the term 'expectation' is used in 'Evaluative sense' and not in an 'anticipatory sense'. It refers to what supervisors/management 'should do' and not to what they 'would do' in a particular work situation.

establishing harmonious relations between the higher echelons and the shop level.

Supervision has been most researched but least understood of all management concepts. What his role consists of — what the supervisor must do, how he fits into the organisation and what is expected of him — is not very clear so far. Variations in role perception and expectations from different segments of the organisation fails to establish a clear pattern for a supervisors role. However, much of the research available on the subject is based on the assumption that supervisors can be characterised in terms of the degree of which they are considerate of the desires of their subordinates. It was once believed that production-oriented supervisors which pressurised employees and which held rigidly to established procedure would yield the best results. Contrary to this belief, however, research in widely different industries in different countries confirmed that the satisfaction of subordinates is positively related to the consideration or employee-orientation of their supervisors, which in turn results in relatively low turnover rate, grievance and absence (Harrison, 1961; Herzberg *et al.*, 1937; Khan, 1960; Likert, 1961). There is further empirical evidence that more considerate, supportives, friendly and employee-oriented the supervisor, the greater the subordinate productivity, motivation and work satisfaction (Dabas, 1958; Davis, 1977; Harrison, 1961; Kendel *et al.*, 1963, Khan, 1960).

The studies conducted in Indian context (Arya, 1982; De, 1975; Desia, 1969; Krishna *et al.*, 1964) have also found that the employee centred supervision has led to greater satisfaction among the workers. Vroom (1964) too has confirmed that the relationship between first line supervisors and the individual workmen is of more importance in determining the attitudes, moral, general happiness and the efficiency of their employees, than any other single factor. In fact satisfaction in all the areas — job management, personal adjustment and social relations — has been found to be higher in employee-centred supervision than the production-centred supervision.

In spite of the vital role being played by the first line supervisor in the organisation, in the situations of conflict and anxiety, many experts suggest that the supervisor has progressively lost his erstwhile authority and status. He finds himself now in changed responsibilities (Agarwal, 1988; Sheth, 1973). He has by and large become a 'buffer' between his superiors and subordinates and, like all bufers, his main job is to take blows. He is exposed to the pressures from the two opposing forces. He has to manage the workers, who being unionised wield lot of power which the supervisor lacks. On the other hand he has to carryout the orders of the management without possessing adequate decision-making powers. The unique challenge of the supervisor is to cope up with these two opposing forces and for this he has to be a 'master and victim of double talk'.

The management has one set of expectations from the supervisors which are mostly technical and production-oriented. These include prevention of wastage, reducing costs, producing more and maintaining discipline at the work place. The pressures brought out by the workers are, on the other hand, largely matters of feeling. But what exactly workers expect from the supervisors? There is not much empirical evidence in India to determine this from the workers point of view.

The present section of the chapter seeks to examine the employees expectations from the supervisors. Workers were given two sets of multiple characteristics, separately of a 'good' and a 'bad' supervisor.* These pertained, in each case, to (1) supervisor's own job, (2) his relations with the workers and (3) his relation with the management. They were asked to rank five characteristics, in each case, in order of preference, which they feel make a supervisor good or bad. The technique of choice scoring has been used to assess the order of preference. Each item has been scored on Likert's Five Point Scale of Summated Ratings. In all five characteristics have been selected and retained in order of priority.

The Good Supervisor

The results of the study regarding the characteristics of a good supervisor, pertaining to his job, his relations with the workers and management, as perceived by the workers, is adduced hereunder.

Table 5.1 presenting the supervisor's characteristics pertaining to his relation with the workers, depicts that the first most important rated quality of a good supervisor is to treat the workers as human beings. This exhibits that workers are more concerned with the treatment they

---

* It is based on the assumption that the characteristics of a 'good' and a 'bad' supervisor are not the opposite poles of the same continuum. Persons who perceive certain factors as good qualities of a supervisor may not perceive the absence of same as undesirable qualities of a supervisor.

receive at the hands of supervisor. A feeling of approval is more likely to result if the boss shows personal interest in subordinates.

TABLE 5.1: Characteristics of a 'Good' Supervisor Pertaining to his Relations with Workers

Rank	Characteristics	Total Score	Percentage of max. possible score
I.	Treats employees as human beings	1,030	82.40
II.	Makes minimum use of authority	950	76.00
III.	Believes in friendly relations	765	61.20
IV.	Takes interest in workers' grievances/problems	618	49.44
V.	Impartial in dealing with workers on the job	462	39.96

Note: Maximum possible Score = N × 5.

While admitting the supervisor's authority over them, the workers' expect him to make minimum use of the same.The authority is two edge sword. The supervisor should examine how to use it and how it affects his influence over his men. Employee behaviour patterns and attitudes towards authority means that supervisors will have to become more flexible in their approach to managing. Workers also anticipate that the supervisor should believe in friendly relations, take interest in their problems and be impartial in dealing with the workers on the job. Co-operativeness and friendliness are, beyond doubt, the prerequisites to impartiality and minimum use of authority. Zechariah (1983) on the basis of his study on Bombay workers suggests: "A supervisor should be one with the workers, tactful with persuasive ideas, informative, tolerant, considerate, forgiving mistakes and not interfering. On the basis of similar findings, Monga (1978) challenges the rationale of Theory X which propagates that only coercion, threats and tight control can deliver the goods.

Regarding the characteristics of a good supervisor relating to his work, the data (Table 5.2) make it obvious that workers attach considerable importance to supervisor's knowing his job well and giving proper work instructions to the workers. The supervisor being closest to his specialised area is expected to know more about its technical aspects than anyone else in his group. The findings substantiate the results of Turner (1955) and Desia (1969) in this context. To be capable enough to exercise good control over the subordinates is the next important characteristic of a good supervisor followed in order of importance by his ability to recognise the merits of the workmen, accept their suggestions relating to work, allocate the workload equitably and objectively and introduce the new comers to the jobs.

TABLE 5.2: Characteristics of a 'Good' Supervisor Pertaining to his Job

Rank	Characteristics	Total Score	Percentage of max. possible Score
I.	Knows his job well and gives proper work instructions	802	64.16
II.	Exercises good control	726	58.08
III.	Recognises the merits of workers and accepts their suggestions	624	49.92
IV.	Objectively and equitably allocates work	512	40.96
V.	Introduces and trains new workers on the job	421	33.68

Among the first five characteristics of a good supervisor regarding his relations with the management (Table 5.3), the first preference reveals that a supervisor should have good relations with the management. They no doubt expect the supervisor to be loyal to the management but at the same time anticipate that he should not mislead the management by biased complaints. Instead, he should project a healthy image of the workers before the management. They look forward to the supervisor being powerful leader so that their recommendations are respected and accepted by the management. This observation is in conformity with that of Agarwal (1982) that a supervisor having good relations with the management can be instrumental in effectively presenting the workers' problems to the management and solving them.

The Bad Supervisor

The first five characteristics of a bad supervisor are presented below separately with the regard to his different roles in the industry.

Table 5.4, reflecting the qualities of a bad supervisor with regard to his relations with the workers, clearly shows that the workers dislike such supervisors who are not considerate to their problems, fair in recommendations, friendly and who are hesitant to take stern action against defaulting workers. The responses obviously indicate that the supervisor should take personal interest in solving the workers' difficulties and grievances, treating them as human beings. Most supervisors fail because they can't interact with those they supervise. They must be able to provide leadership, facilitate workers' performance and communicate properly with them, otherwise they may become the victims of misunderstanding. A supervisor is rightly expected to be not only the best master mechanic but also a specialist in human by engineering who uses a human relations approach in the work situation (Zecharia, 1983).

TABLE 5.3: Characteristics of a 'Good' Supervisor Pertaining to his Relations with Management

Rank	Characteristics	Total score	Percentage of max. possible score
I.	Maintains good relations with Management	1,050	84.00
II.	Never misleads management by biased complaints	856	68.48
III.	Loyal to the management	633	50.64
IV.	His recommendations are respected by the management	581	46.48
V.	Projects healthy image of workers to the management	417	33.36

TABLE 5.4: Characteristics of a 'Bad' Supervisor Pertaining to his Relations with Workers

Rank	Characteristics	Total score	Percentage of max. possible score
I.	Does not consider worker's problems and grievances	796	63.68
II.	Unfair and partial in recommending promotions	742	59.36
III.	Avoids mixing with the workers	644	51.52
IV.	Does not communicate effectively	524	41.92
V.	Does not take stern action against defaulting workers	454	36.32

The breakdown of the responses relating to the work of the supervisor himself (Table 5.5) corroborates the fact that the supervisor's; who do not know to do their job well, are unable to give proper instructions to the subordinates, find faults, are dictatorial and revengeful in nature, dishonest and selfish in their dealings are ranked as the worst kind of supervisors. Workers also do not appreciate a supervisor who is unable to maintain discipline at the work place. The present data strengthen the belief that workers appreciate a supervisor who is knowledgeable, polite, even tempered and morally upright.

TABLE 5.5: Characteristics of a 'Bad' Supervisor Pertaining to his Job

Rank	Characteristics	Total score	Percentage of max. possible score
I.	Does not know his job, unable to locate and correct defects in machines	1,042	83.36
II.	Unable to get work done	758	60.64
III.	Fault finding, dictatorial and of revengeful nature	704	56.32
IV.	Dishonest, selfish, gives false information	544	44.52
V.	Unable to maintain discipline	366	29.28

Perusal of Table 5.6, projecting the workers' opinion about supervisors' relationship with the management, shows that the workers rate a supervisor as worst if he keeps hostile relations with the management, misleads management about workers and pleases them by burdening the workers and stealing their ideas. The study makes it crystal clear that the workers no doubt want the supervisors to project their healthy image to the management but at the same time expect them to be loyal to the management — a finding which is in line with those of some earlier studies in this context (Desia, 1969; Manga, 1978; Turner, 1955).

TABLE 5.6: Characteristics of a 'Bad' Supervisor Pertaining to his Relations with Management

Rank	Characteristics	Total score	Percentage of max. possible score
I.	Keeps hostile relations with management	884	70.72
II.	Misleads management about workers	796	63.68
III.	Pleases management by taking more work from workers	726	58.60
IV.	Steals workers' ideas to have unearned fame	584	46.72
V.	Disobedient to management	397	31.76

From the above analysis it may be concluded that the workers recognise the supervisor's relations with workers as most important aspects of his job. Thus, while expecting the supervisor to be more employee-oriented, the workers want him to behave properly with them, keep them out of trouble, give credit when due to them, convey their fears to the management be honest, friendly, fair and impartial in his dealings, knows his job and exercises fair control. They look to him to carry out his responsibilities to his superiors in a loyal, enthusiastic and sincere way in order to obtain the organisational goals. They like a supervisor who is understanding, not too strict, not too easy, not hot-headed, talks nice and who has no favourites. These reasons express the worker's desire for a certain measure of independence and responsibility and his desire for dignity as a person. What a worker wants more is his opinion and arguments to be listened to with respect and attention. Supervisor should recognise that most employees want to perform acceptably, and that most discipline can be self imposed.

It would be erroneous not to point out that the management and workers also owe their allegiance to the supervisor, and have to share the responsibility of making him a good supervisor. The subordinates have the responsibility of accepting the authority of the supervisor's position, assisting him by carrying out their assignments in a fruitful, productive and efficient manner and keeping him well-informed about the things that might affect the performance of his unit. The management must guide and support the supervisor and give him adequate authority to take decisions particularly in the matters pertaining to the workers and their work. His role as an important member of the management team must be recognised. He must be taken out of the quasi-management ranks and his role must be defined to clear up misunderstanding on the part of his workers and other members of management. A great need exists for upgrading the education, training and development levels of supervisors so that they derive greater satisfaction from their jobs and perform their critical role more effectively and efficiently.

EXPECTATIONS FROM MANAGEMENT

Efficient running of an organisation calls for the whole-hearted co-operation of workers and management. Towards this end, their clear cut understanding of each others roles and expectations play almost a decisive role. "Employer-employee relations", it is recognised, "are to a great extent founded on a sense of reciprocity which shapes and re-shapes them (Monga, 1978: 350). From workers no co-operation is possible if they feel that the management is out of touch with them and is not interested in their problems. They must find, while working in the organisation, the means to satisfy their basic needs. Management should become conscious of their motivational requirements.

The interest in the study of worker's needs dates back to the early part of the 20th century. With the emergence of Human Relations Movement, which sprang up after the famous Howthorne studies of 1920s and 1930s, with its emphasis on good inter-personal relations, conducive work climate and job satisfaction, an important initial stimulous was provided for the study of workers' wants, job attitudes, expectations, aspirations and their relations to human behaviour in organisations. Since then substantial amount of research has been conducted and a number of theories and models have been offered to explain what the workers expect from their management in order to extend their co-operations.

The best known earlier reviews of research studies (Brayfield and Crockett, 1955; Herzberg *et al.*, 1957; Vroom, 1964) have made it possible to see what the workers in the West want from their management. On the basis of these reviews it may be concluded that in the advanced West, where the physical needs of the employees have mostly been met, a set of psychological needs have emerged due to a heavy dose of mechanisation into jobs. The nature of job content factors have acquired a very high significance for the operative employees, as well as managers.

In India, however, no such extensive compilation of studies is available. But the research available on the subject, of whatever nature and magnitude, (see, for example, Ganguli, 1954; Metha, 1978; Singh 1971; Srivastava and Srivastava, 1983) corroborates the fact that the most persistent desire of an average Indian worker is for adequate financial return from his job, besides desire for job security and opportunity for advancement. Lending a confirmation to these findings some recent studies (Kathiroson, 1987; Mukerjee, 1985; Srivastava, 1985) suggest that the Indian poverty-stricken workers are more concerned with the immediate and personal economic gains and that the economic conditions appear to be central source of life satisfaction. It is so because our level of development and socio-cultural values tend to monotonise our motives. Workers consider their jobs as a means through which they can satisfy their basic needs and they look favourable to the management so long as these needs are not threatened.

Now with the growing complexities of business, increased

awareness among workers of their rights and responsibilities, rapidly increasing proportions of work force and fast social changes, the employees' attitudes and expectations have started escalating more than ever before. The growing popularity of what is called 'humanistic psychology', which emphasises fulfilment the self-actualisation and growing cultural emphasis on personal satisfaction, has contributed to this 'revolution of rising expectations'. As against this in spite of the significant improvements in some sectors, the nature and conditions of work have not changed correspondingly. This widening gap between what workers expect and what they get is often the reason for the rejection of work manifested in high rate of absenteeism, labour turnover, poor job performance and deteriorating industrial relations.

In spite of the advancement of various theories on human needs, very little attention has been paid to actual worker responses to the direct question about what the workers want from their management? In the present section an attempt has been made to probe into the factors that make the management 'best' and 'worst' for the workers, in an attempt to ascertain the expectation of workers from management. Following the methodology adopted in the previous section, the respondents were given two sets of multiple characteristics of the 'best' and 'worst' management and were asked to rank any five characteristics, in each case, in order of priority.

The Best Management

In the following paras, the characteristics of the best management pertaining to the workers' salary and service conditions, physical and psychological work environment and welfare facilities are presented.

The detailed analysis of the responses pertaining to the salary and service conditions of workers (Table 5.7) reveals that monetary compensation acquired the highest strength in order of priority of expectations. Workers attach next priority to good service conditions. These findings are in conformity with those of some earlier studies in Indian context (Monga, 1978; Zecharia, 1983; Sharma, 1974). It is logical because most of the other socio-economic and psychological expectations centre around what an employee earns from the job. It indicates the amount of social prestige and social status that an employee can command in society. The other good characteristics that followed in order of importance include adequate profit sharing and bonus, consistent and objective personnel policies, attractive fringe benefits, etc.

TABLE 5.7: Characteristics of a 'Best' management pertaining to his salary and service conditions

Rank	Characteristics	Total score	Percentage of max. possible score
I.	Attractive wages	1,092	87.36
II.	Good service conditions (Promotion, Permanency, Provident Fund, Gratuity etc.)	892	71.36
III.	Profit sharing and bonus	742	59.36
IV.	Consistent and objective personnel	718	57.44
V.	Good fringe benefits	512	40.96

The study, however, does not support the myth that wages constitute the only source of satisfaction for workers. Workers expect a congenial physical and psychological work environment at the work place, where they toil for their 'only remuneration'. The results of the study in this regard (Table 5.8) make it clear that maintaining cordial relations with workers is assigned the first rank. Realising their responsibility towards the organisation, the workers appreciate to get involved and participate actively in the tasks assigned to them. Their desire for proper tools and equipments, training and participation in decision-making is a pointer towards this fact. Scholars almost unanimously agree that people act more responsibly when they are involved in setting their own goals, are accountable for their own behaviour and share the responsibility and rewards for accomplishing organisational goals.

There appears to be gap between expectations and reality in the sphere of welfare facilities, which have been considered to be 'the company commitment to the workers'. Table 5.9 depicts that the proper accommodation facilities near work place, adequate and attractive recreational, educational, medical and canteen facilities are considered as desirable aspects of management. The finding exposes that the workers are conscious of their rights to these necessities and their presence or absence would certainly have a marked influence on the workers' attitudes towards management. The gap needs to be bridged by the management. Even in case of off-the-job life issues of the workers, though exclusively the concern of the State, society and the union, the management has the responsibility of bringing about a match between workers' felt needs and facilities of whatever sort provided by the State and the society.

TABLE 5.8: Characteristics of the 'Best' Management Pertaining to Physical and Psychological Work Environment

Rank	Characteristics	Total score	Percentage of max. possible score
I.	Harmonious relations with working class	1,022	81.76
II.	Ideal and hygienic conditions of work	792	63.36
III.	Participative work culture	754	60.32
IV.	Proper tools and equipments	556	44.48
V.	Good and understanding supervisors	347	27.76

TABLE 5.9: Characteristics of the 'Best' Management Pertaining to Welfare Amenities

Rank	Characteristics	Total score	Percentage of max. possible score
I.	Proper implementation of statutory provisions regarding welfare amenities	942	75.36
II.	Proper accommodation facilities	764	61.12
III.	Good recreational and educational facilities	668	53.44
IV.	Proper and adequate medical facilities	570	45.60
V.	Clean and subsidised canteen facilities	502	40.16

The Worst Management

The detailed breakdown of the responses concerning the characteristics of the 'worst' management, as perceived by the workers, is presented below:

The data reflecting the characteristics of the worst management *vis-a-vis* worker's salary and service conditions (Table 5.10) makes it obvious that inadequate wages and heavy wage differentials, absence of social security measures and fringe benefits followed in that order by the presence of a system of slow and partial promotions, apathetic attitude towards workers' associations and the unhealthy policy of not recognising the merits of the workers and rewarding them for their outstanding performance are the worst possible characteristics of the management as identified by the workers. It appears that the workers want their will to have a great personal meaning.

TABLE 5.10: Characteristics of the 'Worst' Management Pertaining to Salary and Service Conditions

Rank	Characteristics	Total score	Percentage of max. possible score
I.	Inadequate wages, heavy wage differentials	1,055	84.40
II.	Absence of various social security measures and fringe benefits	926	74.20
III.	Slow and partiality in promotions	690	55.20
IV.	Apathetic attitude towards unions	595	47.60
V.	Does not recognise and reward outstanding performance	357	28.50

Insofar as the physical and psychological work environment of workers is concerned, Table 5.11 reveals that a management is considered to be the worst, if it does not provide for conducive working (physical) conditions at the place. Workers also do not appreciate a management which lacks consideration for workers' problems, does not provide adequate training facilities, necessary for job improvement, employees' supervisors having partial, harassing, fault finding and revengeful nature and does not make available proper tools and equipments which are fundamental to job performance.

TABLE 5.11: Characteristics of the 'Worst' Management Pertaining to Physical and Psychological Work Environment

Rank	Characteristics	Total score	Percentage of max. possible score
I.	Poor working (physical) conditions	1,015	81.20
II.	No consideration for worker's victimisation	776	62.08
III.	Absence of training facilities, no chance to improve on the job	655	52.40
IV.	Partial and harassing supervisors	538	43.04
V.	Absence of proper tools and equipments	451	36.08

The proper welfare facilities, though not a substitute for wage increase but having social, economic and civic impact, keep to a greater extent employees contented with their jobs. The responses of the employees (Table 5.12) depict that the worker's dislike a management if it does not take proper measures for workers' safety, does not provide adequate medical, recreational, educational and accommodation facilities — all having a significant impact on the workers' mental make up. The practice of not implementing the statutory provisions regarding the welfare facilities has also been ascertained as the quality of worst management.

TABLE 5.12: Characteristics of the 'Worst' Management Pertaining to Welfare Amenities

Rank	Characteristics	Total Score	Percentage of Max. Possible Score
I.	Inadequate safety measures	990	79.20
II.	Absence of medical facilities	695	55.60
III.	Lack of recreational and educational facilities	635	50.80
IV.	Lack of proper accommodation near work place	497	39.76
V.	Non-implementation of the provisions relating to the welfare facilities	412	32.96

Though the workers vary among themselves in degree of expectations from management, it may be concluded from the above discussion that what the employees are mostly concerned about is economic gain — monetary compensation, relief and reward. The study reveals that the security of service, opportunity for advancement, comfortable working conditions, suitable type of work, better behaved supervisors and better education facilities are some of the main factors reported by the workers as the most desired factors of management. They value their dignity, rights and privileges and expect a congenial work environment and recognition of their jobs from the higher as well as immediate officers. They want to become masters of their immediate environment and feel that their work and they themselves are important — the twin ingredients of self-esteem.

Workers feel somewhat dissatisfied with the managements' way of handling industrial relations problems. This kind of dissatisfaction is reflected in workers' perception that management has apathetic attitude towards workers and their unions and that it does not recognise and reward their merits. Much of the Indian management is not yet convinced of the importance of managements' responsibility for developing good industrial relations. They tend to blame government, labour legislation and unions for the trouble without realising their own fault. At the heart of the failure of the present institution to produce harmonious industrial relations is also the failure to understand one fundamental fact that most of the industrial relation problems are attributed to what Karl Marx called: "alienation of modern industrial worker". While managing human resources, management makes a somewhat unrealistic assumption that we are only dealing with 'economic man' and not the 'whole man' — the man with flesh, blood, emotions, sentiments and deep seated psychological needs. As a result the strategies adopted by the management have, by and large, failed in present day context. The result is low employee commitment and loyalty.

CONCLUSION

The foregoing analysis of the workers' expectations indicates the characteristics which the workers feel make the supervisors and management 'good' or 'bad'. It may be concluded from the discussion that workers expect an employee-oriented behaviour from supervisors and management rather than production centred and technical orientation to human problems. The findings of the study have practical policy implications. These are the indicators of their likes and dislikes and call for the measures to be taken by the supervisors and management for promoting workers' job satisfaction and acquiring their co-operation and confidence which are basic to greater productivity and much needed industrial peace. Accepting these expectations would make their job rather easy, ignoring or floating them would be risky. Non-adherence to these expectations would mean employee frustration, discouragement, anxiety and even bitterness. The study is in agreement with the conclusion of McGregor (1960: 34): "If management understands its men and develops proper environment, its employees will exercise self-direction and self-control in the service of the objectives, to which they are committed".

For getting best out of workers their motivational requirements have to be considered in right perspective. For their effective utilization, management should adopt more progressive measures for making the work humane, interesting and challenging, evolve a proper information system, give the workers fair treatment, make them feel important so that they develop a sense of loyalty. Towards this objective, measures, like, participative management, are not only welcome but may become inevitable for some socio-political reasons. With this perspective in view, the next chapter seeks to examine various aspects of workers' participation in decision-making in the industry under study.

6

WORKERS' PARTICIPATION IN DECISION-MAKING

INTRODUCTION

CONCLUSION EMERGES form the preceding chapter that for the improvement of harmonious labour-management relations concern should be shown not only for the material and economic aspects of employment, but also for the effects of work and work environment on the well-being of workers. Accordingly, considerable attention has been paid, in the recent past, to the improvement of quality of working life. There is a widespread conviction that participation in one form or the other is indispensable in this regard.

There has been a world-wide trend, during the past two decades, towards allocating to the workers a general say in matters affecting or relevant to their working lives. The principle underlying worker participation is that the people who will be affected by decisions should be involved in making those decisions. As such, participation is linked to the concept of industrial democracy and, being one aspect of the worker-management relationship, is usually part of an industrial relations system directed towards the achievement or refinement of an industrial democracy (Bendix, 1978: 1).

A critical review of research in the field and a cross-national experience shows that support for the idea of participation has been rapidly increasing and emanating from diverse sources. Thinkers, such as Comte and Owen, advocated the participation of workers in management for achieving distributive social justice. Karl Marx and Syndicalists, on the other hand, advocated complete control of the enterprise by workers (Sahu, 1985). Even Pope John XXIII (1963: 20) stated:

"The present demand for workers to have a greater say in the conduct of the firm accords not only with man's nature, but also with recent progress in the economic, social and political spheres".

Empirical evidence indicates that workers' participation in management reduces alienation, improves moral and motivation (Wickert, 1954; Beumgartel, 1956; Strauss and Rosemstein, 1970; Patchen, 1970; Poole, 1978), improves productivity (Mair, 1952; Viteles, 1953; Lawrence and Smith, 1955; Morse and Reimer, 1956; Argyle *et al.*, 1958; Juralewicz, 1974; Dachier and Wilpart, 1978; Schuster, 1983), enhances workers' job satisfaction (Tannenbaum and Allport, 1956; Vroom, 1959; French *et al.*, 1960; Lowin, 1970; White and Ruh, 1973; Allutto and Acito, 1974; Lischeron and Wall, 1975a; Lescheron and Wall, 1975b; Poole, 1978), reduces absenteeism (Argyle, 1958; Kartz *et al.*, 1983; Kartz *et al.*, 1985), affects the acceptance and effectiveness of organisational change (Maler, 1952; Bennett, 1955; March and Simon, 1958; McGrager, 1960; Likert, 1961; Lawler and Hackmen, 1969; Scheflen, *et al.*, 1971; Mulder, 1971), reduces power differences in organisations (Mulder, 1971; Mulder and Wilke, 1970; McAllister, 1982) and enhances productive efficiency, fosters industrial harmony and contributes towards employees' personality growth (Likert, 1961; Rosenfield and Smith, 1969; Derber, 1970; Mulder, 1971; Kachalhoffer, 1978). In short, this programme aims at "establishing a peaceful economic system on a democratic basis in order to ensure spontaneous co-operation between workers and management to improve organisational performance and create a general sense of dignified status among workers in the system of national economy" (Gupta, 1981: 199).

In India, since Independence, participative management has remained a major component of the country's Industrial Relations Policy. Several attempts have been made to experiment with various forms of participation, like, works committees (1947), Joint Management Councils (1958), Workers in the Board of Directors in Port Trusts (1963), Nationalised Banks (1970), Public Sector Undertakings (1971), Plant and Shop Councils (1975), and workers' participation in the management of Manufacturing and Minning Industries (1974), Commercial and Service Organizations (1977) and in Manufacturing Industries (1983). But research studies conducted in various parts of the country (for a review of these studies please see Chapter 2) have revealed that there has been very little success in promoting effective working of these participative forums, in spite of the existence of formal, legal and infrastructural facilities and spoon-feeding. With this understanding in view, the present chapter is an attempt to study objectively various vital aspects of the nature and extent of workers' participation in decision-making in the Textile Industry of Jammu and Kashmir.

The specific objectives of the chapter are as under:

(i) To study the composition and working of existing participative schemes.
(ii) To evaluate the effectiveness of these schemes and identify main barriers to participation.
(iii) To assess the existing organisational climate for participative management.
(iv) To identify the main objectives of participation as perceived by workers and management personnel.
(v) To assess the existing and desired degree of workers' influence in different types of decisions, usually taken in an organisation, at various levels.
(vi) To identify the desired mode of involving workers in decision-making at different levels.
(vii) to describe the desired forms of participations as preferred by workers and management personnel.

STRUCTURE AND WORKING OF PARTICIPATIVE FORUMS

In spite of a long and strong tradition of participative decision-making in India, the system has not received due recognition in the State of Jammu and Kashmir — both in the public and private sector enterprises. Though a number of strides has been taken in the recent past to introduce various participative forums in industries, yet the experiences on this account have not been promising except some bipartite committees working in some undertakings and those too with low level of efficiency.

The conditions with regard to participative management are to some extent better in textile industry compared with those in other industries of the State. However, there is no industry-level participative scheme and in none of the undertakings the schemes of involving workers on the Board of Directors, Equity Participation and having parity on the Board have been evolved. The participation is mostly through Joint Committees in all the Organisations under study, apart from the union involvement with management through negotiations and discussions.

Table 6.1 illustrates the details of the forums, composition and functioning of various joint committees in the sample organisations.

TABLE 6.1: Composition and Functioning of Bipartite Committees

Organization	Committees	No. of Members: Representing workers	No. of Members: Representing management	Functions
1	2	3	4	5
I	(1) Works Committee	5	5	Promote welfare facilities and safety of workers, improve work environment, production, productivity matter.
	(2) Joint Management Council	6	6	Promote effective participation of workers and management in vital matters of production, productivity, cost consciousness, working conditions
II	(1) Works Committee	5	5	Select workers for tours outside the State, work allocation, job redesign, maintenance of discipline, physical work environment
	(2) Safety Committee	5	5	Consider problems connected with accidents, suggest preventive measures, frame safety rules
	(3) Sports Committee	3	2	Organise sports and cultural activities, running of sports club
III	(1) Works Committee	5	5	Fix production targets and achievements, consider working conditions, work allocation, maintenance of discipline at lower levels
	(2) Joint Production Committee	6	6	Problems related to the improvement of production/ productivity, plan and achieve production targets, improve methods and layout processes

Contd

TABLE 6.1 *Contd.*

1	2	3	4	5
	(3) Canteen Committee	4	4	Management of Canteens, fix prices of food items, arranging the menus
IV	(1) Works Committee	5	5	Provide for effective grievance resolution machinery, fix and review production targets, improve working conditions, safety measures
V	(1) Works Committee	5	5	Promote working conditions and effective labour welfare, grievance resolution, production, raw-material, work allocation, etc.
	(2) Joint Management Council	6	6	General welfare of workers, training and development policy, eliminate wastes, dispose of grievances, improve industrial relations
	(3) Safety Committee	4	3	Promote safety consciousness, recommend measures for the improvement of medical services, safety policy formulation and review
	(4) Canteen Committee	5	7	Management of canteens, fix prices of eatables, inspect and review functioning of canteens, select contractors
	(5) House Allotment Committee	4	2	Allotment of company houses

Source: Personnel Departments of the Sample organizations.

From Table 6.1 it is clear that in all the organisations studied, works committees have been set up in accordance with the provisions of Industrial Disputes Act, 1947, and in most of the undertakings, these committees have come up in early '60s. In all the units, the committees consist of 10 members, five each representing the management and the workers. The Chairmen of the Committees in all the cases are nominated by the management and Vice-Chairmen are elected by the Committees from among the worker representatives. The works committees in all the units deal with the problems of promoting welfare facilities and safety of workers, improving working conditions, selecting workers for tours outside the State, work allocation, maintaining discipline, grievance resolution, fixing and reviewing production targets, etc. It has been reported that initially there was more enthusiasm amongst the members and the meetings were frequent, but with the lapse of time both the groups have lost their interest in these committees, the meetings became infrequent and enthusiasm seemed to have tapered off.

Joint Management Councils have been introduced as apex bodies both in Organisations I and V to oversee the functioning and progress of the shop-floor level joint committees, co-ordinate their work and set norms for their working. The councils in both the organisations consist of equal number of representatives of management and recognised unions, headed by a chairman (a management nominee) and a vice-chairman (nominee of recognised unions by rotation).

Except Organisations III and V, no other unit has set up a Canteen Committee to look after canteen service. The Canteen Committees in these two organisations consider problems connected with the management of canteens, fixing of prices of food items, arrangement of menus, selection of contractors and inspecting and reviewing the functioning of canteens.

Organisations II and V have established Safety Committees in their respective concerns at the shop-floor level, comprising of representatives from management and unions for promoting safety consciousness, recommend measures for the improvement of medical services, safety policy formulation and review, etc.

Some of the other bipartite committees functioning in sample Organisations are Sports Committee in Organisation II to organise sports and cultural activities with membership from the sports club and management, Joint Production Committee in Organisation III to consider problems relevant to the improvement of production and productivity, planning and achieving production targets, improve methods and layout of processes, etc., and House Allotment Committee, in Organisation V, to allot company houses, lay down guidelines and review policies with respect to allotment of quarters.

In short, these committees mainly aim at facilitating communication between management and workers, encourage production, promote working conditions and welfare measures, secure amity and good relations between management and workers. But the nature of these committees is advisory/consultative. Unfortunately records regarding frequency of meetings, nature and extent of settlements, physical achievements, etc., are not available in any of the sample units, which has rendered the assessment of the functioning and performance of these bipartite committees impossible. However, it has been reported that some recommendations made in various committees have materialised in subsequent implementation, particularly where top executives were involved. But on the whole, the study establishes that the participative management has not been very popular and successful in the industry. The irregularity of meetings, unsatisfactory attendance in such meetings, lack of enthusiasm about the proceedings, ineffective communication regarding these meetings and their proceedings confirm this view. It is disheartening to note that most of the workers even do not know anything about the committees, their representatives, the committee activities and decisions that have been taken by the Committees.

EFFECTIVENESS OF PARTICIPATIVE FORUMS

In order to assess the degree of effectiveness of various joint committees functioning in the sample textile units, nine parameters were selected. The respondents were asked to assert their views on degree of effectiveness as perceived by them in the form of 'high', 'moderate' and 'low'. Table 6.2 provides the results of the study in this regard.

The data in Table 6.2 suggest that a majority of the respondents, from both workers and management, of all the organisations, perceived the existing level of effectiveness of various joint committees in their organisations on almost all selected aspects, to be on the 'lower' side. Another interesting observation being a similarity of perception of both the groups.

With regard to the role of existing participative forums in increasing production, a majority of workers (53.6%) perceived 'low' effectiveness of participative forums as against only 18 per cent of them having described the performance as 'high'. Similarly, majority of the management personnel (58.4%) stated the role of joint committees in increasing production to be on the 'lower' side corresponding to only 18.3 per cent of them mentioning the performance as 'high'. In respect of joint committees' role in improving the quality of production the situation is not much different. As more than half (53.6%) of the workers described the effectiveness of joint committees to be 'low' as against only 23.6 per cent perceiving it as 'high'. Even among management personnel, the perception of 56.6 per cent remained on the 'lower' side as against a minor fraction (16.7%) having described the effectiveness of joint committees to be 'high'.

TABLE 6.2: Effectiveness of Participative Forums as Perceived by Workers and Management Personnel

Issues	Perceived degree of effectiveness (Percentage)					
	Workers (N=250)			Management personnel (N=60)		
	High	Medium	Low	High	Medium	Low
1. Increasing production/ Productivity	45 (18.0)	71 (28.4)	134 (53.6)	11 (18.3)	14 (23.3)	35 (58.4)
2. Improving quality of production	44 (17.6)	72 (28.8)	134 (53.6)	10 (16.7)	16 (26.7)	34 (56.6)
3. Reducing cost of production	59 (23.6)	69 (27.6)	122 (48.8)	14 (23.3)	17 (28.3)	29 (48.6)
4. Eliminating wastage	41 (16.4)	72 (28.8)	137 (54.8)	8 (13.3)	15 (25.0)	37 (61.7)
5. Ensuring safety	39 (15.6)	68 (27.2)	143 (57.2)	13 (21.7)	17 (28.3)	30 (50.0)
6. Improving communication	42 (16.8)	81 (32.4)	127 (50.8)	19 (31.7)	16 (26.7)	25 (41.6)
7. Reducing work stoppages	71 (28.4)	82 (32.8)	97 (38.8)	17 (28.3)	20 (33.3)	23 (38.4)
8. Satisfying workers urge for self-expression	45 (18.0)	79 (31.6)	126 (50.4)	19 (31.7)	17 (28.3)	24 (40.0)
9. Improving Labour-Management relations	65 (26.0)	64 (25.6)	121 (48.4)	19 (31.7)	18 (30.0)	23 (38.3)

Note: Figures in parentheses indicate percentage to total responses.

In assessing the joint committees' role in improving communication, a relatively higher proportion (50.8%) of workers and management personnel (41.6%) have perceived the effectiveness as 'low'. With regard to their role in reducing work stoppages, 38.8 per cent of the workers and 38.9 per cent of management personnel perceived 'low' effectiveness of joint committees.

Pertaining to the role of joint committees in reducing the cost of production more than 48 per cent of the workers and management personnel have viewed the participative forums as 'highly' ineffective. Similarly, more than half of the workers and management representatives described the effectiveness of participative forums in eliminating waste and ensuring safety to be 'low' as against a minor proportion of them perceiving it as 'high'.

Interestingly a majority of respondents from both the groups, i.e., 48.4 per cent of the rank and file and 38.3 per cent of the management representatives, have described the effectiveness of existing joint committees, in improving labour-management relation as 'low' compared to only 26 per cent workers and 31.7 per cent of the management representatives perceiving it to be 'high'. From these observations it clearly follows that participative management has not been very effective in achieving efficiency in different spheres.

BARRIERS TO PARTICIPATIVE MANAGEMENT

In the context of the majority perception of low effectiveness of joint committees, information pertaining to the unsatisfactory functioning of the schemes in the sample textile units, collected through interviewing the respondents, has been presented in the following paras:

During the study, the general complaint emerging from the workers was the "apathy of management" and their fear of giving up power. Most of them are aggrieved about the fact that because of this apathetic attitude of management towards their problems, most of the problems discussed in joint committee meetings remain unresolved. To them administration does not appear to be very enthusiastic about the whole scheme. Interestingly, the foremost cause of the ineffectiveness of the participative forums is perceived by the management to be the "apathy of workers" and their lack of training, education and competence to participate effectively in joint forums. Majority of the management representatives assert that workers, particularly union leaders, give undue importance to the element of 'power' rather than showing unanimity and positive approach to arrive at mutually agreeable solutions. The selection of worker representatives is often a problem.

In general the representatives of workers have been sore over the tendency of management to take unilateral and arbitrary decisions on certain matters, without attempting to resolve disputes through free and frank discussion. Workers have been more critical of the management's unwillingness to disclose some vital information particularly pertaining to production and finance for discussion in the meetings of joint committees. But management considers these matters as the management prerogatives and any attempt on the part of worker representatives to interrupt in these matters is thought to be irrelevant.

In addition to the above barriers, the other major constraints to participative management, as identified both by workers and management personnel, include factors, like, advisory role of joint committees and their inadequate decision-making powers, non-implementation of unanimous recommendations, limited scope of their functioning, poor communication channels, lack of conceptual and role clarity among the participants, absence of enlightened management, worker and union representatives equipped with necessary qualification, training in the specialised technique of participative management, poor industrial relations climate, existence of weak and politically dominated trade unions and lack of leadership among the work-force.

The above results of the study are in tune with most of the other earlier studies conducted in India and abroad (Patchen, 1964; Derber, 1970; Strauss and Rosenstein, 1970; for Indian studies please see Chapter 2).

It is encouraging to find that a vast majority of workers and management representatives hold strong belief that the success of workers' participation in management will depend on the sincerity, depth of conviction and openness of both management and workers. Unless the two sides are convinced at heart and feel enthusiastic about the long term benefits accruing from workers participation in decision-making, it is not possible to make it a success. There is a need for change in the attitude of both management and workers because the schemes of participative management and the question of operationalising these schemes are primarily a matter of attitude orientation. Both the groups must regard workers' participation as a step in the right direction for the overall efficiency of the Organisation in general and for improving the labour-management relation in particular. Management should not fear the fact that if it gives an inch today, it would be a yard tomorrow.

There is a legitimate role of education and training in establishing a participative climate, because the lack of knowledge, training, proper awareness and understanding of the scope and functioning of schemes of participation has given rise to much of the confusion, problems, doubts and misunderstanding between workers and management.

Many scholars hold the view that workers should have formal power in decision-making and participative management should 'really' exist. If the workers have no formal power, it is likely that the participatory structure will function at the level of a communication channel only but unlikely that effective participation will be possible. (Hovels and Nas, 1977; Poole, 1978). An additional danger lies in the mere "appearance of participation" (Havels and Nas, 1977).

In addition to the above measures, the institution of representative participative forums, with regularly scheduled, issue-oriented meetings, will produce conditions conducive to meaningful and productive joint decision-making and adequate, frequent and reliable information sharing, adequate mechanism for implementation of decisions with legislative support, proper co-ordination among different participative forums will go a long way in determining the success of the workers participation in decision-making.

ORGANISATIONAL CLIMATE FOR PARTICIPATIVE MANAGEMENT

Participative management to be possible and effective requires that the organisational climate, existing in the industries, should be conducive for participation. With a view to assess whether the organisational climate existing in the industry under study is favourable for participation or not, workers and management personnel's views on some fundamental items were obtained. The views of workers were collected on five items on a three-point scale, the results of which have been presented in Table 6.3.

TABLE 6.3: Perceived Views of Workers Towards some Fundamental Determinants of Organisational Climate for Participation

Items	Mean scores						
	Organisations					Overall Mean	
	I	II	III	IV	V	M. score	S.D.
1. Workers like their jobs	2.58	2.76	2.59	2.30	2.20	2.47	0.21
2. Their relations with supervisors/ management are cordial	2.42	2.35	2.30	2.32	2.05	2.29	0.13
3. Their relations with co-workers are cordial	2.56	2.50	2.57	2.33	2.32	2.46	0.11
4. Workers have free access to approach management in case of complaints/problems	2.60	2.12	2.20	2.80	2.00	2.34	0.30
5. The top management is supportive	2.20	2.03	2.00	1.95	1.91	2.02	0.10
Average across all items (1-5)	2.47	2.35	2.33	2.34	2.09	2.32	0.17

Note: Scoring scale: Not at all/far from being cordial = 1 to some extent fairly cordial = 2, to a great extent/very much cordial = 3.

The summary of Table 6.3 indicates that in all the units under study the workers have expressed positive views on all the items. This inference can be drawn from the mean scores which with respect to all the items exceed 2.00 implying that all the workers to some extent like their jobs, have free access to management/supervisors, enjoy the support of top management and have fairly cordial relations with their co-workers and superiors — all of these conditions being very important for the participative management to work. The Organisation wise average across all items varies from a minimum of 2.09 in Organisation V (in private sector) to a maximum of 2.47 in Organisation I (in public sector). However, the overall standard deviation (DS = 0.17) indicates that the conditions do not vary substantially and are more or less the same in all the organisations under study.

TABLE 6.4: Perceived Views of Management Personnel Towards some Fundamental Factors Determining the Organisational Climate for Participation

Items	Mean scores						
	Organisations					Overall Mean	
	I	II	III	IV	V	M. score	S.D.
1. Workers are given a share in decision-making	1.78	1.90	1.58	1.66	2.10	1.80	0.18
2. They are informed of the true situation under all conditions	2.30	21.5	1.88	2.10	2.25	2.14	0.15
3. Management does everything to keep the morale of the organisations high	2.16	2.18	1.76	1.98	2.23	2.06	0.17
4. Supervisors/managers are easily approachable	2.24	2.12	2.15	1.90	2.26	2.13	0.13
5. They train and develop workers	2.10	2.11	2.12	2.16	1.87	2.07	0.10
6. They communicate effectively with workers	2.25	2.19	2.26	2.17	2.14	2.20	0.05
7. They show thoughtfulness for others	2.22	2.17	2.15	2.11	1.92	2.11	0.10
8. They support worker when they make mistakes without their fault	2.28	1.95	2.12	2.23	2.16	2.15	0.11
9. They appreciate when workers do a good job	2.31	2.15	2.21	2.15	1.99	2.16	0.10
Average across all items (1-9)	2.18	2.10	2.02	2.05	2.10	2.09	2.12

Note: Scoring Scale: Never = 1, Sometimes = 2, Always = 3.

On the above pattern, the management representatives' views were obtained on nine items on a three-point scale. Table 6.4 illustrates the organisation-wise responses given by the management personnel.

Table 6.4 reveals that management personnel hold the view that the workers in all the organisations are practically not given a share in decision-making (x = 1.80, S.D. = 0.18). With respect to all other items the mean score exceeds 2.00 which indicates that on an average managers inform the workers the real situation, do everything possible to keep the morale of the company high, are easily approachable, counsel, train and develop workers, communicate effectively with workers, show thoughtfulness and consideration for others, support subordinates when they make mistakes without any bad intentions and express appreciation when the workers do a good job — all conditions being favourable for participative style of management. The mean score for all the items taken together varies from the lowest of 2.02 in Organisation III to the highest of 2.18 in Organisation I (both in the public sector), with an overall standard deviation of 0.12.

Thus, in all our samples support for the notion of participation is found, even allowing for the possibility that "managers may show a clear orientation in favour of participation when filling in a questionnaire but may follow a different course of action when faced with the reality of increased decision sharing" (Hespe and Wall, 1976: 419).

OBJECTIVES OF PARTICIPATIVE MANAGEMENT

Critical review of research earlier in this study bears testimony to the fact that one popular barrier to the success of participative management has been the lack of conceptual clarity and incongruent objectives of participative management of those concerned with the functioning of the scheme. In order to ascertain to what extent they are aware of the objectives of participation, the respondents both from the management and rank and file were given 11 alternative objectives and were required to express their views on these alternatives on a five-point scale. Table 6.5 shows the first five objectives of participative management as perceived by the respondents.

The break-up of the responses given in Table 6.5 reveals that amongst the first five objectives identified by both the groups of respondents, there were three common objectives. Both the groups have identified "increase in productivity, improvement in job

TABLE 6.5: Objectives of Participative Management — Perceived Ranking by Workers and Management Personnel

First Five Ranks	Workers (N=250)			Management Personnel (N=60)		
	Objectives	Total score	Percentage of maximum possible score	Objectives	Total score	Percentage of maximum possible score
I.	Increase productivity, improve job satisfaction, and reduce waste	1,025	82.00	Increase productivity, improve job satisfaction, and reduce waste	250	83,33
II.	Provide more peaceful superior-subordinate and union-management relations	830	66.40	Improve team work	191	63.67
III.	Improve the quality of management decision-making	730	58.40	Provide more peaceful superior-subordinate and union management relations	160	53.33
IV.	Improve team work	533	42.64	Increase workers commitment to the organisation	113	37.67
V.	Derive better amenities and service conditions for workers, providing them control over the decision-making process	370	29.60	Improve communication	78	26.00

Notes: 1. Results presented here are the values of all the organisations' studies.
2. Overall ranking is based on percentage of maximum possible scores obtained.
3. Maximum possible score = N × 5.
4. Scoring scale adopted is as follows: Not at all = 1, Slightly=2, Moderately=3, Considerably=4, Completely=5.

satisfaction reduction in waste and decrease in absenteeism" as the number one objective of participative management, the scores obtained being more than 80 per cent of the maximum possible scores for each group. "Providing more peaceful superior subordinate and union-management relations" and "improve team work" were identified to be the other two main objectives by workers and management. With regard to other two objectives, workers feel that "improving the quality of managerial decisions" and "deriving better amenities and service conditions for workers" are two of the first five objectives, whereas management representatives have identified "increase workers commitment to the organisation" and "improve communication" as the other objectives. The other objectives (not tabulated) in order of importance as perceived by both the groups include obtaining a sense of involvement, developing workers to accept change, developing greater trust on management and helping the workers to know the running of an industry and thereby providing a democratic set up.

The results reported above make an interesting revelation that the different categories of respondents have perceived many common aims and objectives of workers participation in management. Although, various schemes of participative management, as stated earlier, have not succeeded in the industry, but these findings provide sufficient evidence to the fact that participative management, if meaningfully designed and utilized, can serve a number of purposes, all geared to improve the organisational effectiveness, efficiency and satisfaction of the workers.

WORKERS' INFLUENCE IN DECISION-MAKING

This section attempts to assess the attitude of workers and management towards different levels and modes of participation and at the same time to explore the relationship between the amount of participation that the workers had (existing) and the amount they should have (desired) as perceived by workers and management personnel. For this purpose a scale consisting of 21 one decision items (see Annexure IV) was adopted from Hespe and Wall (1976) and Wall and Lischeron (1977). Certain modification in decision items were, however, made so as to suit the local conditions. Depending upon the level of management where these decisions are taken and the specific nature of the decision items, these decision items were clubbed into four categories:

a. Distant level participation issues
b. Medium level participation issues
c. Local level participation issues and
d. All level co-operation issues.

To each item, the respondents were required to give two responses on a five-point scale indicating the amount of influence which they felt the workers presently possess and the amount of influence they felt the workers should have. A distinction was made between the existing and desired degree of influence on different issues.

The subjects' responses to each item at each level of participation were summed up to yield average mean score indicating their existing and desired influence for different levels of participation. As a summary of findings, the existing and desired mean scores of workers and management personnel have been presented in Table 6.6 and their differences in Table 6.7 respectively.

TABLE 6.6: Degree of Workers Influence in Different Levels of Decision-making as Perceived by Workers and Management Personnel

Decision areas	Mean score of workers (N = 250)					Mean score of management personnel (N = 60)				
	Existing (Wx_E)	Desired (Wx_D)	Difference (Wx_D-Wx_E)	t-Value	P	Existing (Wx_E)	Desired (Mx_D)	Difference (Mx_D-Wx_E)	t-Value	P
1. Distant level participation	1.79	3.32	1.53	14.41	<.01	1.50	2.15	0.65	3.26	<.05
2. Medium level participation	2.07	3.84	1.77	16.35	<.01	2.82	3.28	0.46	3.12	<.05
3. Local level participation	1.98	3.98	2.00	21.58	<.01	2.73	3.55	0.82	3.63	<.01
4. All level co operation issues	1.88	3.39	1.51	14.80	<.01	2.57	3.07	0.50	2.32	<.05
5. All areas taken together	1.93	3.36	1.70	16.30	<.01	2.14	3.01	0.60	2.55	<.01

Note: For notes please see Table 6.7.

TABLE 6.7: Differences in Mean Responses of Workers and Management Personnel to Workers' Influence in Decision-making

Decision area	Difference between existing mean scores of workers and management personnel ($Wx_E - Mx_E$)	t-value	P	Difference between desired mean scores of workers and management personnel ($Wx_D - Mx_D$)	t-value	P
1. Distant level participation	0.29	1.95	<.05	1.17	6.32	<.01
2. Medium level participation	-0.75	4.36	<.01	0.56	3.20	<.01
3. Local level participation	-0.75	4.50	<.01	0.43	3.03	<.01
4. All level co-operation issues	-0.69	4.75	<.01	0.32	1.75	<.05
5. All areas taken together	-0.48	2.95	<.01	0.62	3.46	<.01

Notes: 1. The score presented in the average mean score for all items in each category of issues.

2. When management personnel's score is more than that of workers (-) sign is used and *vice versa*.
3. Existing scoring scale: No influence = 1, Very little influence = 2, Influence to some extent = 3, Quite a lot of influence = 4, Influence to a great extent = 5.
4. Desired scoring scale: Not at all = 1, Slightly = 2, Moderately = 3, Considerably = 4, Completely = 5.

Distant Level Participation

Distant level participation refers to workers' involvement in higher levels of organisational decision-making, traditionally falling within the scope of top management. The decisions involved are typically less directly relevant to workers' own job activities but of greater concern to the organisation as a whole. As revealed by Table 6.6, the existing mean score across all items of distant level participation is 1.79 indicating that workers had virtually no influence or very little influence in the distant level decision areas. The comparatively higher desired mean score (x = 3.32) exhibited a strong desire of the workers for participation in these decision areas. The difference between the existing and desired mean scores of workers is statistically significant (P < .01).The average mean score of the management personnel (x = 1.50) depicts that they also perceived that the workers had very little influence over distant level participation issues. But they felt that their influence in these decision areas should be much more than what they currently have (x = 2.15). The difference of the average mean scores in this case is statistically significant beyond five per cent level of confidence.

Medium Level Participation

Medium level participation refers to employee involvement in decision areas, normally made at the middle level within the organisational hierarchy, typically involving middle managers. The data reveal that workers have very little influence over the decision areas in the middle level (x = 2.07), but across all the items, majority of workers (x = 3.84) expressed a preference for considerable influence over these decision-making areas. The difference of mean scores, being statistically significant (P < .01), indicates that the ideal influence of workers in the medium level decision areas was far from practice. Management personnel also felt that the workers should have more influence in these decision areas than the existing level. This inference can be drawn from the average desired mean score (x = 3.28) which exceeds the average existing mean score (x = 2.82). The difference of these mean scores is again statistically significant beyond five per cent level of confidence.

Local Level Participation

Local level participation also referred to as immediate level participation (Wall and Lischerson, 1977) occurres when workers take part in decision-making at the lowest level of organisational hierarchy involving supervisors and first line managers. Such decisions concentrate on day to day problems having immediate relevance to workers' own job. In the industry under study, workers had little influence in local level decision areas (x = 1.98) but there existed, among the workers, considerable agreement concerning their desire for local level participation (x = 3.98). The difference between the exiting and desired mean scores across all the local level decision items (P < .01) reflects the overall discrepancy between the degree of influence the workers have and the degree they would like to have at this level. The significant difference (P < .01) between the management personnels' desired mean score (x = 3.55) and existing mean score (x = 2.73) reveals that management personnel too perceived that the workers should have much more influence in these decisions than they possess at present.

All Level Co-operation Issues

Decision-making on certain issues in the organisations, requiring co-operation of workers and management at all levels, such as introduction of new technology and increase of production, has been referred to as "all level co-operation issue participation". Nearly all the workers under study expressed. Their opinion on the first two points of the scale indicating that they had very little or no influence at all in these decision issues (x = 1.88). In contrast to their perception, they exhibited a very high desire for influence in these areas. The management personnels' existing (x = 2.57) and desired (x = 3.07) mean scores in this regard also differed significantly ($P < .05$) implying thereby, that management personnel agree with the workers' view points on this account.

An Overview

Summarising the results contained in Tables 6.6 and 6.7, it can be concluded that workers and management personnel perceive that workers in their organisations had very little influence over all categories of issues. However, both the groups indicated that the level of workers influence should be more than what they currently have, which is evident from the fact that the average desired mean scores in all the categories (except distant level participation in case of management personnel) exceed 3.00. Workers showed maximum desire to participate in medium and local levels' issues and minimum in distant level issues and issues which require co-operation at all levels whereas management personnel also expressed maximum interest to accept workers influence in medium and local level issues. They also expressed substantial interest to accept workers influence in all level co-operation issues. The degree of congruence between the desired level of workers influence as perceived by workers and management personnel in medium level issues, local level issues and all level co-operation issues argue well for the possibility of genuine participation in these issues, excepting distant level issues, which have traditionally been regarded as "jealously guarded prerogatives of management" (Mannon, 1984).

An interesting observation of the study (Table 6.7) is that the perception of management personnel about the existing level of workers' influence was much higher than the workers' own perception about the existing level of influence in all the categories (except distant level issues), the difference being significant (for all issues $P < .01$). In comparison, management personnel desired much less influence than workers in all the categories of decision items. The differences of mean desired influence scores in all the issues between workers and management are statistically significant. ($P < .01 - P < .05$), which confirms the general belief that management does not like much influence by workers in managerial decision-making and more so in distant level decision items.

Several other studies in both socialist and the capitalist countries have also shown a high desire on the part of workers in participative decision-making (Walker, 1972; Patchen, 1970). In Indian context, Kane and Singh (1967), Alexander (1972), Ramssay (1976), Batnagar (1977), Aziz (1978), Arya (1980), Sahu (1981), Bisht (1986), Indira and Harigopal (1985) assert that the interest of workers to participate in management is fairly high in India.

Most of the investigators seem to agree that workers are not interested in participation at higher levels of organisational decision-making, but want more participation in decisions which affect their own work (Morse, 1953; Katz, 1954; Blauner, 1964; Holter, 1965; Foster, *et al.*, 1970; Hespe and Wall, 1971; Hespe and Little, 1971). In Indian context, that if we have to give an organisational form to the idea of labour participation in management, with a view to make a success of it, the beginning will have to be made gradually starting from the production level and create at the shop floor level a sense of identification with the organisation. Only after this new attitude has been successfully developed at the shop floor level, should the participation in management be extended to the next higher level. If we begin from the top straight away without adequate preparations and without remoulding the attitudes of both labour and management, the board level will become the venue of such acrimonious battles on the 'division of cake' that there would be neither the atmosphere nor the opportunity to attend in a collective manner to the problems of 'producing the cake' itself (Patil, 1976: 52)

Contrary to the above views, Schregle (1976) feels that "workers' participation in initiatives, to be successful, must come from all levels and from all sides, if possible simultaneously. The problem is to co-ordinate their various limitations properly and weld them into a coherent whole". There are still quite a few commentators who believe that there is much less evidence of widespread and intense interest of workers in participating in management decision-making and conclude that educating workers to think in participative terms is essential before more progress could be achieved (Haire, *et al.*, 1966; Derber, 1970; Guest and Fatchett, 1974).

DESIRED MODE OF INVOLVEMENT IN DECISION-MAKING

With a view to measure, the mode of participation/involvement desired at each level, a scale was used which required the respondents to indicate one of the following six alternative ways of involving workers in decision-making, they preferred, for each of 21 decision issues:

(a) this is a management prerogative,
(b) information sharing,
(c) consultation,
(d) joint decision-making,
(e) collective bargaining, and
(f) workers say to be accepted.

Collective bargaining has been incorporated as one of the alternatives by various scholars because through collective bargaining workers can influence the management decisions at least with regard to their interest related items (Schregle, 1976; Mills, 1978; Sahu, 1980; Mannon, 1984; Lall, 1984).

Table 6.8 illustrates the summary of the results for each category of issues.

The results of the responses in Table 6.8 depict that except for distant level decision issues, both the groups have preferred for joint decision-making and consultation. Majority of the workers (36.4%) and management personnel (61.7%) considered the distant level participation issues as management prerogative. But both the groups showed considerable desire for joint decision-making and consultation in medium level issues, local level issues and issues which require co-operation at all levels, indicating that greater amount of involvement of workers in these important issues of immediate interest

TABLE 6.8: Desired Mode of Involvement/Participation in Decision-making in Different Categories of Issues (Only First Four Ranks in Terms of Percentage of Respondents have been Tabulated)

Categories of issues	Workers (N=250)			Management Personnel (N=60)		
	Ranks	Mode of involvement	Percentage preferred	Ranks	Mode of involvement	Percentage preferred
(a) Distant level participation issues	1	Management prerogative	36.4	1	Management prerogative	61.7
	2	Consultation	29.2	2	Information sharing	20.0
	3	Information sharing	20.8	3	Consultation	8.3
	4	Joint decision-making	9.6	4	Joint decision-making	9.7
(b) Medium level participation issues	1	Joint decision-making	46.4	1	Joint decision-making	46.7
	2	Collective bargaining	31.2	2	Consultation	23.3
	3	Consultation	12.8	3	Collective bargaining	15.0
	4	Workers say to be accepted	6.4	4	Management prerogative	11.7
(c) Local level participation issues	1	Joint decision-making	51.6	1	Joint decision-making	52.7
	2	Consultation	28.8	2	Information sharing	16.6
	3	Information sharing	12.4	3	Consultation	15.0
	4	Collective bargaining	6.0	4	Collective bargaining	10.0
(d) All level co-operation issues	1	Consultation	41.6	1	Consultation	45.0
	2	Joint decision-making	26.4	2	Management prerogative	21.6
	3	Information sharing	19.2	3	Information sharing	16.7
	4	Management prerogative	6.4	4	Joint decision-making	13.3

Notes. 1. Results presented here represent the values of all the organisations studied.
2. For details of the decision areas please see Annexure IV.

to workers is possible. Medium level and all level co-operation issues have also been considered to be the management prerogatives by 11.7 per cent and 21.6 per cent management personnel, respectively. But the rest agreed to allow collective bargaining and information sharing at these levels in addition to joint decision-making and joint consultation. Except 6.4 per cent workers in medium level participation none from both the groups of respondents opted for "workers say to be accepted". A sizable percentage of worker respondents have also preferred workers' participation at various levels through collective bargaining and information sharing.

From the above analysis it clearly follows that neither the workers, nor the management were in favour of full control of workers in any category of decision area. Management, however, does not want to share the decision-making powers in respect of various policy issues in distant level participation as well as in introducing new technology and increasing productivity – all of which have overall organisational implications. Interestingly, the workers' views also support this to a considerable extent. But they are in favour of information sharing and consultation in these decision areas. But if in due course the success of participation is desired, it cannot be restricted to immediate level and local level issues only. It has been widely accepted that once participation has its proper footing in medium level and local level issues, it is expected that a climate will be created in the organisation for consultation or joint decision-making in distant level issues also. To start with, management should take care to have effective information sharing on decision items of distant level issues also (Alexander, 1972; Schrigle, 1976; Sahu, 1980; 1981; Lall, 1984; Mannon, 1984), a finding corroborated by the findings of our present study.

DESIRED FORMS OF PARTICIPATIVE MANAGEMENT

In the present study in order to assess the desired forms of participation in decision-making, as preferred by workers and management personnel, a total of seven different forms of participation, both formal and informal, were given and the respondents were asked to indicate on a five-point scale as to what extent they preferred these forms taking into consideration the whole gamut of decisions generally taken in an organisation, the results of which have been exhibited in Table 6.9.

TABLE 6.9: **Desired Forms of Participative Management as Perceived by Workers and Management Personnel**

	Alternative forms	Workers (N=250)			Management Personnel (N=60)		
		Score	Percentage of max. score	Rank	Score	Percentage of max. score	Rank
1.	Having one or two workers nominated to the Board of Directors	830	66.4	II	93	31.0	VI
2.	Workers' purchasing shares and representing in the Board	752	60.2	III	103	34.3	V
3.	Having parity in the Board	324	25.9	VI	71	23.6	VII
4.	Having workers representatives in various joint committees at different levels	962	76.9	I	215	71.7	I
5.	Union officials/ representatives only representing in various joint committees	531	42.5	V	178	59.3	II
6.	Various suggestion schemes	272	21.8	VII	122	40.6	IV
7.	Informal face to face sharing of decision-making at work place, job enrichment, participative style of supervision, etc.	581	46.5	IV	155	51.7	III

Note: Scoring Scale: Do not prefer at all = 1, prefer slightly = 2, moderately = 3, considerably = 4, completely = 5.

An analysis of Table 6.9 reveals that both workers and management personnel have identified "workers' representatives in joint committees" at different levels as the first preferred form of participation. Workers showed strong desire for the workers' representation on the board and equity participation (as the 2nd and 3rd preference, respectively). But the management personnels' support was least for these forms of participation. The idea of having parity in the board has received very poor response from both the groups of respondents. Management gave second preference to the representation of union officials/representatives in various joint committees whereas workers gave fifth rank to this form presumably because they do not find union representatives to represent in join committees feasible in the existing state of poor, uneducated and political unionism in the textile industry of the State. Both the groups have given much importance to informal face to face sharing to decision-making at work place. A sizable number of management representatives also preferred participation through various suggestion schemes, but the workers prefer it as the last alternative only.

It is clear from the above account that the management in the State's textile industry does not prefer involving the workers in equity participation, but on the other hand, the workers do have a feeling that unless they own major share of the company, their views at the board level may not have much meaning. Supporting these viewpoints, Sherwani (1976), Tandon (1976) and Rao (1977) feel that the workers ownership (equity participation) is the best form of workers participation because through such a participation there will be no tension between management and workers, no strikes and a realisation amongst workers of the benefits of productivity and profitability, development of a sense of involvement and participation in the affairs of the company.

However, as rightly put, "whatever steps are taken to involve workers' representatives in the decision-making process at higher management levels, they must be supplemented by arrangements for associating rank and file workers with decisions that are taken at the shop floor level and that affect them directly (Sahu, 1985). However, workers' participation at shop floor level and other informal methods of participation must not be seen in isolation but as a part of a more general process of workers' participation at various levels, including, where appropriate, works councils, workers' representation on the Company Boards and, above all, collective bargaining." (Schregle, 1976).

CONCLUSION

The summary of the results of the investigation cited above indicates that though various schemes of workers participation in decision-making, mostly consisting of joint committees, have been set up in all the organisations under study, but the schemes have not shown desired results due to various constraints. But it is heartening and encouraging to find that a vast majority of both workers and management continue to attach high hopes with the scheme. The workers and management personnel perceived most of the common objectives and as per their perception, the organisational climate existing in the industry is also quite conducive for participation, implying that participative management if properly and sincerely designed and utilized can achieve the desired success.

There is near unanimity between the workers and management representatives that workers have a low degree of influence in decision-making at all levels and it is revealing to find that both the groups exhibit a strong desire for involving workers in decision-making particularly at medium and local levels of organisational hierarchy. Except distant level participation issues both the groups desired to arrive at decisions through joint consultation and information sharing. While as both the groups feel that distant level participation issues are "management prerogative". Under the existing conditions both the groups of respondents preferred to have joint committees at different levels involving worker representatives rather than union representatives.

Workers' participation in decision-making, as one of the viable methods of establishing cordial labour-management relations, to be successful, needs sincerity and openness of both the participants. The participative forums should be used as joint decision-making forums and not as consultative forums only. Further, proper training and education of workers, change in the attitude of participants, adequate legal and government support, timely implementation of recommendations, effective grievance machinery, proper communication system will go a long way in determining the success of workers' participation. The success stories of participative management in TISCO, BHEL, Central Coal Fields etc., should be given wide publicity in the industry. Production and productivity, working conditions, employee welfare, shop floor relation matters, training and development and employee relations are the possible fields in which workers' participation can be tried with success.

The scholars are almost unanimous on the fact that one of the seriously disturbing factors for the success of participative management is weak, multiple and politicalised trade unionism. As such united, strong, trained and responsible trade unions with sound leadership are indispensable for creating permissible environment for participation. Such vigorous, well-organised and recognised representative unions will avoid any division between the negotiative and consultative functions of the unions. Further, till a strong system of participative management is evolved, trade unions would continue to play an increasingly important role in settling the dispute through negotiations and discussions with the management. With this understanding in view, the next chapter of the study is devoted to the study of various aspects of the trade unionism in the textile industry of the State.

7

TRADE UNIONISM

INTRODUCTION

THE TYPE and character of Industrial relations scene obtaining in any country, region or the industry is determined by certain related institutions — the employers' and employees' organisations and the State policy. Therefore, any study of industrial relations in proper perspective needs to be undertaken against the background of these actors. The study of the growth and development of trade unions, being the most important aspect of the Industrial Relations System, is much more pertinent.

The right to unionise on the part of workers and to strive for their socio-economic betterment, either through negotiations or militant methods, is today not only guaranteed by legislation but also duly accepted and recognised by all the sections of society both in democratic and communist countries of the world. There is a firm and widespread conviction about the absolute necessity of trade unions for fostering and maintaining harmonious relationship between labour and management.

The trade union movement now covers all the categories of workers — gazetted and non-gazetted, low-paid and high-paid, blue-collar and white-collar and even policemen in the uniform. Our democratic constitution, international acknowledgement of human rights, enormous growth in the size of labour force with the growing industrialisation, steady process of urbanisation and spread of education, have mainly contributed to such an enormous boost to trade unionism.

A critical review of research (see Chapter 2) amply demonstrates that the analysis of trade unionism and its different aspects, enjoy an enviable position among the issues discussed in the literature on industrial relations in India. But no attempt has so far been made to study the nature and extent of trade unionism in Textile Industry of

Jammu and Kashmir State. The present study intends to make a modest attempt in this direction, the objectives of which have been set as follows:

1. To examine the State level trade union background by exploring its origin, growth and structure.
2. To trace the genesis, growth, structure and extend of trade unionism in Textile Industry of Jammu and Kashmir.
3. To make a motivational analysis of union membership and explore its correlates.
4. To ascertain the extent of participation and involvement of union members in union activities and examine its determinants.

GROWTH AND STRUCTURE OF TRADE UNIONISM IN JAMMU AND KASHMIR

A Historical Perspective

The origin and growth of labour movement in Jammu and Kashmir State is traceable as far back as 1865, when the Shawl Weavers of Kashmir organised themselves to revolt against their *Karakhandars*. On 29th April, 1865, the shawl weavers marched out in procession towards 'Zaldagar' (a locality in Srinagar) to forward their memorandum of demands to the authorities. But before the processionists had ended their deliberations, the cavalry swooped on the unarmed and unguarded labourers, surrounded them and then charged with guns and spears. After some deaths, the processionists ran towards a bridge, where they were trapped. It is stated that 29 of them were drowned in the marshy canal, four of their leaders were arrested and imprisoned till their death (Jalali, 1972: 33). Thus, this first sign of labour movement was immediately suppressed.

The labour rising of the silk factory in Kashmir in 1924, because of severe socio-economic grievances, marked another important milestone in trade union history of the State (Fazli, 1980: 28). The rising was, however, ruthlessly crushed, partly because of the excessive use of military force and partly due to the lack of leadership among the working class, absence of an organisation structure, cohesion, solidarity and discipline among the working class.

Like their counterparts in British India Provinces, the labouring class in the State could not evolve an organised movement due to the governmental ban on the formation of associations. Besides poverty, backwardness and illiteracy were so abysmal that they just could not organise themselves into unions and subscribe to them. The leadership also did not play effective role in the growth and development of an organised and institutional labour movement in the State. This state of affairs continued till 1937.

In Jammu and Kashmir State, the workers were organised for the first time under the "Mazdoor Sabha", which came into being in the middle of 1937, through the efforts of a group of young comrades whose mental outlook and political connections were in contact with some Indian socialists, like, comrade Bedi (Khan, 1980: 336). A large number of workers became its members irrespective of religion, caste and creed. Silk factory workers' strikes on 19th August and 7th September of 1937 on the factory premises, the rally on 13th September, 1937 at Partap Park, Srinagar, in which about five thousand workers participated, the important meeting on 18th September, 1937, in Srinagar, in which the significance of the labour movement in the State was highlighted, were some of the demonstrations held under the banner of Mazdoor Sabha (Khan, 1980).

On 4 October, 1937, the Sabha organised a grand joint procession of the industrial workers and peasants. The special feature of the procession was the demonstration of red banners and flags for the first time. The banners contained new slogans and demands of purely economic character, such as "A labour is a human being", "Slavery is curse", "We want two-time meals", "Slavery does not profess any religion", "Give bread to the hungry and clothes to the naked". These slogans reflected hitherto deeply repressed aspirations of workers.

The activities of the Mazdoor Sabha in Kashmir markedly influenced the workers of the Jammu province. The beginning of 1938 saw the establishment of the labour union in Jammu for the first time. By the end of January 1938, The union had enrolled more than 160 regular workers (Mattoo and Gani, 1987). In short, Mazdoor Sabha, with all the sufferings it had to undergo, made a creditable contribution to the trade union movement of the State and assumed a great momentum as a force to be reckoned with.

While in rest of the country, factory system of oraganisation led to the creation of trade unionism, an altogether different situation is found in the case of Jammu and Kashmir State. The trade union movement in the State owes its origin to the Nationalist Movement which came into being after 1938. The organised working class formed the strongest organ of the National Movement, led by National Conference, between 1940-50, under the banner of Central Labour Union which was created in 1942 (Mattoo, 1976). Another important development of early '40s was the organisation of trade unions by the working class in silk factory, the Karan Singh Woollen Mills, the Municipal Workers and Workers in many other establishments. Early in 1944, a control organisation known as Kashmir Mazdoor Union was established to co-ordinate and lead all its constituent trade unions (Raina, 1978: 12).

Although the Jammu and Kashmir Trade Unions Act, 2006 (Svt.) was already enacted to govern the legal position of trade unions in the State, yet the same was not enforced till 1953, when it was amended and brought at par with the Central Trade Unions Act of 1926. The scope of the Act was further widened by an Amending Act of 1961, as a result of which it became obligatory on the part of employers to accord recognition to the trade unions. Accordingly "Water Workers Union" in Kashmir was the first union registered in the State in 1953, followed by "Hanjian Kashmir Valley Food Control Union", Srinagar, in the same year.

The above developments clearly reveal that the unity among the workers was no doubt visible to a large extent much before Independence, but the unions existing during the period in the State were weak both financially and organisationally. The movement was rather slow as compared to the development of the movement in other States of the country. This slow growth of trade unionism in the States was attributed to a host of adverse conditions, such as the industrial backwardness lower level of education, workers' unlettered and unconsciousness of their rights and utility of collective strength, absence of efficient and independent leadership, pressure of unemployment, unsympathetic attitude of authorities, absence of legislation promoting labour organisation and above all the higher degree of political domination of trade unions.

The Present Scenario

The trade unionism in the State of Jammu and Kashmir saw a phenomenal growth after the State took to economic planning. Increasing industrialisation, expanding proportion of labour force from within and outside the State, increasing cost of living, growing trade union consciousness, increasing rate of literacy among the workers are some of the most effective causes that led to a tremendous growth in trade unionism in the State. The trade unions have increased enormously both in number and membership. As against just 17 registered trade unions in 1954, the number has gone up to 626 in 1986, with a corresponding increase in membership from 2,922 to 60,332 during the same period. The data pertaining to the period under study, i.e., 1970-1986, are set out in Table 7.1.

TABLE 7.1: Growth of Trade Unions and Their Membership, 1970-86

Year	No. of registered unions (N)	Index number of registered (1970=100)	Union member-ship (M)	Index of union membership (1970=100)	Average membership per union
1970	212	100	32,800	100	155
1971	237	112	34,345	105	145
1972	250	118	35,988	110	144
1973	285	134	37,879	115	133
1974	325	153	42,053	128	129
1975	361	170	45,735	139	127
1976	376	177	46,374	141	123
1977	391	184	46,848	143	120
1978	417	197	48,204	147	116
1979	434	205	49,370	150	114
1980	466	220	52,274	159	112
1981	502	237	53,849	164	107
1982	516	243	54,600	166	106
1983	539	254	55,692	170	103
1984	560	264	57,247	174	102
1985	597	282	58,925	180	99
1986	626	295	60,332	184	96

Source: Jammu and Kashmir Handbook of Labour Statistics, Department of Labour, Govt. of Jammu and Kashmir, Srinagar, March 1986, p.68.

Table 7.1 clearly depicts that the index of the number of registered unions as well as their membership has been steadily going up. The trade unions, during the period of 17 years, have increased by more than 295 per cent. In absolute terms the number rose from 212 in 1970 to 626 in 1986. The trade union membership swelled up from 32,800 to 60,332 during the same period, registering an increase by 184 per cent with 1970 as the base year. However, the trend in the average membership of unions, which is the most important determinant of the strength of unionism has been continuously declining. As the Table 7.1

indicates, the average membership of the registered unions which was 155 in 1970 declined to 96 in 1986. This steady decline is mainly due to the substantial increase in the number of unions without proportionate increase in membership. "Relatively faster growth in the number of small unions is the result of two unrelated tendencies. One is the fragmentation of membership, due to the formation of rival unions in the same bargaining territory. The other is the creation of plant unions, particularly in the medium and small scale enterprises" (Johri, 1967: 60). These statistics, therefore, indicate that while the population of trade unions in the State has grown enormously, the degree of membership has lagged behind. The overall effect has been the expansion by size and in space, but a general weakening of quality.

Inter-industry and Inter-district Variations in Unionisation

The industry-cum-district-wise distribution of trade unions in Jammu and Kashmir is provided in Table 7.2 The districts have been ranked from the highest to the lowest for the number of unions on register in 1986.

Table 7.2 interestingly reveals that the "Miscellaneous group" of industries, consisting of a large number of small units, like handicrafts, industrial estates, shops and establishments, printing and publicity, leather and leather products, migrant workers, etc., has the highest degree of unionisation and accounted for over 26 per cent of the total registered union in 1986. Next to it in order of importance are Engineering and Construction, Transport and Automobile, Textiles Banking, Insurance and Allied Services, which account for 12.9 per cent, 12.8 per cent, 12.5 per cent and 11.3 per cent of the total number of unions, respectively. In manufacturing sector, textile industry is highly unionised and enjoys substantial proportion of the total membership of trade unions in the State. The other sectors including minerals, cements, chemicals and drugs, food and hotels, forests and furniture have also been unionised to a large extent.

In view of the performance of individual districts of the State, as revealed by Table 7.2, Srinagar emerges as having the highest degree of unionisation which accounts for more than 50 per cent of the total unions on register in 1986, followed by Jammu district with about 20 per cent share of total unions. This is due to the high rate of industrialisation, high rate of literacy and union consciousness and the fact that almost every sector of employment is unionised in these

TABLE 7.2: Industry-wise and District-wise Distribution of Trade Unions, 1986

Districts	Industry									
	Textiles	Engineering and construction	Food, drinks and hotels	Minerals, chemicals and drugs	Banking Insurance & allied services	Agriculture forests and furniture	Transport and automobiles	Miscellaneous group	Total	Percent to the total
1. Srinagar	43	28	20	35	45	19	40	89	319	50.9
2. Jammu	14	10	8	14	21	6	18	36	127	20.3
3. Baramulla	2	7	4	—	4	2	14	20	53	8.5
4. Anantnag	3	8	6	1	1	3	4	8	34	5:4
5. Pulwama	8	2	—	9	—	7	2	3	31	4.9
6. Udampur	—	14	—	2	—	1	—	1	18	2.9
7. Kathua	6	4	—	—	—	—	—	3	13	2.1
8. Poonch	2	2	2	—	—	2	1	3	12	1.9
9. Budgam	—	2	5	—	—	—	—	—	7.	1.1
10. Doda	—	2	—	—	—	2	—	1	5	0.8
11. Rajouri	1	—	3	—	—	—	—	—	4	0.6
12. Kupwara	—	1	—	—	—	—	—	1	2	0.3
13. Leh	—	—	—	—	—	—	1	—	1	0.2
14. Kargil	—	—	—	—	—	—	—	—	—	—
Total	78	81	45	64	71	42	80	165	626	100
Percentage to the total	12.5	12.9	7.2	10.2	11.3	6.7	12.8	26.4	100	

Source: Compiled from the official records of Registrar of Trade Unions in Jammu and Kashmir, Srinagar.

districts. Districts of Baramulla, Anantnag and Pulwama can be described as low unionised districts in terms of overall trend of unionisation. In these districts the trade union penetration is significantly less while the remaining districts happen to be the least unionised districts of the State.

Role of Central Organisations of Workers

Different Central organisations of workers such as INTUC, AITUC and BMS have started taking active interest to organise the workers of the State, on their respective lines. The data on the number of unions affiliated to these organisations and their verified membership in 1981 is reported in Table 7.3 However, industry-wise and year-wise position of these Central trade union centres in the State is not possible due to the paucity of relevant data.

TABLE 7.3: Central Trade Union Organisations and Their Verified Membership in Jammu & Kashmir

Sl. No.	Trade union organisations	No. of union affiliated	Verified memb-ership
1.	B.M.S.	6	4,364
2.	A.I.T.U.C.	3	174
3.	I.N.T.U.C.	1	248

Source: Master Reference Book on Labour Statistics, Labour Bureau, Chandigarh, 1984, pp. 322-25.

Table 7.3 presents a peculiar feature of trade union affiliation in the State. In spite of greater strides of national trade union federations, majority of the unions in the State have not affiliated themselves to any of these centres. Only a few trade unions are affiliated to BMS and AITUC which are mainly confined to Jammu and its suburb areas. INTUC, which dominates the trade union movement in entire India has not any substantial hold on the Trade Union Movement of the State, where as HMS and UTUC have not even made their beginning.

It is agreed that "the links between the national federations and regional/local unions are very important in a federal system not only because the regional and local unions get the lead and the support from the national federations in the time of struggle but also because these provide policy guidelines to the regional/local unions so that there will be uniform policy followed by the trade unions affilliated to a particular federation which ensures better solidarity among the group of unions (Nagaraju, (1981: 107). But as is evident from the above account, the Central trade union centres have yet to gain ground in the State.

The trade Union Movement in Jammu and Kashmir is controlled by a State level federation, called the State Central Labour Union, which was established in 1942. This central apex body is quite often politically in line with the State Government. With the change of political party ruling the State, there have been changes in this union also. Even now, there are two rival State Central Labour Unions, under the control of two factions of National Conference. The presence of these two unions under different political groups has always been a source of trouble most of the industries in the State particularly in the State sector. But the magnitude of the problem that is posed by the rivalry between the political factions in Jammu and Kashmir is very much less or almost insignificant compared to that in industries located in West Bengal, Bihar or even other States of the country (Karim, 1972: 269).

An Evaluation

It may be observed from the above discussion that Trade Union Movement in Jammu and Kashmir is passing through an evolutionary stage. Unions in general are free from many evils which have otherwise plagued the Trade Union Movement of the country. Militancy, violence and inter-union rivalry did not creep in the ranks of unions, which reflects the infant character of the movement, which has to be encouraged and protected. Today almost all major manufacturing industries, trades and occupations have been unionised. But a large number of workers in the unorganised sector has generally remained outside the fold of trade unionism. This is obvious from the fact that the work-force in the manufacturing and service sectors of the State according to 1981 census was of the order of 7.21 lakh. But the total union membership in 1981 accounted for only 53,840 leaving a gap of non-unionised membership of over 6,67,000.

Industry-cum-region unions are rarely found in the State. The main reasons for the absence of such unions of the type found in Bombay, Ahmedabad, Kanpur, Sholapore, Madras and other industrial centres in India, are the lack of concentration of certain industries in particular areas. A large number are primary unions, or, what they are called in American terminology, the "locals" or plant level unions. The overwhelming majority of the trade unions is very small in size, which is one of the major weaknesses of the State Trade Union Movement.

There is, however, some difference between the activities of the unions in old units and the new ones. The newer units, where labour coming from outside the State is employed in large numbers, have been more restive than the older units and violent troubles have taken place due to the greater degree of their exposure to union activities outside the State.

Industrial peace in the State has so far been bought by concessions, which does not allow the trade unions to grow on sound lines. Free intervention by the courts and other governmental agencies has created a state of legal freeze and political confusion in the labour-management relations. Unions are indulgent in the court action and political bargains than resorting to the field programmes directed towards sound union growth. Though, in the initial stages of labour movement, the assistance of political leaders and parties was indispensable, but now it appears that becoming leaders of unions has become a fashion among the politicians and professional leaders, who dominate the trade union leadership in the State. Therefore, efforts have to be made to replace professional leaders by the workers' leaders through the "Workers-Education Scheme".

In short, the Trade Union Movement in the State is a developing one and its future will depend on the degree of industrialisation, the type of leadership, changes in political climate, attitude of the employers and authorities, which will go a long way in moulding the future course of Trade Union Movement in Jammu and Kashmir.

TRADE UNIONISM IN TEXTILE INDUSTRY

A Brief Retrospect

The history of Trade Union Movement in Jammu and Kashmir reveals that the unionism in Textile Industry has grown parallel to that of the State. In fact, the Textile Industry has throughout occupied a predominant position in the Trade Union Movement and has given a lead to the entire State in this respect. The origin of this Trade Union Movement in the Textile Industry in 1865, the first ever labour rising of its kind was organised by the Shawl Weavers of Kashmir, also marks the beginning of trade unionism in the State (Jalali, 1972: 33).

The strike by the workers of Government Silk Factory in Kashmir in the summer of 1924 in protest against the insufficiency of wages, the corruption of the officials and tyranny of the inspecting staff performed a pioneering task in organising the working class of the State (Khan, 1980: 18). When, after the severe economic depression caused by the First World War, the textile workers of the State were required to do double the work at 20 per cent reduced wages, the burden of securing the much needed justice for the workers fell on the shoulders of a group of intellectually advanced young socialists, who organised the workers of the State under 'Mazdoor Sabha' in 1937. As elsewhere, it was the textile industry which provided the platform for the Sabha. The events of August 19, 1937, September 7, 1937, and October 4, 1937, corroborate this fact (Khan, 1980). When in 1938, trade unionism was extended to Jammu province again the stage was provided by the textile industry.

Up to '40s almost all the textile units of the State were well organised and till '40s, the industry continued to be highly unionised not only in the Jammu and Kashmir State but also in the entire textile sector of the country. The Labour Bureau's Survey Report, supporting this viewpoint, states that where as in Jammu and Kashmir, all or most of the workers in every textile factory surveyed were found to be members of trade unions, the overall percentage for the country, as a whole, was of the order of only 35 per cent. Next to the State, the percentage of factories, where workers were found to be members of trade unions was highest (53%) in Bombay. In Punjab and Mysore the percentage was only about 33 per cent (Govt of India, 1964: 89). Again in 1969, the percentage of workers who were union members was highest (93%) in Kashmir followed by Bombay city and its suburbs (55%) and Mysore (51%). The lowest figure was in respect of Amritsar (38%) (Govt of India, 1969: 89).

The Present Position

The textile industry being the largest industry, still continues to be most unionised in the entire manufacturing sector of the State. The industry has retained its traditional strong hold in various centres where it happens to be well organised. As reported earlier, at present (1986) out of a total of 626 registered trade unions in the State, 78 unions operate in the textile industry, accounting for about 12.5 per cent of the total trade unions. The unions in the industry also account for the substantial proportion of trade union membership in the State.

The district-wise analysis shows that the industry is highly unionised in Srinagar, as a majority of 43 unions (51.13%) are operating in this district, which has been and still continues to be one of the important woollen and silk textile centres of the country. It is followed by Jammu, which reports 14 textile trade unions. The other districts where textile trade union penetration is relatively low include Pulwama (8), Kathua (6), Anantnag (3), Baramulla (2) and Poonch (2).

The textile trade unions share the general features of the trade unions in the State, i.e., a smallness in size, organisational weaknesses, financial constraints and political domination. All the unions operating in the industry are plant level unions and the industry-cum-region unions are rarely found. Almost all the State sector textile unions are affiliated to State Central Labour Union (SCLU). While the unions operating in the private sector units take guidance from various Central Trade Union Organisations.

TABLE 7.4: Trade unions in sample textile units by their membership and affiliation, 1987

Organisation		Name of the trade union	Year of registration	Membership as per the subscriptions paid	Affiliation
I	(1)	"...Silk Weaving Factory Workers Union..."	1953	385	S.C.L.U.
	(2)	"...Silk Weaving Factory Staff Union..."	1971	61	J.K.E.F.
II	(1)	"...Silk Factory Workers Union..."	1972	299	S.C.L.U.
III	(1)	"...Woollen Mills Mehnatkash Union..."	1975	125	S.C.L.U.
	(2)	"...Woollen Mills Mehnatkash Mazdoor Congress..."	1977	88	I.N.T.U.C.
	(3)	"...Woollen Mills Staff Union..."	1985	77	J.K.E.F.
IV	(1)	"...Woollen Mills (old) Labour Union".	1953	162	S.C.L.U.
	(2)	"...Woollen Mills (old) Employees Union."	1970	54	J.K.E.F.
V	(1)	"...Textile Mill Workers Union..."	1975	285	B.M.S.
	(2)	"...Textile Mill Employees Union..."	1978	250	Independent
	(3)	"...Textile Mill Mazdoor Union..."	1978	382	S.C.L.U.
	(4)	"...Textile Mills Industrial Workers' Union..."	1982	180	A.I.T.U.C.

Sources: (1) Office of Registrar of Trade Unions, Govt. of Jammu & Kashmir, Srinagar.
(2) Offices of the respective trade unions.

After a brief historical sketch of the early trade unionism in the industry and its present scenario, the present section professes to cast some light on the features of trade unions in the sample textile units. Table 7.4 gives a consolidated position of the trade unions in all the units under study.

It may be observed from the above data that trade unions in the organisations do not present an example of high order multiple trade unionism. There are two trade unions each in two of the units — I and IV — three unions in Organization III and one in Organisation II. In comparison, there has been a mushroom growth of unions in Organisation V which provides a structure of multiple trade unions, with a majority of four unions.

Table 7.4 reveals that unions have been established separately for industrial and non-industrial workers. The industrial unions cover all the categories of workers — skilled, semi-skilled and unskilled — and are affiliated to various trade union federations (SCLU being the dominant). The non-industrial trade unions commonly known as 'Staff Unions' represent all the administrative, sales and service employees and owe allegiance to the Jammu and Kashmir Employees Federation (JKEF) — a State-level association of low paid employees. However, both types of unions have been found working with solidarity. All the unions working in the sample organisations have been recognised except ". . . Woollen Mills Mehnatkash Mazdoor Congress" in Organisation III and ". . . Textile Mills Industrial Workers Union" in Organisation V.

With the exception of only a few, all the trade unions existing at present in the sample units have been operating right from the inception of the respective plants, some of them from early '40s. The year of registration, however, does not conform to the year of establishment of these trade unions.

In the absence of proper membership records and irregular collection of subscriptions, it has been impossible to trace the exact membership of the different unions for various years. However, the membership of the unions, as existing at the end of 1987, has been used to study the degree of unionisation in the sample units. Table 7.5 reports the results of the study in this context.

The overall degree of unionisation, to the extent of 60.31 per cent as revealed by the above data confirm the earlier finding that the textile industry of the State is highly unionised. The degree of unionisation in much more than that reported in Kanpur Cotton Textile Industry, i.e.,

48 per cent (Shrimali, 1970: 30) and also that in Ahmedabad Textile Industry (Sharma 1980: 44), which are the pioneer industries and were also pioneer in the trade unionism. However, it is less than that of Textile Industry in Punjab, i.e., 88.1 per cent (Asdhir, 1987: 78). Organisation wise, highest intensity of unions has been reported in Organisation II (91.44%), followed in that order by Organisation III (90.34%), Organisation IV (88.16%) and Organisation I (86.94%). Comparatively Organisation V experienced the lowest degree of unionisation (44.11%), presumably because of the multiple union structure at the plant. This finding confirms the hypothesis that higher the number of trade unions, lower is the degree of unionisation in the enterprise and *vice versa*.

TABLE 7.5: Membership of Unions and the Degree of Unionisation, 1987

Organisation	No. of trade unions	Total union membership (u)	Total No. of employed (N)	Degree of unionisation (u/N×100)
1	2	3	4	5
I	2	446	513	86.94
II	1	299	327	91.44
III	3	290	321	90.34
IV	2	216	245	88.16
V	4	1,097	2,487	44.11
Average (x)	2.4	469.6	778.6	60.31

Sources: (1) For column 2 and 3 Table 7.4.
(2) For column 4 Personnel Departments of respective units.

The overall analysis of the trade unionism in textile industry of the State brings to light the following characteristic features:

1. The textile trade unionism is characterised by small size unions, functioning on plant basis and suffering from very loose organisational structure. The union endeavour to create real, capable and independent bargaining strength and help in the establishment of harmonious-labour management relations has largely remained unaccomplished.
2. The financial position of the unions is very precarious and has been the main factor contributing to the union's inability to

undertake any worthwhile welfare programme for the members. The major portion of the union income is spent in legal cases. The main source of unions' income is the membership subscription which varies from one to three rupees per workers per month. Apart from the regular subscriptions, it is also customary in most of the cases to collect lump sum amounts from the union members in the form of donations.

3. The Jammu and Kashmir Trade Union Rules, 1972, provide for a statutory recognisation of a trade union as "representative union". In the textile industry statutory recognition is granted to a representative union on plant-wise basis and the industry-wise recognisation is rare.
4. A characteristic feature of the trade unionism in Jammu and Kashmir in general and in its textile industry in particular is the excessive interference of political parties in the union affairs. During the survey, it has been observed that more than 65 per cent of the respondents are not appreciative of political affiliation of unions. It is because of this reason that some of the workers have adopted the passive attitude towards union affairs. But, interestingly, majority of the office bearers justify their political affiliation by stating that unions badly need political influence for bringing pressure upon the Government/management for the redressal of their grievances.
5. The other problem in no way less viciousis is the domination of union leadership by outsiders to a large extent. The leadership of the major unions has remained with the people, other than from the rank and file, having strong political leanings. Though only about 20 per cent of the leaders are involved in politics directly, an overwhelming majority of the rest takes political stand indirectly. A core section of the management personnel felt that because of the frequent interference of various outside agencies in the day-to-day labour matters hardly any room is left for the management to take decisions and exercise powers freely and independently. This state of affairs instead of achieving industrial peace has at times created an atmosphere more conducive for labour unrest.
6. An interesting and encouraging feature of the union activity in the industry is that by and large the union-management relations are cordial. Unions have been reported avoiding militant approach and attitude as far as possible. Unions take very active interest in

the matters of production, sales, materials, etc., and quite often suggest improvements in the operation of the units.

WORKERS' INVOLVEMENT AND PARTICIPATION IN TRADE UNIONS

From the extensive review of research on industrial relations (See Chapter 2), it clearly follows that only a few objective studies have been carried out to empirically investigate who join the unions and why? and among those who join who participate more actively in union activities. Such a study is very useful to assess the strength of trade unions, their capacity to bargain, the workers commitment to unionism and industrial way of life, the process of democratisation at the grassroots level and to determine the process of social change.

The following sections of the study seek to analyse the involvement and participation of rank and file in unions, their union interest, membership behaviour against the socio-economic background of workers, motivational analysis of union membership, the degree of union participation in relation to various factors influencing it.

Extent of Unionisation

During the study it has been found that almost all the workers in all the organisations under study were aware of the existence of trade unions in their respective organisations. Majority of 208 (83.20%) workers interviewed were union members and most of them for past about ten years, which depicts a higher degree of unionisation among the textile workers of the State. Only 42 (16.80%) did not join any union. A large majority of workers were members of those unions, which are affiliated to State Central Labour Union (68%), followed by the INTUC (20%).

The distribution of union members and non-members *vis-a-vis* other variables is presented in Table 7.6 and the association between union membership and its correlates in Table 7.7.

The data corroborate the fact that the workers who are in the age group of 25 to 35 years (87%) and 35 to 45 (96%) were union members in large proportion than those who are too young, i.e., below 25 years or too old, i.e., above 45 years of age. As such, age is to a greater extent associated with the union membership ($P < .01$).

TABLE 7.6: Extent of Unionisation *vis-a-vis* Personal Attributes of Workers

Personal Attributes/Groups	Union members		Non-members		Total	
	f	%	f	%	f	%
1	2	3	4	5	6	7
1. *Age*						
Below 25 years	88	84	17	16	105	100
25 to 35 years	45	87	7	13	52	100
35 to 45 years	43	96	2	4	45	100
45 years and above	32	67	16	33	48	100
Total	208	83	42	17	250	100
2. *Skill*						
Skilled	65	81	15	19	80	100
Semi-skilled	103	92	9	8	112	100
Unskilled	40	69	18	31	58	100
Total	208	83	42	17	250	100
3. *Rural-urban background*						
Rural	20	44	25	56	45	100
Urban	165	93	12	7	177	100
Semi-urban	23	82	5	18	28	100
Total	208	83	42	17	250	100
4. *Education*						
Illiterates	105	82	23	18	128	100
Up to 10 years of schooling	93	85	17	15	110	100
More than 10 years of schooling	10	83	2	17	12	100
Total	208	93	42	17	250	100
5. *Length of service*						
Below 10 years	118	83	25	17	143	100
10 to 20 years	40	95	2	5	42	100
20 to 30 years	23	82	5	18	28	100
30 years and above	27	73	10	27	37	100
Total	208	83	42	17	250	100
6. *Marital status*						
Married	135	83	28	17	163	100
Unmarried	73	84	14	16	87	100
Total	208	83	42	17	250	100

Contd.

TABLE 7.6 *Contd.*

1	2	3	4	5	6	7
7. *Political activism*						
Yes	65	93	5	7	70	100
No	143	79	37	21	180	100
Total	208	83	42	17	250	100
8. *Wage level*						
Below Rs. 700	23	53	20	47	43	100
Rs. 700 to Rs. 1,000	137	93	10	7	147	100
Rs. 1,000 & above	48	80	12	20	60	100
Total	208	83	42	17	250	100

TABLE 7.7: Association Between Union Membership and its Correlates

Correlates of union membership	χ^2	df	P
1. Age	15.29	3	< 0.01
2. skill	14.44	4	< 0.01
3. Rural-urban background	55.86	2	< 0.01
4. Education	0.13	2	N.S.
5. Length of service	7.52	3	< 0.10
6. Marital status	0.13	1	N.S.
7. Political Activism	6.88	1	< 0.01
8. Wage level	40.15	2	< 0.01

Notes: 1. "N.S." stands for "Not significant".
2. Based on Corresponding Contingency Table 7.6.

Similarly 81 per cent skilled and 92 per cent semi-skilled workers joined unions as compared to 69 per cent unskilled workers and thus union membership is also positively associated with skill level acquired by the workers (P < .01). A higher proportion of urban (93%) and semi-urban (82%) workers were union members than rural ones (44%). It is interesting to note that as many as 56 per cent of the rural workers working in the industry are largely unskilled and unaware of union philosophy. The significant association between union membership and rural-urban background is supported by χ^2 value (P < .01). In the same way there is statistically significant relationship between length of service and union membership, as 17 per cent of workers having put in less than 10 years of service and 27 per cent of workers who are very old having 30 or more years of service as compared to the middle service group, did not join any union. The results reveal a higher degree of association between union membership and political activism ($P < .01$), as 93 per cent of the politically active workers were members of one or the other union. Further, a higher degree of association is found between union membership and wage level ($P < .01$).

However, it is significant to observe that union membership is not statistically related with education and marital status as union membership is evenly distributed between illiterates and literates and between married and unmarried. The above findings are logical because as workers mature in age, skill, experience and came up with urban taste and outlook, they look forward for the unions to help them protect their interests.

Union Membership: A Motivational Analysis

Why do workers join or refrain from joining any union? This question has an important bearing on the landscape of labour-management relations. Scholars on the subject have propounded various personal, socio-economic, psychological and organisational reasons for workers' joining or not joining the unions. Ganguli (1960), Rose (1952), Chamberlin (1935) and Viteles (1953), presenting similar viewpoints, find that economic needs expressed in the desire for higher wages, job security, fringe benefits, bargaining power are the most commonly stated factors, which play a significant role in leading the workers to join unions. Golden and Ruth (1942) and Barbash (1951), on the other hand, maintain that the workers join unions not only for economic motives, but also for equally compelling psychological and social ones. Relatively little efforts have been made by the Indian scholars to explore the subject (for brief review of these studies please refer to Chapter 2).

We give in the following paras a comprehensive list of reasons given by the sample textile workers to explain why they join or not join the trade unions.

Why do Workers Join the Unions?

With a view to analyse the motives of workers in joining the unions, they were given a set of 12 alternative reasons, deriving their basis from theoretical as well as empirical studies on the phenomenon and were asked to select three of them in order of priority which accounted for their joining the unions. Of these, nine reasons have been selected and retained in order of importance. The reasons given by 208 union members, along with their total scores and ranks assigned, have been presented in Table 7.8.

TABLE 7.8: Workers' Major Reasons for Joining the Unions

Sl No.	Reasons	Unionists (N=208) Priorities			Total scores	Percentage of total scores obtained	Rank
		I	II	III			
I.	Secure higher wages, fringe benefits, bonus, etc.	48	23	28	218	18.23	III
II.	Job security	18	30	45	159	13.29	IV
III.	Protection against victimisation	43	33	28	223	18.65	II
IV.	Obtain better working conditions/welfare amenities	13	30	13	112	9.36	V
V.	Fair promotion and advancement	16	8	13	77	6.44	VI
VI.	For working class strength and solidarity	33	53	28	233	19.48	I
VII.	Labour-management co-operation	10	9	25	73	6.10	VII
VIII.	Pressure from fellow workers	13	10	11	70	5.85	VIII
IX.	Because all are members	5	3	10	31	2.60	IX

Notes:
1. Results presented here represent the responses of the union members of all the organisations.
2. Overall ranking is done on the basis of percentage age of total scores.
3. Scoring is done as per the following scale. Priority 1st = 3 , 2nd = 2, 3rd = 1.

As revealed by Table 7.8, majority of the workers joined the unions for working class strength and solidarity(Rank I), followed by reasons like protection against victimisation (Rank II), secure higher wages, fringe benefits, bonus, etc. (Rank III), job security (Rank IV) and obtain better working conditions and welfare amenities (Rank V). The desire for fair promotion and advancement, labour-management cooperation and pressure from others have been the other but only minor motives for workers in joining the unions. The first five motives ranked in the present study are to a greater extent in agreement with some earlier studies conducted in India by Vaid (1965), Sinha and Pai

(1963), Panday and Vikram (1969), Laldas (1980) and Sharma (1980). As such it emerges that an average Indian workers joins union mainly for the economic motives and security needs. But the findings are quite contrary to those of some Western scholars who have laid great emphasis on social, psychological and political needs of workers in joining unions (Golden and Ruttenberg, 1942; Krech and Crutechfuled, 1948; Mills, 1976).

TABLE 7.9: Reasons for Workers' not Joining any Union

Sl. No.	Reasons	Non-Unionists (N=42) Priorities			Total scores	Percentage of total scores obtained	Rank
		I	II	III			
1.	Fear of victimisation	10	6	2	44	19.56	III
2.	No knowledge of any union	2	—	1	7	3.11	VIII
3.	Unions doing nothing for workers	11	10	5	58	25.78	I
4.	No confidence in union leaders	5	15	10	55	24.44	II
5.	Temporary nature of job	2	2	10	20	8.87	IV
6.	No difficulties — getting good salary and facilities	2	3	2	14	6.22	VI
7.	Got the job on the promise of safe conduct and loyalty	5	2	—	19	8.44	V
8.	Having family, cannot take the risk of joining any union	2	—	2	8	3.56	VII

Note : Same as for Table 7.8.

Why Workers do not Join the Unions?

On the above pattern, the grounds on which 16.80 per cent workers desisted from joining any union have been analysed in Table 7.9.

It is revealed by the above data that majority of the non-members had not joined any union because of their dissatisfaction with the functioning of the unions. They felt that "the unions in general do not do anything substantial for the workers" (Rank I) and that "they had no faith and confidence in the union leadership" (Rank II). The following statements reflect the non-members' discontentment with the unions and their leaders.

"Unions are formed for the welfare of the workers, but they are

welfare organisations in name sake only."
"Neither the unions nor their leaders perform their duties honestly"
"Union activists are politicians and work for their own ambition with the union label."
"Politicians befool innocent workers".

It is interesting to observe that the "fear of victimisation" also kept a fairly large number of workers away from unions (Rank III). The temporary nature of job and the fear of being branded disloyal to the organisation were the other stated reasons for not joining the unions. In comparison only a smaller number of workers did not join unions because they were generally satisfied with their jobs and had no substantial grievances against the management and again only a small number of non-members had no knowledge of the existence of any union. Most of the earlier Indian studies on the subject support the findings of the present study.

WORKERS' PARTICIPATION IN TRADE UNION ACTIVITIES

Degree of Union Participation

For the sound growth of trade unionism, an active involvement and participation of rank and file in union activities is indispensable. In view of the prevalence of illiteracy, inexperience, rural-background and general dissatisfaction of workers and weak trade union movement, it was hypothised that there is a lower degree of union participation by the members. This hypothesis is, however, rejected as the members participated more actively in the union activities, as revealed by Table 7.10.

Table 7.10 depicts that a majority of 61 per cent of the union members paid union dues regularly and there has been no member who did not pay union dues, as and when required. Forty per cent of the members always attended union meetings and only 7 per cent never attended any meeting. Although 68 per cent participated in union elections, only 12 per cent of them always worked for enrolling new members. The relatively, higher union participation is also revealed by the fact that when a call for strike is given, majority of the workers (78%) always participate in it.

TABLE 7.10: Indicators of Workers' Participation in Union Activities

Sl. No.	Union Activities	Responses							
		Always		Some time		Never/No response		Total	
		f	%	f	%	f	%	f	%
1.	Payment of union dues	127	61	81	39	—	—	208	100
2.	Collecting funds for unions	28	13	155	75	25	12	208	100
3.	Attending union meetings	84	40	110	53	14	7	208	100
4.	Participating in union elections	142	68	41	20	25	12	208	100
5.	Making new members	25	12	101	49	82	39	208	100
6.	Taking part in strikes/ *dharnas*	163	78	36	17	9	5	208	100
7.	Reading union notices/ pamphlets	61	29	121	58	26	13	208	100
8.	Going in support of unions to conciliation/ tribunals etc.	35	17	124	60	49	23	208	100

It is significant to note that only a limited number of union members (17%) always represented their unions before the Industrial Relations Machinery, helped unions in collecting funds (13%) and read union notices and pamphlets (29%), indicating thereby that these do not figure among the prominent activities which the members perform for their unions. These findings lead us to the all important conclusion that the union members always participate actively in almost all the important union activities as "union members" and rarely or never take part in such activities which are likely to affect, unnecessarily, their working as "workers". These observations, however, do not agree with those of Seth (1968); Panday and Vikram (1969), Crouch (1966), Sharma (1974) and Dayal and Sharma (1976), which showed that the Indian workers on an average show an apathetic attitude towards the union activities.

UNION PARTICIPATION AND ITS CORRELATES

A higher degree of membership participation in union activities reflects a higher level of support to the union and thereby adds to its effectiveness, strength and vigour and *vice versa*. What makes some union members active and others passive is an important question and researchers have examined various aspects of participation, attempting to find their correlates. In earlier studies, demographic variables were found to be important determinants of union particiation. But in most recent studics attitudinal, behavioural and perceptual variables have received more attention (Checko, 1985); Colchin and Hyclek, 1984; Huszeze, 1983; Monga and Maggu, 1981; Sharma, 1987).

In the present study with a view to assess the level of members' participation in unions, an index of union participation was prepared on the basis of the response of the respondents. The distribution of the respondents in terms of the degree of participation shows that only 14 per cent of the union members showed relatively low, 46 per cent moderate and 40 per cent considerably higher degree of union participation.

The degree of union participation shown by the members *vis-a-vis* their socio-psychological and personal variables is presented in Table 7.11 followed by the nature and magnitude of these correlates in Table 7.12.

TABLE 7.11: Degree of Union Participation *vis-a-vis* Other Variables

Variables/Groups	Degree of participation			
	Low	Medium	High	Total
1	2	3	4	5
1. *Union Interest*				
Low	12	8	6	26
Medium	10	49	35	94
High	7	39	42	88
Total	29	96	83	208
2. *Age*				
Below 25 years	15	35	38	88
25 to 35 years	3	28	14	45
35 to 45 years	4	25	14	43
45 years and above	7	8	17	32
Total	29	96	83	208

Contd.

TABLE 7.11 *Contd.*

1	2	3	4	5
3. *Skill Level*				
Skilled	5	26	34	65
Semi-skilled	14	54	35	103
Unskilled	10	16	14	40
Total	29	96	83	208
4. *Rural-urban background*				
Rural	6	10	4	20
Urban	19	75	71	165
Semi-urban	4	11	8	23
Total	29	96	83	208
5. *Length of service*				
Below 10 years	18	66	34	118
10 to 20 years	4	17	19	40
20 to 30 years	4	5	14	23
30 years and above	3	8	16	27
Total	29	96	83	208
6. *Education*				
Illiterate	17	49	39	105
Up to 10 years of schooling	10	45	38	93
More than 10 years of schooling	2	2	6	10
Total	29	96	83	208
7. *Marital status*				
Married	21	64	50	135
Unmarried	8	32	33	73
Total	29	96	83	208
8. *Political Activism*				
Yes	6	25	34	65
No	23	71	49	137
Total	29	96	83	208
9. *Wage Level*				
Below Rs 700	3	6	14	23
Rs 700 to Rs 1,000	21	72	44	137
Rs 1,000 and above	5	18	25	48
Total	29	96	83	208

TABLE 7.12: Association Between Union Participation and its Correlates

Sl. No.	Correlates of	χ^2	df	P
1.	Union interest	24.28	4	<.01
2.	Age	13.66	6	<.05
3.	Skill level	9.54	4	<.05
4.	Rural-urban background	6.63	4	N.S.
5.	Length of service	17.57	6	<.01
6.	Education	5.11	4	N.S.
7.	Marital status	1.64	2	N.S.
8.	Political Activism	6.09	2	<.05
9.	Wages	12.09	4	<.02

Notes: 1. 'N.S.' stands for 'Not significant'
2. Based on corresponding contingency Table 7.11

Union Interest

The above cross-examination of union interest and union participation reveals the promising result that there is statistically significant association between the two variables ($P < .01$). About 47 per cent of the union members who are highly interested in unions also participate in union activities to a greater extent and 46 per cent of those who possess lower degree of union interest also participate in union activities marginally. It suggests that interest in unions as expected is directly converted in active union participation. Sinha (1984) also found that those members, who had shown high interest in unions, had high participation in union activities. This observation is, however, not supported by Sharma (1971), Ammassari (1964) and Sharma (1981), who found negative relationship and a gap between interest in unions and member's participation in union activities.

Age and Experience

Both age and length of service were found significantly related to union participation. The workers who were too young and less experienced or too old having more experience showed considerably lower degree of union participation. The studies of Seth (1969), Glick, *et al.* (1977), Arya (1980), Mattoo and Gani (1987) and Sharma (1987) also find that senior and older members participate in unions actively than junior and younger ones. As rightly expressed by Seth (1969):

> "Young workers who are at the initial stages of their career may be cautious to avoid any threat to their jobs and hence modest in union involvement. At the opposite extreme, workers who are very old and who have put in long period of service in the job may not feel concerned much with the unionism in view of the duration already spent on the job and the approaching and of their career."

Sharma (1974) also notes that higher the experience in industrial life, the lower is the level of commitment to unionism.

Skill and Education

The relationship between skill and degree of union participation is found to be statistically significant ($P < .05$) which suggests that the desire to participate in union activities tends to increase as one acquires more and more skill. In contrast, education does not correlate with union participation. It indicates that more educated members may find satisfaction from their jobs and may not need to participate in union activities. Anderson (1979), Rees (1962), Arya (1980) and Sharma (1971) also report a similar gap between education and union participation.

Rural-Urban Background

Though rural-urban background and union participation do not appear statistically associated, yet a notable difference is revealed in the distribution of the degree of participation between the rural and urban workers. Relatively higher and moderate levels of participation are shown by 71 and 75 urban workers, respectively, as compared with just four and 10 rural workers. Sayles and Strauss (1953) have also found that those with the rural background are less involved in their unions than those brought up in politically sophisticated urban environment.

Marital Status

The data reveal that the members being married or unmarried does not bear a significant relationship with union participation, in spite of the fact that a greater degree of union participation is shown by married than unmarried workers. This observation is in keeping with those of Arya (1980), Sinha (1984), Mattoo and Gani (1987) and Seth (1969) but quite contrary to the findings of Sharma (1971), Tannenbaum and Kahan (1958) and Sharma (1987) who found that the active union member was more likely to be married.

Political Activism

Affiliation of a worker to any political organisation, directly or indirectly, has considerable influence on the workers' level of participation in union activities. The χ^2 value bears out this relationship between the two variables ($P < .01$). More than 90 per cent members who are associated with political parties participate in union activities comparatively to a higher or moderate extent. In the absence of any other corroborative evidence this finding cannot be compared with others.

Wage Level

The hypothesis that union members with lower wages participate in union activities more actively holds true in the case of present study, as a higher degree of positive relationship is observed between the union participation and wage level. Arya (1980) and Singh (1971) also found that pro-union groups of workers were more dissatisfied with wages and other financial incentives.

Other Correlates

There are certain other variables which, though not analysed in the present study, have been found strong determinants of membership participation in union activities by scholars. These include social interaction and community involvement, job satisfaction, organisational climate, commitment to work, family structure, occupational status, exigencies of unionism and union leadership, union identification, size and the type of union, antagonistic attitude of management, job security, caste stratum and the desire for participative management (Basu Sharma, 1987; Monga and Maggu, 1981; Seth, 1969; Sharma, 1971; Farm and Danseareau, 1956; Stagner, 1956; Glick, *et al.*, 1977; Strauss, 1956; Faunce, 1962 and Sinha, 1964).

CONCLUSION

An overview of the findings, emerging from the present chapter, strongly suggests that though the Labour Movement in Jammu and Kashmir started much earlier than the Political Movement, its growth on modern lines synchronises with the growth of Political Movement particularly after 1937. Up to 1947, it was a movement of nationalism with union label. After Independence, particularly after the planning period, the trade unionism in the State started growing both in number and size. At present the labour force is reasonably organised in the form of trade unions.

The textile industry, which has throughout dominated the trade union scene of the State, has reported higher degree of unionisation not only as compared to the State as a whole but also much higher than that reported in textile industries of Ahmedabad and Kanpur.

Workers have shown relatively higher degree of interest and have positive attitude towards unions in that they consider unions to be "important" and "essential" aspects of their working lives. This higher degree of union interest is translated in active participation in union activities. The economic needs in the form of desire for higher wages and better fringe benefits, effective redressal of grievances and need for protection and security against powerful management seem to motivate the workers much in joining the unions. Union participation appears to be higher among the workers who are comparatively young, experienced, skilled, politically active and those earning less wages.

The characteristics feature of the Industrial Relations System in the State is that industrial peace has been achieved by concessions from time to time, which has retarded the development of trade unions on sound lines. Most of the well organised trade unions are affiliates of political parties. In any discussion of trade unionism in Jammu and Kashmir, the name of State Central Labour union dominates like a huge *banyan* tree. Because of the higher degree of illiteracy, the rural background and outlook and the abject poverty of the working class, the politicians have succeeded not only in exercising a political control over the unions but also in using them as 'pawns on the chess board' of power politics. The unstable political situation in the State seems to favour such a climate of political unionism.

Trade unionism in textile industry is also characterised by domination of outside leadership. Most of the union leaders are local professionals who are more pre occupied with their own interests rather than safeguarding the interests of workers. Though Gandhiji did not oppose the outside leadership in trade unions, yet he emphasised that such leaders should not take to politics and should stick to truth, give proper guidance and work for the amelioration of the workers (Majumdar, 1973: 50).

The above account leads us to the all important conclusion that Textile Trade Unionism in Jammu and Kashmir is characterised by small size and plant level unions, organisationally weak, financially eroded and politically dominated.

8

CONCLUSIONS, SUGGESTIONS AND POLICY IMPLICATIONS

THE TEXTILE industry is one of the oldest and important industries in Jammu and Kashmir State in terms of volume of employment, production, capital investment and its share in the State revenue. The industry has witnessed a significant growth in the recent past. The development of the industry has given rise to some industrial conflicts which are a matter of serious concern, especially at this juncture when the industrial progress in the State is tardy, resources are limited, the pressure of population is increasing and the industrial progress is the prime need. It is, therefore, very important to examine the causes of industrial unrest in the industry with a view to take remedial measures to ensure industrial peace.

With the above backdrop in view, the present investigation, into a largely unexplored area, has been undertaken to examine the state of labour-management relations in textile industry of Jammu and Kashmir and probe objectively into the factors that help or obstruct the maintenance and development of harmonious relations between labour and management in the industry and on the basis of the findings of the study offer policy recommendations for achieving much needed industrial peace. The major focus of the study has been on exploring the nature and extent of industrial conflicts, working of dispute handling machinery, degree of job satisfaction of workers, nature and extent of workers' participation in decision-making and growth and structure of trade unionism.

The textile industry has been selected for the purpose of this study because of its being the oldest, largest, highly dispute-prone and most unionised industry in the State. To keep the frame of analysis intact and give a proper direction to the study, a set of working hypotheses has been set up. The research approach employed to substantiate the given hypotheses consists of (1) literature survey; (2) field study;

(3) attitude analysis and (4) study of records.

Based on the objectives, hypotheses and methodology outlined the empricism of labour-management relations in the industry under study has been examined in eight broad chapters. These include the background of the research design and the critical review of theoretical and empirical literature, which form the subject matter of the first two chapters. An attempt has been made in the present chapter to recapitulate the major findings of the study to draw conclusions and analyse critically the implications of these findings for the purpose of discerning the future direction of labour-management relations in the textile industry of the State.

CONCLUSIONS

Nature and Extent of Industrial Conflicts

An analysis of the strike activity in Jammu and Kashmir State reveals that comparatively a marginal number of industrial disputes has been reported. During 1970-86, there have been on an average about four industrial disputes per year involving around 2,357 workers and resulting in a loss of more than 10, 641 man-days. The production and employment loss due to these strikes, given the lower level of industrial development in the State, has been of substantial order.

Compared with all other States and Union Territories, Jammu and Kashmir takes the 4th lowest rank in terms of conflict proneness. The lowest conflict prone situation of the State is attributed to various factors including the lowest level of industrialisation, weak trade unionism and frequent and excessive State intervention disputes.

The textile industry has been comparatively the most conflict prone industry and accounts on an average for about 15 per cent of the disputes reported in the State. This propensity of conflicts has increased overtime with the growth of the industry and expansion of trade unionism in it. The first ever labour insurrection in the history of the industrial relations of the State took place in its textile industry as early as 1965. Since then a number of disputes have taken place in the industry, which have performed a pioneering task in creating the basis for the industrial relations system in the State.

Though there has been a dispute on every conceivable issue that can emerge in the day to day operation of an enterprise, the demand for higher wages, bonus, allowances, etc., has been the principal cause of industrial disputes, accounting on an average for about one-third of the total number of disputes in the State. Evidence suggests that many other direct and indirect variables, like, alienation of industrial work-force, their social needs etc., influence industrial relations but the incidence of disputes due to wages and allowances continue to be high, despite the efforts of the Government to solve the problems of wage earners, through the appointment of wage-boards, commission etc., including Chatterji Wage Commission in 1973 and Rajan Wage Review Committee in 1980. It establishes that the economic environment existing in the State adversely affects the industrial relations scene.

The study unfolds a grim story of the economic, working and living conditions of textile workers in the State, which have had a marked influence on their health, efficiency and quality of working lives. Though the per capita annual earnings of workers in the State have increased by 338.40 per cent during 1970-83. It has always lagged behind the national average in this respect. On the other hand, the consumer price index for industrial workers has gone up by 227 per cent which has been the highest compared with the national growth rate of about 189 per cent during the same period. As a result benefits accruing to the workers though continuous struggle have been entirely negated and eroded.

The workers have been found working in appalling working and living conditions. Majority of them work continuously in standing positions in poor lighting, ventilation, cleanliness and conservancy conditions and are exposed to undesirable dust, fumes, gases and steam. They are deprived of the wholesome drinking water, washing and bathing facilities, canteens, rest pauses, medical and accommodation facilities. The welfare activities, undertaken by the State Government, following its vague labour policy, have not been able to bring about any appreciable change in the vast working class.

The findings of the study lead us to the conclusion that through the number of disputes in the State and textile industry is apparently very small, yet if we analyse the number of workers involved and man-days lost due to these disputes, in view of the lower level of industrialisation there is no doubt about the fact that these strikes would continue to be great impediments in industrial development of the State if appropriate measures for their proper handling are not taken in time.

Workers' Job Satisfaction

The presence of poor physical and psychological work environment in the textile industry, as reported above, has made a significant difference in the attitude and morale of the workers and has consequently led to much of their job dissatisfaction and general lack of commitment to the industry.

In the present study, with a view to measure the level of job satisfaction of workers, a scale developed and standardised by Ganguli (1954), consisting of 30 internally consistent statements and measuring nine dimensions of the job satisfaction, has been used. A perusal of the index of overall job satisfaction reveals that the scores of job satisfaction are skewed on the negative side, indicating thereby that the textile workers of the State do not possess favourable attitude towards their jobs. Majority (40.8%) of the workers show lower degree of job satisfaction. In comparison, a lesser percentage (34%) is moderately satisfied and a still lesser percentage (25.2%) is satisfied with their jobs. A comparative analysis of the results of the study and other research evidences on the subject, in India, reveals that most of the studies, conducted in different parts of the country, largely support the findings of the present study.

The study brings out clearly the association of a variety of personal background factors and different behavioural variables with workers' job satisfaction. Comparatively very young and old age group workers are either highly or moderately satisfied with their jobs. Majority of the workers in the middle experience group shows a very low degree of job satisfaction as compared with the groups at the low extremes of work experience. Statistically, the level of skill seems to have a decisive influence on the degree of job satisfaction. Wage level has been found to be important variable influence job satisfaction. The hypothesis that higher the number of dependents, lower the degree of job satisfaction also holds true in the case of present study. The relationship between other background factors and job satisfaction was not so close as to reach the accepted level of significance. Certain trends were, however, noticeable. Those who belonged to very low education level tended to show greater satisfaction. Workers' martial status does not bear any significant relationship with the degree of job satisfaction.

There is sufficient evidence that a satisfied worker is very regular in his attendance and is perceived to be more productive and generally adjusted with his supervisor. A worker dissatisfied with his job, in contrast, is often rigid inflexible, irregular, less productive and unrealistic in his choice of goals. The management to make better utilization of human resources would have to follow progressive measures to make work humane challenging and interesting.

Workers' Expectations

For healthy industrial relations, spontaneous co-operation between the working class and management both at the top and supervisory levels and towards that end their clear cut understanding of each other's roles and expectations, plays almost a decisive role. There is a strong conviction that if the supervisors and managers know as to what the workers expect from them and are able to comprehend to their expectations, it would certainly reduce the labour-management tensions.

The workers under study look forward to the supervisors to treat them as human beings and make minimum use of authority. They expect them to recognise their merits and accept their suggestions relating to their work. They feel that a competent supervisor is one who knows his job well and gives proper work instructions to his team. The supervisor being closest to his specialised area is expected to know much about its technical details than anyone else in his grade. The workers anticipate the supervisors to carry forward their responsibilities to their management in a loyal, enthusiastic and sincere way and view workers' viewpoints to management in right perspective. Such supervisors are disliked who are not considerate of workers' problems, fair in recommendations and those who indulge in fault findings, dictatory, revengeful and selfish practices.

With regard to the workers' expectations from management, monetary compensation acquired the highest strength in order of priority in expectations. The study, however, does not lend support to the myth that wages constitute the only source of satisfaction for workers. Workers' value, their dignity and prestige and expect recognisation of their job, ideal and hygienic, physical and psychological work environment, proper job security, involvement in organisational decision-making, adequate profit sharing, consistent and objective personnel policies and above all their will to have greater personal meaning. Slow and partial promotion schemes, to apathetic attitude towards trade unions and industrial relations problems are identified to be worst possible characteristics of the management. Workers do not appreciate a management which lacks consideration for workers' problems and does not provide adequate training accommodation, medical, recreational and educational facilities — all having significant bearing on the workers mental make up.

In sum, the workers expect an employee-oriented behaviour from their supervisors and managers rather than production centred orientation to human problems. The findings having practical policy implication, are the indicators of worker's likes and dislikes and call for the measures to be taken by the management and supervisors for promoting worker's job satisfaction in ensuring greater productivity and peaceful industrial relations. Ignoring these expectations would be rather risky. In order to be more effective in coping up with these expectations, they must practically alert as to how these will affect the management's people. They should recognise that most employees want to perform acceptably and that most discipline can be self-imposed. They should be an expanded base of technical, human relations and systems knowledge if the best out of workers.

Workers' Participation in Decision-making

The system of workers' participation in decision-making has not been very popular and successful in the industry. The participation is mostly through joint committees such as Work Committees, Joint Management Councils, Safety Committees, Canteen Committees, Sports Committees and Joint Production Committees. These Committees mainly aim at facilitating communication between labour and management, encouraging production, promoting working conditions and welfare measures and securing amity and good relations between management and workers.

The assessment of the degree of effectiveness of these joint committees establishes that the participative management forums have not been very effective and successful. A majority of workers and management personnel have also perceived low effectiveness of participative forums. The factors attributing to such a state of affairs include advisory role of the committees, their limited scope, poor implementation of joint decision, defective institutional arrangements, poor communication and more so the lack of sincerity and apathetic attitude of the participants.

It is quite revealing that vast majority of workers and management personnel attach high hopes with the schemes. Workers have shown considerable interest to participate in decision-making process of the organisation and the management has also shown willingness to accept the workers' involvement in decision-making in various levels. There is considerable unanimity with regard to the main objectives of participation. The organisational climate, existing in the industry, is also conductive for participation as perceived by workers and management personnel.

Workers and management personnel perceived that workers, in their organisations, have very little influence in decision-making, but both the parties desire that the level of workers influence should be more than what they currently have. They desire maximum level of influence of workers in local, medium and co-operation level decision-making issues and minimum in distant level issues. Both the group desire to arrive at decisions at various levels through joint consultation and information sharing, except at distant level participation issues which they consider to be management prerogatives.

Regarding the desires forms of participation, both the groups prefer to have joint committees at various levels of organisation, having workers' representatives either directly or through unions. Workers showed some desire for board level participation, where as it was the least preferred by management personnel. Management feels that at the present stage of development, workers' participation in decision-making process at the board level may not be much purposeful.

The findings of the study lead us to the conclusion that both, workers' and management, have developed their strong faith in participative management. They consider it highly utilitarian and mutually beneficial. If various barriers to participation are removed and participation utilized meaningfully, it can help in improving the quality of decision-making, organisational effectiveness efficiency and satisfaction of workers.

Trade Unionism

The origin and growth of labour movement in the textile industry of Jammu and Kashmir is traceable as far back as 1865 and since then it has grown parallel to that of the State. In fact, the textile industry has throughout occupied a predominant position in the trade union movement and still continues to be the most unionised one. In 1986, the industry accounted for about 12.5 per cent of the total number of registered trade unions in the State. These union also account for a substantial proportion of the trade union membership.

The degree of unionisation reported in the sample units is much more than that reported in the Kanpur Cotton Textile Industry and Ahmedabad Textile Industry. It is encouraging to find that there is a firm and widespread conviction among the employees about the absolute necessity of trade unions. A majority of workers interviewed (83.20%) is union members. The economic needs in the form of desire for higher wages, better fringe benefits, proper working conditions, effective representation of grievances, adequate protection, job security and working class strength and solidarity seems to motivate the workers much in joining the unions. The study of non-members' responses about the reasons for not joining any union reveals that majority of them was dissatisfied with the functioning of union and their leadership.

Union members always participate actively in almost all the important union activities which they as union members deem necessary. The index of the degree of union participation indicates that 46 per cent of union members showed moderate and 40 per cent considerably higher degree of union participation. An analysis of the degree of union participation *vis-a-vis* their socio-psychological and personal variables indicates that union participation is higher among those workers who are comparatively young, skilled, politically active, interesting in unions and earning less wages. The rural-urban background, education and martial status of the workers do not seem to affect the degree of union participation.

The management has apparently shown favourable attitude towards trade unions. But the attitude seems to be somewhat lukewarm. Despite holding a favourable attitude towards trade unions and their leaders in general, for one reason or the other, the sign of considerable apathy and reservation among managers to accept the workers' decisive role in settling disputes are noticed in the study.

On the whole, the textile trade unions show the general features of trade unions in the Ctate i.e., small size, loose organisation structure, financial constraints, high degree of politicalisation and domination of outside leadership. Almost all the unions operating in the industry are plant-level unions and the industry-cum-region unions of the type found in Bombay, Ahmedabad and Kanpur are rarely found. But the unions in general are free from many evils which have otherwise plagued the trade union government of the country. By and large, the union-management relations are cordial. Militancy, violence and inter-union rivalry have not crept into the ranks of unions which reflect the infant character of the trade union movement, which has to be encouraged and protected.

Dispute Handling

In Jammu and Kashmir State the Industrial Relations Machinery, consisting of both the machinery for direct and third party settlements, is modelled by and large on the prevailing policy in the country as a whole. Before Independence, the State has virtually no set policy on labour and the industrial relations were conditioned on eco-political necessities rather than on sound traditions. There is no evidence on record that could reflects the Government's concern to redress the workers' grievances and built-up healthy labour-management relations. With the spreading spectrum of industrialisation and growing labour movement in the State, the Government started realising its responsibility in maintaining harmonious industrial relations. It took upon itself the key-role of an active third party in Industrial Relations System.

In all the organisations under study the formal three-tier grievance procedure existed, through which workers sought redressal of their grievances. Most of the grievances related to promotion, pay fixation, working hours, transfers, work assignments, disciplinary action and various other production problems. A majority of the workers (48%) felt that the grievances of workers.

In spite of an increasing trend of workers, having been benefited by standing orders, a glance over the declining index of response ratio reveals that the progress of standing orders certification has been far from satisfactory. In the textile industry up to 1985, 12 industrial units with employment of 5,711 workers were covered under the Act, but out of these only 10 units with employment of 5,405 has certified the standing orders. Further in most of the cases, it has been observed that standing orders have remained the 'letters of law' and have 'hardly been observed in spirit'.

Collective bargaining, with a very long past history has been shaping the labour-management relationship in the industry. Various bipartite and tripartite collective agreements concluded have proved very helpful in avoiding many of the major strikes and in maintaining, as far as possible, peaceful labour-management relations in the industry. But the process has not been as successful and effective as that witnessed in Ahmedabad Textile Industry and Cotton Textile Industry of Kanpur. Various reasons responsible for such a state of affairs have been, among others, the weak bargaining power of the unions, easy accessibility of conciliation and adjudication machinery, small size of the majority of industrial establishment and frequent State intervention.

The State Industrial Relations Machinery, in the absence of a sound industrial relations policy, has not succeeded in fulfilling its stated legal responsibility and has failed to pave the way for establishing cordial relationship between labour and management. The State has bought industrial peace by concessions from time to time which has hindered the development of a fully matured industrial relations system.

The low and decreasing percentage of settlements and the high and increasing percentage of failure, coupled with the majority perception of respondents, suggests that the conciliation machinery in the State has failed to deliver the goods. The recommendatory nature of conciliation, insincere and causal approach of disputants, availability of compulsory adjudication, lack of proper selection, absence of training and doubtful integrity of the conciliation officers have been mainly responsible for such a situation.

Non-availability of the required data has made the study of the working of arbitration and adjudication machinery very difficult. However, on the basis of the responses of disputants, it can be concluded that the workers of these systems has been ineffective and their processes lengthy and cumbersome. The longer time taken by the government in making reference, the lengthy judicial procedure followed, the low an decreasing percentage of settlements, the high and increasing rate of delay, and absence of any deterrent punishment for violation of awards have rendered the arbitration and adjudication machinery very ineffective.

The important conclusion is that though the direct measures of dispute handling have, by and large, been able to create a conductive environment for peaceful labour relations, the industrial relations machinery is still characterised by the State intervention, which the Government considers a must to keep the production running and undisturbed so as to achieve rapid economic growth. However, majority of the respondents, both workers and management personnel, show their strong favour for joint consultation and negotiations followed by conciliation. Both the groups show almost equal inclination against voluntary arbitration and adjudication. Some workers were in favour of getting their grievances redressed through strikes, but most of them preferred strikes as a last resort only.

SUGGESTIONS AND POLICY IMPLICATIONS

A number of suggestions have been put forth in connection with various aspects of policy and practice in the relevant chapters. Many of them are of fundamental nature and importance and are summarised below along with some other principal recommendation having broad policy implication:

1. The study draws attention to the fact that wage discontent, poor working conditions and welfare amenities continue to be the major considerations in industrial conflicts. Unless these basic causes are removed, no amount of other improvements will help in establishing harmonious relations between labour and management. Wages bonus and allowance conflicts invite macro-solutions, since these cannot be settled in a large number of cases at the plant level. There should be an overall wage policy and as a matter of policy the cost of living of workers should be linked with the rise in prices and wages should be revised from time to time taking into consideration the local conditions and capacity of the industry to pay.
2. Considering that the increase in money earnings has not led to an increase in real wages and that the improvements in wages alone can neither satisfy the workers nor cause job mobility and work commitment among them, the non-wage incentives should receive more attention than they have hitherto received. These facilities in the form of dress items, subsidised housing and canteens, family planning, recreational activities, transport, education, health care assistance, etc., would go a long way in improving the economic lot of workers. The provision of these facilities, it is proved, is less inflationary than cash payments.
3. Certainly no amount of efforts will help in the mitigation of hardships of textile workers of the State, unless steps are simultaneously taken to raise the average productivity of the industry, which has, so far, been the main limiting factor. The wherewithal for financing the incentives must come out of the

economic surplus created by workers themselves, with the co-operation of the management, otherwise the progress as would be forced upon the industry will cause no more than a once-over change with no promise for setting into motion a self-generating virtuous spiral of growth. The productivity of the workers cannot go up unless the machinery is improved, better arrangements are made for material handling, labour efficiency is increased, technical knowhow is made available, market fluctuations and under-capacity utilization are removed, idle time is curtailed and pace of work increased and management education and development is taken up on priority basis.

4. The study has identified some worker groups which are dissatisfied with their jobs. The management would have to be particularly vigilant about the motivational requirements of these workers for their effective utilization. It should adopt more progressive measures for making the work more humane, interesting and challenging; evolve a proper information system and give the workers fair treatment so that they feel important and develop a sense of belongingness. Effective grievance handling procedure, participative management, code of conduct and similar measures based on mutual trust and confidence can be helpful in creating a conductive environment for good industrial relations, provided these are properly implemented and sincerely followed. But at the same time it has to be borne in mind that as long as the basic needs of the workers are not satisfied no amount of sophisticated techniques of management would provide them with any intrinsic satisfaction.
5. Industrial relation is never a one-sided game but depends for its maintenance, on the mutual understanding, faith and good-will of all the actors in industrial relations system. The positive approach of one party towards the whole issue needs to be favourably responded by the other. If only workers and management learn to co-exist and mutually accommodate each others' attitudes and responses, the drift in industrial relations can be arrested. They have to realise that their interests are inextricably interwoven and that, instead of depending on outside help, they have to help themselves and in that lies the solution of the problem of industrial conflicts.

The workers should recognise their moral obligation to do a good day's for a good day's wages, take genuine interest in their work to accomplish company's production targets, develop an uninhibited attitude towards management, join hands with it in times of crisis, assess realistically the difficulties of management and resort to peaceful and constructive means in order to establish long lasting industrial peace.

The role of the trade unions also requires complete re-orientation. From the traditional, militant and agitational attitude, they have to switch over to the role of welfare organisations, looking after all aspects of labour welfare; covering not only the monetary aspects of their career but also social aspects embracing such wider issues as education and training as well.

Management must ensure fair treatment to all the workers without fear or favour. The everchanging needs of the work-forced should be kept in mind and met fairly and spontaneously. Where as the State as third party, must represent the social interest and provide infrastructure through its economic and social policies and Industrial Relations Machinery for stable labour relations.

6. For the effective conflict resolution and dispute handling, four principles, enunciated by first Central Pay Commission, are suggested for the guidance of the parties. These are:

   (i) in the adjustment of differences between labour and management the best course is to prevent the differences from developing into disputes,
   (ii) even when the difference has developed into a dispute, it is desirable to secure its settlements by negotiations between the two parties,
   (iii) if, however, it becomes necessary to secure outside help, it must rather be for the purpose of mediation and consultation rather then for adjudication and
   (iv) if all attempts of consultation fall, adjudication should be sought by voluntary settlements rather than by compulsory reference.

7. There is an important need for the formulation of sound and healthy Industrial Relations Policy based on constructive and collaborative attitude, development of confidence and good faith between the labour and management. The industrial relations

policy should aim at ensuring fair wages, good working conditions and realistic terms of employment and also speedy resolution of disputes by instituting effective statutory machinery, with encouragement to voluntary procedures in conformity with the importance of industrial democracy.

8. The success of participative management will depend on the sincerity, depth of conviction and openness of both management and workers. Unless the two sides are convinced and feel enthusiastic about the long term benefits accruing from workers' participation it is not possible to make a success of it. There is a need for change in the attitude of both management and workers; because the schemes of participative management and the question of operationalising these schemes are primarily a matter of attitude orientation. Proper training and education of workers, effective communication in the form of information sharing, peaceful industrial relations climate, existence of single but strong trade unions, effective grievances settlement procedure, consisting bridging of the social distance between the representatives of workers and management, timely implementation of the recommendations, Government support, etc., will go a long way in determining the success of participative management. The success stories of TISCO, BHEL, Central Coal Fields, etc., in participative management should be given wide publicity in the industry.
9. There should be strong, stable and well-organised trade unions as a pre-condition for successful collective bargaining process. Proper union leadership will strengthen the union-management relationship. In order to reduce the dominance of outsiders, legislative measures are necessary. These measures should limit the number of outsiders who can be office bearers in the unions. It will be better to allow the outsiders as only the members of the executive committees of the unions, leaving important positions to be filled up from among the workers.

There should be a Central trade union organisation in the textile industry of the State in the pattern of Ahmedabad Textile Labour Association, to be called as Jammu and Kashmir Textile Labour Association, to which all the textile workers and their plant labour unions should be affiliated. Because the success of Ahmedabad Textile Labour Association has made trade unionists to realise the importance of organising workers on the basis of craft. This will not only ensure the working class strength and solidarity but also web out the political impact and political interests being served by the working class.

10. To ensure industrial peace, inside the industry, all the labour enactments should be implemented readily. Some efforts have to be made and care taken to see that the implementation is sincere and honest and that unnecessary technical interpretation of the 'letter of law' is not adopted for the sake of convenience. The key factor in establishing good relations is a spontaneous acceptance of legal responsibility in this respect.
11. A tripartite evaluation and monitoring cell should be established at the State level having representatives from the Ministry of Labour, trade unions and employers management associations. The cell with the support of behavioural scientists and labour experts, for proper guidance and expertise, should evaluate the working and implementation of labour welfare schemes, participative management forums, labour legislation and industrial relations policy.
12 One of the main factors responsible for the deplorable labour conditions is the poor performance of the State Labour Department. The present set up of the department was created long back and marginally strengthened in 1969. The existing set up of the labour department at regional level, headed by Deputy Labour Commissioners, was sanctioned as early as 1961. At that time there were only few labour laws to administer, in the State and the industrialisation was also negligible. Now we have got 26 labour laws, over 700 registered factories, about 60 thousand shop and commercial establishments, apart from huge forest and construction works where lakhs of workers are employed. The entire task of implementation of the labour laws and Labour Welfare Schemes is entrusted to this department, which does not have the necessary infrastructure and as such is burdened with these responsibilities. The available enforcement machinery in the department has proved no match to the task entrusted to it. The department, therefore, needs reorganisation and re-orientation on priority basis. The 7th Five-Year Plan outlay of Rs. 44 lakhs provided for the entire labour sector is not sufficient. Adequate funds should be provided for strengthening of the department, if effective enforcement of labour laws is to be made possible.

There are no separate departments of personnel/industrial relations in most of the textile units and as a result the redressal of personnel problems has no priority. The personnel/industrial relations departments should be set up in the units separately to deal with all matters concerning industrial relations in the industry.

CONCLUDING OBSERVATIONS

The overall conclusion emerging from this study is that apparently a marginal number of industrial conflicts has been reported in the textile industry of Jammu and Kashmir State. But this does not necessarily mean that the labour-management relations in the industry are very cordial and constructive. Being the predominant industry in the State, the poor industrial relations in textile industry has and would adversely affect the overall effectiveness and efficiency of industrial relations scenario. What is required is a good infrastructure for the management of industrial conflicts so that the situation does not go beyond limits.

The study has highlighted some pre-requisites for the maintenance of harmonious labour-management relations. The investigator has reasons to believe that the conclusions of the study, along with the suggestions, if rightly perceived and properly implemented may facilitate the task of settling industrial disputes and promoting industrial peace. However, industrial relations problems are living and dynamic and there can be no final and permanent solution to them. Hence, there is always need for research and indepth study in the area so as to bring out, from time to time, the factors responsible for the success or failure of industrial relations scene under different situations and contexts. The present study has brought out some research gaps which have considerable bearing on industrial relations. It is suggested, therefore, that more detailed investigations into these vital issues need to be taken up by separate comparative and contextual studies.

APPENDICES

APPENDIX I

FACULTY OF COMMERCE & MANAGEMENT STUDIES, UNIVERSITY OF KASHMIR, SRINAGAR

Labour-Management Relations in Textile Industry of J&K State
Interview Schedule for Workers

(All the information will be treated as strictly confidential)

Sl. No. of Schedule: ....
Date of Issue: ....
Date of Return: ....

Personal Data

1. Name of the organisation:
2. Name of the worker:
3. Designation:
4. Age:
5. Location: Urban———, Rural———, Semi-Urban———,
6. Regional background: Kashmir———, Jammu———, outsider———,
7. Education: No/yes, If yes, state the level of education:
8. Marital Status: Married/Unmarried
9. Date when joined the factory:
10. Nature of work: Skilled/Semi-skilled/Unskilled
11. Wage/Salary: Monthly Rs.———
12. Total No. of dependents: ———
13. Training Yes/No
14. Member of any political party: Yes/No

15. No. of absentees in the last month ———

Workers' Satisfaction from Job

1. How far are you satisfied with your present wages?
   Not at all/Slightly/Moderately/Considerably/Completely.
2. How do your wages compare with those in similar other Industries in the State?
   Low/Slightly Low/Equal/Slightly high/High.
3. How interesting do you find your work?
   Not at all/Slightly/Moderately/Considerably/Completely.
4. It is said that Public/Private Sector workers do not work hard, what is true in your factory?
   Not work hard/Work hard to a little extent/To some extent/To a lot of extent/To a great extent.
5. To what extent your job is secured in the factory.
   Not at all/Slightly/Moderately/Considerably/Completely.
6. What are the chances of your promotion in the company Low — Slightly low/Average/Slightly high/High.
7. How far are you satisfied with the supervisory behaviour,
   Not at all/Slightly/Moderately/Considerably/Completely.
8. How far are you satisfied with the management behaviour,
   Not at all/Slightly/Moderately/Considerably/Completely.
9. To what extent are you satisfied with the various working conditions in the factory.
   Not at all/Slightly/Moderately/Considerably/Completely.
10. To what extent are you satisfied with various personnel policies?
    Not at all/Slightly/Moderately/Considerably/Completely.
11. To what extent are you satisfied with the various welfare facilities?
    Not at all/Slightly/Moderately/Considerably/ Completely.
12. On the whole are you satisfied with your job?
    Not at all/Slightly/Moderately/Considerably/Completely.

Workers' Expectations

1. You know that a supervisor plays an important role in modern industries. What can make him a good supervisor. From the following list tick (√) three important qualities of a good

supervisor with regard to his relations with workers in order of priority:

(i) Co-operativeness
(ii) Minimum use of authority
(iii) Believes in friendly relations
(iv) Does not exploit works weaknesses
(v) Impartial in dealing with workers'.

2. From the following tick (√) any three qualities of a good supervisor with regard to his work:

(i) Knows his job well
(ii) Trusts subordinates
(iii) Capable to exercise good control
(iv) Recognises the merits of the workers
(v) Believes in delegation of authority
(vi) Accepts suggestions from workers
(vii) Effective in solving workers' problems
(viii) Makes interest in his work
(ix) Others (allows freedom to work or rest, influences decisions allows to work according to capacity).

3. From the following list tick (√) any three qualities of a good supervisor with regard to his relations with the Management:

(i) Maintains good relations with management
(ii) Never misleads management by biased complaints
(iii) Tactful in dealing with management
(iv) Obedient to management
(v) His recommendations are respected
(vi) Fights for the cause of workers
(vii) Projects healthy image of workers to the management

4. What can make a supervisor a bad supervisor ? From the following list tick (√) three important features of a bad supervisor with regard to his relations with workers:

(i) Not bothers about workers' problems
(ii) Partial in recommending promotions

(iii) Avoids mixing with workers
(iv) Rude behaviour
(v) Exploits workers' weaknesses
(vi) Complaints about minor issues.

5. From the following tick (√) three important features of a bad supervisor with regard to his relations with work:

(i) Does not know his job
(ii) Unable to give proper instructions
(iii) Does not like listening to workers
(iv) Tries to conceal his lack of knowledge
(v) Finding fault with workers and never satisfied with them
(vi) Unable to get work done
(vii) Not interested in his work
(viii) Unnecessarily interferes with the work of others
(ix) Unduly punishes the workers

6. From the following tick (√) three important features of a bad supervisor with regard to his relations with management:

(i) Maintains bad relations with management
(ii) Misleads management about workers
(iii) Pleases management by taking more work from workers
(iv) Steals workers' ideas to gain unearned fame
(v) Any other (please specify)

7. From the following tick (√) three important features of a bad supervisor with regard to his personal behaviour:

(i) Dictatory behaviour
(ii) Nasty way of talking to workers
(iii) Selfish
(iv) Hot tempered
(v) Indulges in unfair practices
(vi) Unable to maintain discipline
(vii) Others (irresponsible, revengeful, talkative).

8. What makes management the best management. From the following list tick (√) three important qualities of a best

management with regard to the salary and service conditions:

(i) Pays well
(ii) Good service conditions, such as promotions, permanancy, provident fund, training, etc.
(iii) Encourages participation
(iv) Good fringe benefits and bonus
(v) Consistent policies
(vi) Lesser hours of work, equitable distribution of work according to capacity

9. From the following list tick (√) three important qualities of best management with regard to physical and psychological work environment:

(i) Cordial relations with labour
(ii) Ideal working conditions
(iii) Economically sound company and good reputation
(iv) Proper tools and equipments
(v) Good and understanding supervision
(vi) Hygienic conditions of work
(vii) Others (specify by name)

10. From the following list tick (√) three important features of best management with regard to welfare facilities:

(i) Adequate welfare facilities
(ii) Proper accommodation
(iii) Good recreational and educational facilities
(iv) Proper medical facilities
(v) Any other (please specify)

11. What makes the Management the worst management. From the following list tick (√) three important features of worst management with regard to salary and service conditions:

(i) Low pay
(ii) Absence of provident fund and other social security measures
(iii) Slow and partiality in promotions

(iv) Lack of fringe benefits and bonus
(v) Unhealthy attitude towards unions
(vi) Strictly getting work done
(vii) Involvement in unfair labour practices

12. From the following list tick (√) three important features of worst management with regard to physical and psychological work environment:

(i) Poor working conditions
(ii) No consideration for workers' victimisation
(iii) Partial and harassing supervisors
(iv) Absence of proper tools and equipments
(v) Economically poor company, bad reputation
(vi) Others (no chance to improve or learn, discouraging unions, absence of proper training)

13. From the following list tick (√) three important characteristics of worst management with regard to the provision of welfare facilities in the factory:

(i) Absence of proper welfare facilities
(ii) Absence of medical facilities
(iii) Absence of recreational and educational facilities
(iv) Absence of proper accommodation
(v) Any other (please Specify)

Trade Unionism

1. Are you a member of any trade union: Yes/No
2. If yes, please mention the name of the union:
3. How interested are you in unions in general:
   Not at all/a little/Average/Very much
4. About unions in general, is your opinion favourable or not.
   Favourable/Unfavourable/Indifferent
5. Would you consider unions
   Necessary/Unnecessary/can't say
6. To what extent you participate in union activities:
   Not at all/a little average/to a great extent
7. If you are a member, why did you join the union. From the

following give any three reasons in order of priority:

(i) Get higher wages, fringe benefits, bonus, etc.
(ii) Provide job security.
(iii) Safeguard against victimisation
(iv) Obtain better working conditions and welfare facilities
(v) Fair promotion and advancement
(vi) Workers' unity and solidarity
(vii) For labour-management co-operation
(vii) Majority wanted it Pressure from fellow workers
(ix) Because all are members
(x) Any other (please mention)

8. If you are not a member of any union, please state, from the following, three reasons for not joining any union in order of priority:

(i) No knowledge of any union
(ii) Fear of victimisation
(iii) No need to join any union, unions doing nothing for workers
(iv) No confidence in union leadership
(v) Can't afford union membership
(vi Temporary nature of job
(vii) No difficulties, getting good salary & other benefits
(viii) Got job on the promise of safe conduct and loyalty to the company
(ix) Having family, can't take the risk of joining any union
(x) Any other (please mention)

9. If you are a member what work do you do for the union?

(i) Payment of union dues:	Never	Sometimes	Always
(ii) Collecting funds for union:	"	"	"
(iii) Attending union meetings:	"	"	"
(iv) Participating in union elections	"	"	
(v) Making new members:	"	"	"
(vi) Taking part in strikes	"	"	"
(vii) Reading union notices:	"	"	"
(viii) Going in support of			

union to tribunals/
conciliation/etc.

(ix) Any other (please mention)

10. Do you think that unions fulfil the interests of leaders and not the workers:
    Agree/Undecided/Disagree.
11. Should there be only one union in a factory or more than one:
    One/More than one.
12. What are the factors responsible for the failure of unions in meeting with the desired objectives?

    (i) Disunity of workers
    (ii) Unjustified demands
    (iii) Non-co-operative attitude of management
    (iv) Incompetent leadership
    (v) Any other.

Workers' Participation in Management

1. Do you like your own job?
   Very much-3, to some extent-2, Not at all-1.
2. How is your relationship with your supervisors/managers
   Cordial-3, fairly cordial-2, Not cordial-1.
3. How is your relationship with your co-workers?
   Cordial-3, fairly cordial-2, Not cordial-1.
4. To what extent are you free to approach supervisors/managers?
   Fully-3, To some extent-2, Not at all-1.
5. To what extent is your top management supportive
   Fully-3 To some extent-2, Not at all-1.
6. Should workers be given a right to participate in Management decision-making?
   Never/Seldom/to some extent/Usually/Always.
7. Does management encourage workers' participation?
   Never/Seldom/To some extent/Usually/Always.
8. To what extent will workers participation be successful in future?
   Not at all/To a little extent/To some extent/Quite a lot of extent/To a great extent.

9. Are you a member of any committee in your Company Yes/No
10. If yes, please mention the name of the committee______
11. If no, then would you like to become member of any committee: Yes/No
12. How far are the following committees useful in your company (if existing)?

		Useful	Moderately	Useless
a.	Works Committee			
b.	Joint Committee	"	"	"
c.	Production Committee	"	"	"
d.	Safety Committee	"	"	"
e.	Grievance Committee	"	"	"
f.	Medical Committee	"	"	"
g.	Sports Committee	"	"	"
h.	Canteen Committee	"	"	"
i.	Any other Committee (Please mention)	"	"	"

13. How far have the above committees been effective in the following areas:

		High	Moderate	Low
a.	Increasing production			
b.	Improving quality of production	"	"	"
c.	Reducing cost of production	"	"	"
d.	Eliminating wastage	"	"	"
e.	Ensure safety	"	"	"
f.	Improve communication	"	"	"
g.	Reducing work stoppages	"	"	"
h.	Improve labour-management relations	"	"	"
i.	Satisfy workers urge for self expression	"	"	"

14. At present do you have any influence in the following decision areas?

a. Formulation of overall organisation policies and their implementation:
No influence/Very little/To some extent/Quite a lot/To a great extent.

b. Formulation of marketing policy of the company:
No influence/Very little/To some extent/Quite a lot/To a great extent.

c. Operation of sanctioned Budgets:
No influence/Very little/To some extent/Quite a lot/To a great extent.

d. Allocation of profits between investments, reserves/etc.:
No influence/Very little/To some extent/Quite a lot/To a great extent.

e. Expansion and diversification of business of the company:
No/Very little/To some extent/Quite a lot/To a great extent.

f. Formulation of recruitment policy of executives/officers of the company:
No influence/Very little/To some extent/Quite a lot/To a great extent.

g. Formulation of recruitment policy of workers:
No/Very little/Some extent/A lot/A great extent.

h. Development of training programmes for the workers:
No/Very little/Some extent/A lot/Great extent.

i. Formulation of promotion policy for workers:
No/Very little/Some extent/A lot/Great extent.

j. Principle of taking disciplinary action against workers:
No/Very little/Some extent/A lot/Great extent.

k. Formulation of wage policy and other benefits for workers:
No/Very little/Some extent/A lot/Great extent.

l. Practice of handling grievances of workers:
No/Very little/Some extent/A lot/Great extent.

m. Policy for rewarding workers for good work:
No/Very little/Some extent/A lot/Great extent.

n. Policy for determining rate of bonus for the workers:
No/Very little/Some extent/A lot/Great extent.

o. Arrangement for workers housing:
No/Very little/Some extent/A lot/Great extent.

p. Determining welfare programmes/facilities for workers:
No/Very little/Some extent/A lot/Great extent.

q. Maintaining good working conditions:
No/Very little/Some extent/A lot/Great extent.

r. Provision for safety measures:
No/Very little/Some extent/A lot/Great extent.

s. One's own work (sequence/method/co-ordination and evaluation of work):
No/Very little/Some extent/A lot/Great extent.

t. Introduction of new technology:
No/Very little/Some extent/Great extent.

u. Increasing production:
No/Very little/Some extent/A lot/Great extent.

15. To what extent you desire to participate in the following decision areas:

a. Formulation of overall organisational policy and their implementation:
Not at all/Slightly/Moderately/Considerably/Completely.

b. Formulation of marketing policy:
Not at all/Slightly/Moderately/Considerably/Completely.

c. Operation of sanctioned budgets:
Not at all/Slightly/Moderately/Considerably/Completely.

d. Allocation of profits between investments/reserves/etc.:
Not at all/Slightly/Moderately/Considerably/Completely.

e. Expansion and diversification of business:
Not at all/Slightly/Moderately/Considerably/Completely.

f. Formulation of recruitment policy for managers/officers:
Not at all/Slightly/Moderately/Considerably/Completely.

g. Formulation of recruitment policy of workers
Not at all/Slightly/Moderately/Considerably/Completely.

h. Development of training programmes for the workers:
Not at all/Slightly/Moderately/Considerably/Completely.

i. Formulation of promotion policy for workers:
Not at all/Slightly/Moderately/Considerably/Completely.

j. Principle of taking disciplinary action against workers:
Not at all/Slightly/Moderately/Considerably/Completely.

k. Formulation of wage policy & other benefits for workers:
Not at all/Slightly/Moderately/Considerably/Completely.

l. Practice of handling grievances of workers:
Not at all/Slightly/Moderately/Considerably/Completely.

m. Policy of rewarding workers for good work:
Not at all/Slightly/Moderately/Considerably/Completely.

n. Policy of determining rate of bonus for workers:
Not at all/Slightly/Moderately/Considerably/Completely.

o. Arrangement for workers housing:
Not at all/Slightly/Moderately/Considerably/Completely.

p. Determining welfare programmes/facilities for workers:
Not at all/Slightly/Moderately/Considerably/Completely.

q. Way of maintaining good working conditions for workers:
Not at all/Slightly/Moderately/Considerably/Completely.

r. Provision for safety measures for workers:
Not at all/Slightly/Moderately/Considerably/Completely.

s. One's own work (sequence,method, co-ordination and evaluation of work):
Not at all/Slightly/Moderately/Considerably/Completely.

t. Introduction of new technology:
Not at all/Slightly/Moderately/Considerably/Completely.

u. Increasing productivity:
Not at all/Slightly/Moderately/Considerably/Completely.

16. Taking into consideration all the above decision areas which one of the following ways of involving workers in decision-making you prefer

(i) This is a management prerogative
(ii) Information sharing
(iii) Consultation
(iv) Joint decision-making
(v) Collective bargaining
(vi) Workers say to be accepted

17. In your opinion, to what extent can workers' participation in management be helpful in achieving the following objectives:

(i) To maintain industrial peace:
Not at all/Slightly/Moderately/Considerably/Completely.

(ii) To increase production:
Not at all/Slightly/Moderately/Considerably/Completely.

(iii) To obtain a sense of involvement:
Not at all/Slightly/Moderately/Considerably/Completely.

(iv) To receive more monetary benefits:
Not at all/Slightly/Moderately/Considerably/Completely.

(v) To improve team work:
Not at all/Slightly/Moderately/Considerably/Completely.

(vi) To increase employee commitment to organisation:
Not at all/Slightly/Moderately/Considerably/Completely.

(vii) To improve quality of management decisions:
Not at all/Slightly/Moderately/Considerably/Completely.

(viii) To develop workers to accept change:
Not at all/Slightly/Moderately/Considerably/Completely.

(ix) Improve communication:
Not at all/Slightly/Moderately/Considerably/Completely.

(x) Derive better amenity and service conditions for workers:
Not at all/Slightly/Moderately/Considerably/Completely.

(xi) To help workers to control the organisation:
Not at all/Slightly/Moderately/Considerably/Completely.

18. There are different forms of participation in management decision-making which of the following forms you prefer and to what extent:

(i) Having one or two workers nominated to the Board of Directors:
Do not prefer at all/Prefer Slightly/Moderately/Considerably/Completely

(ii) Workers purchasing shares and representing in the Board:
Not at all prefer Slightly/Moderately/Considerably/Completely.

(iii) Having worker representatives in various joint Committees:
Not at all/Slightly/Moderately/Considerably/Completely.

(iv) Through union officials/representatives only representing in various Joint Committees:
Not at all/Slightly/Moderately/Considerably/Completely.

(v) Through suggestion Schemes:
Not at all/Slightly/Moderately/Considerably/Completely

(vi) Through face to face decision-making at work place:
Not at all/Slightly/Moderately/Considerably/Completely.

(vii) Any other scheme (Please mention the name, and extent to which you prefer).

19. The scheme of workers' participation has not met with desired success so far. In your opinion to what extent have the following factors been responsible for such failure:

    (i) lack of supportive climate in the organisation:
    Not at all/Slightly/Moderately/Considerably/Completely.
    (ii) Poor communication:
    Not at all/Slightly/Moderately/Considerably/Completely.
    (iii) Workers fear of victimisation by the management:
    Not at all/Slightly/Moderately/Considerably/Completely.
    (iv) Managers fear of giving up power:
    Not at all/Slightly/Moderately/Considerably/Completely.
    (v) Lack of adequate education/training of workers to participate:
    Not at all/Slightly/Moderately/Considerably/Completely.
    (vi) Lack of desire of workers to participate:
    Not at all/Slightly/Moderately/Considerably/Completely.
    (vii) Attitude of trade unions in the factory:
    Not at all/Slightly/Moderately/Considerably/Completely.
    (viii) Multiplicity of unions:
    Not at all/Slightly/Moderately/Considerably/Completely.
    (ix) Lack of leadership among work, force:
    Not at all/Slightly/Moderately/Considerably/Completely.
    (x) Lack of proper industrial relations climate:
    Not at all/Slightly/Moderately/Considerably/Completely.
    (xi) Lack of clarity of concept of participation:
    Not at all/Slightly/Moderately/Considerably/Completely.
    (xii) Any other (please specify giving the extent).

20. What steps should be taken to make workers' participation a success:

    1.
    2.
    3.

Conflict Resolution and Promotion of Industrial Peace

1. What have been the main causes of disputes in your plant so far. Please give in order of priority:

1.
2.
3.

2. Which method of dispute settlement you favour. Please give in order of priority.

   1. Strikes
   2. Mutual Negotiations
   3. Conciliation
   4. Court
   5. Voluntary Arbitration
   6. Any other (please mention).

3. What is the attitude of management towards your grievances: Sympathetic/Unsympathetic/Indifferent.
4. Do you think that if the workers represent their cases directly and not through unions it would improve relations with management:
   Never/Sometimes/Always.
5. Do you find that personal discussions with management are better for maintaining cordial relations with management:
   Never/Sometimes/Always.
6. To what extent can workers participation in management maintain cordial labour-management relations:
   Never/Sometimes/Always.
7. Will workers or union leaders consultation, while framing standing orders, be helpful in maintaining good industrial relations:
   Never/Sometimes/Always.
8. Do you think that higher wages, bonus and profit sharing schemes can lead to cordial relations:
   Never/Sometimes/Always.
9. Do you think that co-partnership is helpful for maintaining good industrial relations:
   Never/Sometimes/Always.
10. What are your suggestions for improving the industrial relations in your establishment. Please give in order of priority:

   1
   2.
   3.
   4.
   5.
   6.
   7.
   8.
   9.
   10.

APPENDIX II

FACULTY OF COMMERCE & MANAGEMENT STUDIES, UNIVERSITY OF KASHMIR, SRINAGAR

Labour-Management Relations in Textile Industry of J&K State
Interview Schedule for Management

(All the information will be treated as strictly confidential)

Sl. No. of Schedule: ....
Date of Issue: ....
Date of Return: ....

Personal Data

1. Name:
2. Age:
3. Designation:
4. Department:
5. Length of Service:
6. Education:

Trade Unionism

1. To what extent do trade unions co-operate with the management in your plant:
   High/Moderate/Low.
2. Do you find the trade unions co-operative in carrying out the production programmes in your plant:
   Yes/To some extent/No.
3. Do the majority of workers in your establishment follow their trade union leaders blindly or disassociate themselves if they consider unions' stand unjustified:
   Yes/Sometimes/Never.

4. Do you feel that the majority of the workers force the trade unions to take stiff attitude towards the management:
   Often/Sometimes/Never.
5. What in your opinion is the influence of trade union leaders on the workers:
   Good/Fair/Bad.
6. What is your opinion about the trade union leaders:
   a) Sincere: No/To some extent/Yes.
   b) Popular: No/To some extent/Yes.
   c) Capable: No/To some extent/Yes.
   d) Selfish: No/To some extent/Yes.
7. What is the role of political leaders in trade unions:
   Useful/Unuseful/To some extent/Harmful.
8. Do the workers in your plant by and large participate in trade union activities:
   Participate to a great extent/Sometimes/Never.
9. What are the major issues of disagreement between the unions and management in your plant (please specify):
   1.
   2.
   3.

Workers' Participation in Management

1. Do you feel that workers should participate in decision-making:
   Never/Seldom/To some extent/Usually/Always.
2. To what extent will workers' participation in management be successful in future:
   Not at all/To a little extent/To some extent/Quite a lot of extent/To a great extent.
3. In your organisation are the workers given a share in decision-making:
   Never/To some extent/Always.
4. Are workers informed of the situation under all circumstances:
   Never/To some extent/Always.
5. Management does everything to keep the company's morale high.
   Never/To some extent/Always.
6. Supervisors/Managers are easily approachable:
   Never/To some extent/Always.

7. Management consults, trains and develops workers:
Never/To some extent/Always.
8. Management communicates effectively with workers:
Never/To some extent/Always.
9. Management shows thoughtfulness for others:
Never/To some extent/Always.
10. Management supports workers when they make mistakes without any bad intentions:
Never/To some extent/Always.
11. Management appreciates when workers do a good job:
Never/To some extent/Always.
12. In your organisation do the workers have any influence in the following decision areas at present:

    a. Formulation of overall organisation policies and their implementations:
    No influence/Very little/To some extent/Quite a lot/To a great extent.
    b. Formulation of marketing policy of the company:
    No/Very little/Some extent/Quite a lot/Great extent.
    c. Operation of sanctioned budgets:
    No/Very little/Some extent/Quite a lot/Great extent.
    d. Allocation of profits between investments, reserves, etc.:
    No/Very little/Some extent/Quite a lot/Great extent.
    e. Expansion and diversification of business:
    No/Very little/Some extent/Quite a lot/Great extent.
    f. Formation of recruitment policy of executives/officers of the company:
    No/Very little/Some extent/Quite a lot/Great extent.
    g. Formation of recruitment policy of workers:
    No/Very little/Some extent/Quite a lot/Great extent.
    h. Development of training programmes for the workers:
    No/Very little/Some extent/Quite a lot/Great extent.
    i. Formation of promotion policy for workers:
    No/Very little/Some extent/Quite a lot/Great extent.
    j. Principle of taking disciplinary action against workers:
    No/Very little/Some extent/Quite a lot/Great extent.
    k. Formation of wage policy and other benefits for workers:
    No/Very little/Some extent/Quite a lot/Great extent.

l. Practice of handling grievances of workers:
No/Very little/Some extent/Quite a lot/Great extent.

m. Policy of rewarding workers for good work:
No/Very little/Some extent/Quite a lot/Great extent.

n. Determining rate of bonus for the workers:
No/Very little/Some extent/Quite a lot/Great extent.

o. Arranging for workers housing:
No/Very little/Some extent/Quite a lot/Great extent.

p. Determining welfare programmes/facilities for workers:
No/Very little/Some extent/Quite a lot/Great extent.

q. Maintaining good working conditions:
No/Very little/Some extent/Quite a lot/Great extent.

r. Provision for safety measures:
No/Very little/Some extent/Quite a lot/Great extent.

s. Ones own work (sequence, method, co-ordination and evaluation of work):
No/Very little/Some extent/Quite a lot/Great extent.

t. Introduction of new technology:
No/Very little/Some extent/Quite a lot/Great extent.

u. Increasing Productivity:
No/Very little/Some extent/Quite a lot/Great extent.

13. To what extent you desire the workers of your company to participate in the following decision areas:

a. Formation of overall organisational policy and their implementation:
Not at all/Slightly/Moderately/Considerably/Completely.

b. Formation of marketing policy:
Not at all/Slightly/Moderately/Considerably/Completely.

c. Operation of sanctioned budget:
Not at all/Slightly/Moderately/Considerably/Completely.

d. Allocation of profits:
Not at all/Slightly/Moderately/Considerably/Completely.

e. Expansion and diversification of business:
Not at all/Slightly/Moderately/Considerably/Completely.

f. Formation of recruitment policy for managers/officers:
Not at all/Slightly/Moderately/Considerably/Completely.

g. Formation of recruitment policy of workers:
Not at all/Slightly/Moderately/Considerably/Completely.

h. Training programmes for the workers:
Not at all/Slightly/Moderately/Considerably/Completely.
i. Formation of promotion policy for workers:
Not at all/Slightly/Moderately/Considerably/Completely.
j. Taking disciplinary action against workers:
Not at all/Slightly/Moderately/Considerably/Completely.
k. Formation of Wage Policy and other benefits for workers:
Not at all/Slightly/Moderately/Considerably/Completely.
l. Handling grievances of workers:
Not at all/Slightly/Moderately/Considerably/Completely.
m. Rewarding workers for good work:
Not at all/Slightly/Moderately/Considerably/Completely.
n. Determining rate of bonus for workers:
Not at all/Slightly/Moderately/Considerably/Completely.
o. Arrangement for workers housing:
Not at all/Slightly/Moderately/Considerably/Completely.
p. Determining welfare programmes/facilities for workers:
Not at all/Slightly/Moderately/Considerably/Completely.
q. Maintaining good working conditions:
Not at all/Slightly/Moderately/Considerably/Completely.
r. Provision for safety measures:
Not at all/Slightly/Moderately/Considerably/Completely.
s. Ones own work (sequence, method, co-ordination, evaluation of work):
Not at all/Slightly/Moderately/Considerably/Completely.
t. Introduction of New Technology:
Not at all/Slightly/Moderately/Considerably/Completely.
u. Increasing productivity:
Not at all/Slightly/Moderately/Considerably/Completely.

14. To what extent can workers' participation in management be helpful in achieving the following objectives, if implemented properly:

a. To maintain industrial peace:
Not at all/Slightly/Moderately/Considerably/Completely.
b. To increase production:
Not at all/Slightly/Moderately/Considerably/Completely.
c. Obtain a sense of belonging:
Not at all/Slightly/Moderately/Considerably/Completely.

d. Receive more monetary benefits:
Not at all/Slightly/Moderately/Considerably/Completely.

e. Improve team work:
Not at all/Slightly/Moderately/Considerably/Completely.

f. Increase employee commitment to organisation:
Not at all/Slightly/Moderately/Considerably/Completely.

g. Improve quality of managerial decisions:
Not at all/Slightly/Moderately/Considerably/Completely.

h. Develop workers to accept change:
Not at all/Slightly/Moderately/Considerably/Completely.

i. Improve Communication:
Not at all/Slightly/Moderately/Considerably/Completely.

j. Derive better welfare and service conditions for workers:
Not at all/Slightly/Moderately/Considerably/Completely.

k. Help workers to control the organisation:
Not at all/Slightly/Moderately/Considerably/Completely.

15. There are different forms of involving workers in decision-making process which of the following forms you prefer and to what extent:

a. Having one or two worker(s) nominated on the Board of Directors:
Not at all/Slightly/Moderately/Considerably/Completely.

b. Workers purchasing shares and representing on the Board:
Not at all/Slightly/Moderately/Considerably/Completely.

c. Having worker representatives in various joint committees:
Not at all/Slightly/Moderately/Considerably/Completely.

d. Through union officials/representatives only representing in various Joint committees:
Not at all/Slightly/Moderately/Considerably/Completely.

e. Through suggestion Schemes:
Not at all/Slightly/Moderately/Considerably/Completely.

f. Through face to face decision-making at work place:
Not at all/Slightly/Moderately/Considerably/Completely.

g. Any other Scheme (please mention the extent to which you prefer).

16. So far, the schemes of participative management have not met with desired success. In your opinion, to what extent have the following factors been responsible for such failure:

    a. Lack of supportive climate in the organisation:
    Not at all/Slightly/Moderately/Considerably/Completely.
    b. Poor Communication:
    Not at all/Slightly/Moderately/Considerably/Completely.
    c. Workers fear of victimisation by the management:
    Not at all/Slightly/Moderately/Considerably/Completely.
    d. Managers fear of giving up power:
    Not at all/Slightly/Moderately/Considerably/Completely.
    e. Lack of adequate education/training of workers to participate:
    Not at all/Slightly/Moderately/Considerably/Completely.
    f. Lack of desire of workers to participate:
    Not at all/Slightly/Moderately/Considerably/Completely.
    g. Attitude of Trade Unions in the factory:
    Not at all/Slightly/Moderately/Considerably/Completely.
    h. Multiplicity of unions:
    Not at all/Slightly/Moderately/Considerably/Completely.
    i. Lack of leadership among work-force:
    Not at all/Slightly/Moderately/Considerably/Completely.
    j. Lack of proper industrial relations climate:
    Not at all/Slightly/Moderately/Considerably/Completely.
    k. lack of clarity of concept of participation:
    Not at all/Slightly/Moderately/Considerably/Completely.
    l. Any other reason (please specify giving the extent).

17. What steps should be taken to make workers participation a success?

    1.
    2.
    3.

Conflict Resolution and Promotion of Industrial Peace

1. What have been the chief causes of disputes in your plant so far (give in order of priority):

1.
2.
3.

2. What method of dispute settlement you favour. Please give in order of priority:
   1. Strikes
   2. Mutual Negotiations
   3. Conciliation
   4. Court
   5. Voluntary Arbitration
   6. Any other (please mention).

3. To what extent, is the bargaining power of management in your plant:
   High/Moderate/Low.
4. Are the unions helpful in solving disputes:
   Never/Sometimes/Always.
5. Do you feel that disputes could be more easily settled if there were no trade unions:
   Yes/No.
6. Do you find that personal discussion with workers' representatives and mutual consultation are better for maintaining cordial labour-management relations:
   Never/Sometimes/Always.
7. In the light of your experience to what extent do you think that workers participation in management can maintain cordial industrial relations:
   Always/Sometimes/Never.
8. Do you think that workers or union leaders' consultation while framing standing orders can be helpful in maintaining harmonious industrial relations in the establishment:
   Always/Sometimes/Never.
9. Do you think that higher wage, bonus, profit sharing scheme can lead to cordial industrial relations:
   Always/Sometimes/Never.
10. Do you think that co-partnership is helpful for maintaining cordial industrial relations:
    Always/Sometimes/Never.
11. What are your suggestions for improving the industrial relations on your establishment. Please give in order of priority:
    1. 2. 3. etc.

APPENDIX III

LIST OF LABOUR LAWS IN FORCE IN JAMMU & KASHMIR STATE

(a) Central Legislation

1. The Workmen's Compensation Act, 1923.
2. The Trade Unions Act, 1926.
3. The Children (Pledging of Labour) Act, 1933.
4. The Payment of Wages Act, 1936.
5. The Employers Liability Act, 1938.
6. The Employment of Children Act, 1938.
7. The Weekly Holidays Act, 1942.
8. The Industrial Employment (Standing Orders) Act, 1946.
9. The Industrial Disputes Act, 1947.
10. The Minimum Wages Act, 1948.
11. The Employees State Insurance Act, 1948.
12. The Factories Act, 1948.
13. The Working Journalists (Conditions of Service and Miscellaneous Provisions) Act, 1955.
14. The Motor Transport Workers Act, 1961.
15. The Maternity Benefit Act, 1961.
16. The Payment of Bonus Act, 1965.
17. The Payment of Gratuity Act, 1972.
18. The Equal Remuneration Act, 1976.
19. The Contract Labour (Regulation and Abolition) Act, 1970.
20. The Inter-State Migrant Workmen's Act, 1979.
21. The Sales Promotion Employees (Condition of Service) Act, 1976.
22. The Bonded Labour (Abolition) Act, 1976.

(b) State Legislation

1. The J&K Employees Provident Fund Act, 1961.
2. The J&K Shops and Establishments Act, 1966.
3. The J&K National and Festival Holidays Act, 1974.

APPENDIX IV

A DETAILED DESCRIPTION OF THE DECISION AREA

Category	Decision Items
Distant level Decision Areas (D)	D_1 - Formulation of overall organisational policy and their implementation.
	D_2 - Formulation of marketing policy.
	D_3 - Operation of sanctioned budgets.
	D_4 - Allocation of profits between investment, reserves, etc.
	D_5 - Expansion and diversification of business.
	D_6 - Formulation of recruitment policy of executives/officers.
Medium Level Decision Areas (M)	M_1 - Formulation of recruitment policy of workers.
	M_2 - Development of training programmes for the workers.
	M_3 - Formulation of promotion policy for workers
	M_4 - Principle of taking disciplinary action.
	M_5 - Formulation of policy of pay/allowance and other benefits for the workers.
	M_6 - Practice of handling grievances of workers.
	M_7 - Policy for rewarding workers for good work.
	M_8 - Way of determining rate of bonus to be paid to the workers.

Category	Decision Items
Local Level Decision Areas (L)	L_1 - Arrangement for workers housing.
	L_2 - Determining welfare programmes/ facilities for workers.
	L_3 - Way of maintaining good working conditions.
	L_4 - Provision for safety measures.
	L_5 - Ones own work (sequence, method, co-ordination and evaluation of work).
All Level Co-operation Issues (C)	C_1 - Introduction of new technology.
	C_2 - Increasing productivity.

Source: Adopted from Hespe and Wall (1976) and Wall and Lischeron (1977).

PERCENTAGE POINTS OF THE 't' DISTRIBUTION

	α					
φ	.20	.15	.10	.05	.01	.005
1	1.376	1.963	3.078	6.314	31.821	63.657
2	1.061	1.386	1.886	2.920	6.965	9.925
3	.978	1.250	1.638	2.353	4.541	5.841
4	.941	1.190	1.533	2.132	3.747	4.604
5	.920	1.156	1.476	2.015	3.365	4.032
10	.879	1.093	1.372	1.812	2.764	3.169
15	.866	1.074	1.341	1.753	2.602	2.947
20	.860	1.064	1.325	1.725	2.528	2.845
25	.856	1.058	1.316	1.708	2.485	2.787
30	.854	1.055	1.310	1.697	2.457	2.750
40	.851	1.050	1.303	1.684	2.423	2.704
60	.848	1.046	1.296	1.671	2.390	2.660
120	.845	1.041	1.289	1.658	2.358	2.617
∞	.842	1.282	1.645	2.326	2.576	2.576

Source: This table is abridged from Table 3 of Taro Yammi: *Statistics — An Introductory Analysis*. Harper and Row, New York, 1970. p. 878.

PERCENTAGE POINTS OF THE χ^2 DISTRIBUTION

	P					
ϕ	.90	.50	.10	.05	.01	.005
1	0.0158	0.455	2.71	3.84	6.63	7.88
2	0.211	1.386	4.61	5.99	9.21	10.60
3	0.584	2.37	6.25	7.81	11.34	12.84
4	1.064	3.36	7.78	9.49	13.28	14.86
5	1.610	4.35	9.24	1.07	15.09	16.75
6	2.20	5.35	10.64	12.59	16.81	18.55
7	2.83	6.35	12.02	14.07	18.48	20.3
8	3.49	7.34	13.36	15.51	20.1	22.0
9	4.17	8.34	14.68	16.92	21.7	23.6
10	4.87	9.34	15.99	18.31	23.2	25.2
15	8.55	14.34	22.3	25.0	30.6	32.8
20	12.44	19.34	28.4	31.4	37.6	40.0
25	16.47	24.3	34.4	34.7	44.3	46.9
30	20.6	29.3	40.3	43.8	50.9	53.7
50	37.7	49.3	63.2	67.5	76.2	79.5
80	64.3	79.3	96.6	101.9	112.3	116.3
100	82.4	99.3	118.5	124.3	135.8	140.2
$Z\alpha$	-1.28	0.000	1.282	1.645	2.33	2.58

Source: This table is abridged from Table 4 of Taro Yammu: *Statistics — An Introductory Analysis*, Herper & Row, New York, 1970, p.879.

BIBLIOGRAPHY

Acharji, Nilma: *Trade Union leadership profile*. Ambica Publications, New Delhi, 1980.

Acharya, H.G.: *Standardisation of wages in the Ahmedabad Cotton Textile Mill Industry*. Rawat, Ahmedabad, 1959.

Agarawal, A.P.: *Gheraos and Industrial Relations*, Bombay, 1968.

Agarwal, D.K.: Problems of Delay in Labour Judiciary. A Case Study. *Indian Journal of Industrial Relations*, 3(1), 1967: pp. 49-59.

Agarwal, K.G.: *Supervision-Man and leader*. N.L.I., New Delhi, 1988.

Agarwal, K.P.: "Productivity Fair Wage and Capacity to Pay in Indian Cotton Mill Industry, D. Litt. thesis, Agra University, Agra, 1960.

Agarwal, M.C.: "Expectations of management and Workers from Supervisors." *Indian Jr. of Ind. Relations*. 17(4), 1982, pp. 573-76.

Agarwal, O.P.: "Industrial Relations in Madhya Pradesh — Worsening situation and its remedy." *Indian Journal of Commerce*, 24, 1971, pp. 104-14.

— "A Study of Industrial Relations in the Cotton Textile Industry of Madhya Pradesh", Ph.D. thesis, Jiwaji University, Gwalior, 1971.

Aggarwal, M.L.: "Trade Unions in India. Trends and a Gandhian perspective." *Indian Journal of Lab. Economic*, XXVI(4), 1984, pp. 400-8.

Akhauri, R.K.: "Labour in Coal Industry in India". Doctoral Dissertation, 1966 in Murthy, B.S. *Trade Unionism in Orissa State (1938-1943)*, unpublished Doctoral Dissertation, Berhampur University, Berhampur, 1970.

Akhtar, S.S. and D.M. Pestonjee: "A Study of Intrinsic and Extrinsic Motivational factors". Souvenir of Business Administration Course, St. Joseph, Bangalore, 1969.

Alexander, K.C.: "Participative Management: The Indian Experience," Sri Ram Centre, New Delhi, 1972.

Alutto, J.A. and F. Acito: "Decision, participation and source of job satisfaction: A study of manufacturing personnel". *Academy of Management Journal*, 17(1), 1974, pp. 160-7.

Ammassari, P.: "Worker's satisfaction and occupational Life: A study of automobile worker in Italy, 1964" in B.R. Sharma: "Union Involvement", *Indian Journal of Industrial Relations*, 6(4), 1971, pp. 335-56

Anand, Prakash: "Labour Relations and the Rule of Law". *Monthly Commentary on Indian Economic Conditions*, 8(4), 1967, pp. 33-43.

Anderson, J.C.: "Local Union Participation – A re-examination". *Industrial Relations*, 18, 1979, pp. 18-31.

Argyle, Michael, Godfrey Gardner and Frank Ciotti, "Supervisory methods related to productivity, Absenticism and Labour Turn Over". *Human Relations*. 11(1), 1958, pp. 23-40.

Arya, P.P.: "Nature and Extent of worker's participation in decision-making" *Indian Jr. of Industrial Relations*, 16(1), 1980, pp. 45-72.

——. "Worker's Involvement in trade unions." *Indian Journal of Lab. Economics*, XXIII (3), 1980, pp. 115-39.

——. *Labour-Management Relations in Public Sector Undertaking*, Deep and Deep, New Delhi, 1982.

Asdhir, Vijay: *Industrial Relations in India*. Deep and Deep, New Delhi, 1987.

Ash, P.: "The SRA Employee Inventory – a statistical Analysis." *Personnel Psychology*, 7, 1954, pp. 337-364.

Ashraf, Mohd. Sidiq: "Political Affiliation of Industrial workers – An Area Study," *Indian Journal of Industrial Relations*, 10(2), 1974.

Ayyar, S.V.: "Report on Industrial Relations – Case Studies of the Allwyn Metal Works Ltd. and the Praga Tools Corporation Ltd., Hyderabad." The Indian Institute of Economics, Hyderabad, 1967.

Aziz, Abdul: "Aspects of Trade Unionism in Karnataka." *The Economic Times*, XIV(241), 5th Nov. 1974.

——. "Trade Unions and worker's participation in management with reference to Karnataka," *The Indian Journal of Labour Economics*, 20, 1978, pp. 187-99.

——. "Worker's participation in management in Karnataka", *Southern Economics*, 17(13), 1978.

Balaji, C.: "Organisational Commitment of Job Satisfaction which explains Intent to Quite Better," *Indian Journal of Industrial Relations*, 24(3), 1988, pp. 311-28.

Bali, Rajeshwara Rao: "Worker's attitude to work – A study of Refugee workers". *Indian Journal of Industrial Relations*, 3(2), 1967, pp.183-92.

Balu, P.M.: *The Nature of Organisation*, New York, 1971.

Bamzi, P.N.K.: *A History of Kashmir*. Mitro Polition, Delhi, 1973.

Banerjee, R.N.: *Industrial Awards and Industrial Relations in India*, New Age Publication, Calcutta, 1963.

Barbash, J.: "Why workers join union" in R. Dubin: *Human Relations in Administration*, Prentice Hall, 1951.

Barker, A.F.: "A Report on the Cottage Textile Industries of Kashmir and their perspective development." England, 1933.

Basu, Gopal and D.M. Pestonjee: "Executives and the satisfaction cycle." *Indian Journal of Industrial Relations*, 9, 1974, pp. 507-15.

Basu, Sharma: "Determinants of Membership participation in Union activities". *Indian Journal of Industrial Relations*, 22(4), 1987, pp.454-69.

Baumgartel, H.: "Leadership, Motivations and Attitudes in Research Laboratories". *Journal of Social Issue*, 53, 1956, pp. 361-66.

Baveskar, B.S.: "Sociology of Politics" in *Survey of Research in Sociology and Social Anthropology*, 11, I.C.S.S.R., Popular Parkashen, Bombay, p. 74.

Bendix, D.W.F.: "Limits to co-determination-Industrial Democracy in the Federal Republic of Germany, 1945-1977" *LexPatria*, Johanesburg, 1978.

Bennet, E.B.: "Discussion, Decision, Commitment and Consensus in group decision". *Human Relations*, 6, 1955, pp. 251-73.

Bhatia, O.P.: "India's Experiment in Joint Management Council", *Indian Labour Journal*, XII(II), 1971, pp. 611-20.

Bhatnager, Deepti: "Workers desire for participation: An Empirical study". *Productivity*, XIII(4), March 1977, pp.578-98.

Bhatnager, S. and P.C. Sharma: "Role and Effectiveness of Labour Welfare Officer in Industrial Relations," *Indian Journal of Industrial Relations*, 19(4), 1984, pp. 507-11

Bhattacharya, D.: "Trends of wages in India, 1973-1900." *Artha Vijnana* 7(3) 1965, 202-22.

Bisht, N.S.: *Participative management in India*, Shri Publishing House, Delhi, 1986.

Blauner, R.: *Alienation and Freedom: The Factory Worker and His Industry*. University of Chicago Press, Chicago, 1964.

Blum, M.L. and J.C. Naylor: *Industrial Psychology – its theoretical and social foundations*. Harper and Row, New York, 1968.

Bograte, M.V.D.: "Dynamics of political unions: A study of Calcutta Dock Unions." *Indian Journal of Industrial Relations*, 4(2), 1968, pp.199-214.

——. : "Trade Unionisms in Indian Ports – A Case study of Calcutta and Bombay", Sri Ram Centre, Delhi, 1970.

Bose, R.N.: "Gandhian Technique and tradition in Industrial Relations." All India Institute of Social Welfare and Business Management, Calcutta, 1956.

Bose, Bires, C.: "Bipartite Negotiations, when, how and why?" *Productivity*, 8(1), 1967, pp. 71-6.

Bose S.K. "A psychological approach to productivity movement." *Indian Journal of Psychology*, 2, 1958, pp. 195-204.

Brayfield, A.H. & Crockett: "Employee Attitude and Employee Performance". *Psychological Bulletin*, 52, 1955, pp. 396-424.

Brown, I.: "Trade Unionism in India". *Indian Journal of Social Work*, 10(3), 1949, pp. 205-17.

Budania, A.L.: "Industrial Relations in Private Sector of Rajasthan," unpublished thesis, University of Rajasthan, Jaipur, 1971.

Carlson, R.E. *et al.*: "The Measurement of Employee Satisfaction." Minnesota Studies in Vocational Reliabilisation, XIII, Minneapolis, Industrial Relations Centre, University of Minnesota, 1962.

Chamberlin, E.M.: "What Labour is thinking?" *Personnel Journal*, 14, 1935, pp. 118-25.

Chandra, S.: "Trade Unionism in a Developing Economy". Doctoral Dissertation, Patna University, Patna, 1966.

Chatterjee, A.: "Satisfaction and productivity – A Study of Moral and Team work in industry with respect to productivity". Doctoral Dissertation. Indian Institute of Science, Bangalore, 1961.

—— and E.V. James: "An Investigation into the problem of Effective Supervisor", *Journal of Indian Academy of Applied Psychology*, 2, 1965, pp. 8-12.

Chatterjee, D.: "Arbitration". *Industrial Relations*, 18, 1966, pp. 3-6.

Chatterjee, N.N.: "Industrial Relations in Public Enterprises in India", *Decision*, 10(2), 1983, pp. 109-42.

Chattapadhya, S.N. and Venkateshwara: "Aspiration of Industrial personnel". *Indian Journal of Psychology*, 95(1), 1972, pp. 39-52.

Chaturvedi, J.P.: "Collective Bargaining as I see it". *Industrial India*, 27(10), 1976, pp. 31-34.

Chaudhary, A.S.: "Inplant Union Leaders in Public Sector, Background and Attitudes". *Indian Journal of Industrial Relations*, 16(1), 1980, pp. 133-42.

Chaudhuri, K.K.: "Employment, Industrial Disputes and Participation – the case of India". *Decision*, 8(2), 1981, 99-107.

Chaudhuri, S.K.: "Relevance of long term settlement in the changing circumstances" *Industrial Relations*, XXVI(4), 1974, pp. 134-39.

Chawda, V.K.: "State Intervention. A determinant of Industrial Relations in India". *Indian Journal of Labour Economics*, 12(4), 1971, pp. 70-73.

Checko, Thomas, I.: "Member participation in Union Activities – Perception of Union Priorities, performance and satisfaction". *Journal of Labour Research*, VI, 1985, pp. 363-73.

Colchin, Michael, G. And Hycilck Thomas: "Participation in Union Activities – A multivariate Analysis". *Journal of Labour Research*, 1984, pp. 254-62.

Cruch, H.A.: *Trade unions and politics in India*. Manaktalas, Bombay, 1966.

Dabas, Z.S.; "The dimensions of moral: An item factorisation of S.R.A. employees Inventory". *Personnel Psychology*, 11, 1958, pp. 217-34.

Dachler, H.P. and B. Wilpert: "Conceptual dimensions and boundaries of participation in Organisation. A critical evaluation". *Administrative Science Quarterly*, 23, 1978, pp. 1-39.

Daleda, V.N.: "Industrial Relations and Unions in India with special reference to public enterprises". *Indian Journal of Commerce*, XXIX(107), 1976, pp. 90-94.

Darshan, Kour: "Subjective Factors in Industrial Unrest". Ph.D. thesis, Agra University, 1963.

Das, Anand Kumar: "The conditions of labour in Sugar Industry in Western U.P"., an unpublished thesis of Agra University, 1971.

Das, G.S.: "Some Aspects of Union Involvement of the Bank Employees". *Decision*, 12(1), 1985.

Das, Nabagopal: *Experiments in Industrial Democracy*. Asia, Bombay, 1964.

Dass, Mohan, S.R.: "Anatomy of trade union leadership". *The Economic Times*, Bombay, Oct. 9, 1967.

——.: "Delays in Industrial Adjudication – A Study of the organisations and their behaviour". Indian Council of Social Science Research New Delhi, 1979.

——.: "Behavioural Factors in Indian Industrial Relations". *Indian Management*, 13(7), July, 1974, pp. 29-31.

Datar, B.N.: "Earnings of Employees in Manufacturing Industries during 1961". *Indian Labour Journal*, 5(11), 1964, pp. 963-95.

——.: "The Australian and Indian Industrial Relations System: A Comparison". *Indian Journal of Industrial Relations*, 4(1), 1968, pp. 105-18.

Datta, S.: "A Study of Incentives as Expressed by the Attitudes of different types of employees". Unpublished dissertation, University of Calcutta, Calcutta, 1959.

Davis, Kieth: *Human Behaviour at work* Tata McGraw-Hill, New Delhi, 1977.

Dwson, W.A.: *An Introductory Guide to Central Labour Legislation*. Asia, Bombay, 1967.

——.: "Unionism in Western India Textile Industry". Doctoral Dissertation, University of Wisconsin, Madison, U.S.A., 1971.

Daya, E.: "Freedom of Association and Industrial Relations in Asian Countries". *International Labour Review*, 1955.

Dayal, Ishwar: "Strategy for Industrial Relations in the Public Sector". *Industrial and Engineering Annual*, Bombay, 1969.

——.: "Prerequisite of worker involvement in work organisation". *Manpower Journal*, 12(2), 1976.

Dayal, Ishwar and B.R. Sharma: *The strike of supervisory staff in State Bank of India*. Progressive Corporation, Bombay, 1970.

——.: "Draft Report on Employer: Employer Relations in Banks". IIM, Ahmedabad, PTI and II, 1970, "Management of Trade Unions", Sri Ram Centre, New Delhi, 1976.

Deodhar, S.B.: "Industrial Relations at the plant level – A study with an emphasis on the role of management in some selected units in Greater Bombay and Thana Regions". Unpublished Ph.D. thesis, University of Bombay, 1978.

De, Nitish, R.: "Contents and Discontents of work commitment". *Lok Udyog*, April, 1975.

——.: "Process consultation for effective industrial relations". *Economic Times*, May 27, 28, 1977.

——.: "A balance-sheet of worker participation in the formal sector in developing countries". Towards Continuing Education, IV(9), 1984, pp. 179-91.

De Nitish, R. Suresh Srivastava: "Gheraos in West Bengal". *Economic and Political Weekly*, 2(49), 1967.

Deber, M.: "Cross currents in workers participations". *Industrial Relation*, 1970: pp. 123-26.

Desai, K.G. "A comparative study of Motivation of Blue Collar and White Collar workers". *Indian Journal of Social Work*, 28(4), 1968, pp. 379-87.

——.: "A study of workers expectations from supervisors and management". *Indian Journal of Social Work*, 30(2), 1969, 105-115.

Devasasayam, A.: "Empolyer-Employee tension in Industry". *Indian Journal of Social Work*, 12(3), 1951, pp. 297-306.

Dhingra, O.P.: "Participative pre-disposition of public sector managers". *Lok Udyog*, V(12), 1972, p. 1204.

——, and H.V. Chellapa: "Cases in Industrial Relations". Sri Ram Centre, Delhi, 1971.

——, and V.K. Pathak: "Organisational culture and Managers". *Indian Journal of Industrial Relations*, 1973, pp. 387-405.

*Dolke, A.M.: "A study of managerial practices, managerial motivations and satisfaction in textile industry". Ahmedabad Textile Industry's Research Association, 1975.

Donald, P. Schwah and J. Waldace More Jr.: "Correlates of Employees satisfaction with pay". *Industrial Relations*, 13(1), 1974.

Dubey, B.L., K.K. Uppal, S.K. Verma and Padma Dwividi: "Job satisfaction and need Hierarchy Among Bank Officers". *Indian Journal of Lab. Economics*, XXVI(1&2), 1983, pp. 86-91.

Dufty, N.F.: *Industrial Relations in India*. Ailied, Bombay, 1964.

Edward, E.L. and W.P. Layman: "Antecedent Attitudes of Effective Managerial Performance" Organisational Behaviour and Human Performance, 2, 1967, pp. 122-43 in D.W. Organ. *The Applied Psychology of Work Behaviour*. Business Publications, U.S.A. 1987.

Elliot, J.D.: "Increasing office productivity through job enlargement". in *The Human side of the office managers' job*. American Management Association, New York, 3-15, 1953.

Employers Federation of India. "Collective Agreement – Trends in the sixties", 1971.

Farm, W.H. and Danseareau, H.K.: "Union member orientations and patterns of social integrations". *Industrial and Lab. Relations Review*, XI, 1956.

Farris, G.F.: "A predictive study of turnover". *Personnel Psychology*, 24, 1971.

Faunce, W.A.: "Size of locals and union democracy". *American Journal of Sociology*, 68, 1962, pp. 291-98.

Fazli, Manzoor A.: *Socialist ideas and movements in Kashmir (1919-1947)*, Eurek Publications, New Delhi, 1980.

Fonescca, A.: "Contribution of the trade Unions to Development". *Indian Journal of Industrial Relations*, 4(3), 1965.

Foster, M., E.L. Hilgendore and B.L. Irving: "An overview of Industrial Democracy and worker participation". Report of the Human Resource Centre. The Tavistock Institute of Human Relations, London, 1970.

French, John, R.P., Joachim Israel and Dagfina As: "An Experiment on participation in a Norwegian Factory – Interpersonal dimensions of decision-making". *Human Relations*, 13, 1960, pp. 3-19.

Friedlender, F.: "Job characteristics as satisfiers and dissatisfiers". *Journal of Applied Psychology*, 48, 1964, pp 388-92.

Ganguli, H.C.: "An Enquiry into incentives for workers in an Engineering Factory". *Indian Journal of Social Work*, 15(1), 1954, pp. 30-40.

——.: "Relations of Union membership to attitude of Industrial workers". *Indian Journal of Social Work*, 15(3), 1954.

——.: "A Study of the effect of Union membership on the Industrial moral". *Indian Journal of Psychology*, 29, 1954, pp. 45-60.

——.: "A Study of some variables affecting attitudes of industrial workers". *Indian Journal of Psychology*, 30, 1955, pp. 45-60.

——.: "Attitude of union and non-union employees in Calcutta Engineering Factory". *Journal of Applied Psychology*, 40, 1956, pp. 78-82.

——.: "Effect of union membership on attitudes of industrial workers". *Indian Journal of Social Work*, 15, 1964, pp 189-99.

——.: "The structure of Indian trade union and its characteristics", unpublished study, 1960 in D. Sinha and U. Pal, "Motivational Analysis of Union membership". *The Indian Journal of Social Work*, XXIII(4), 1963, pp. 343-49.

——.: *Industrial Productivity and Motivation*. Asia Publishing House, Bombay, 1961.

Ganguly, T.: "The workers attitude towards the management". *Indian Journal of Psychology*, 28, 1953, pp. 29-37.

——.: "Study of tension through an attitude survey in a large steel industry". *Alumni Association Bulletin*, 1, 1954, pp. 82-85.

——.: "Group participation as an effective technique to improve the industrial worker's attitude and moral: An Experiment". *Indian Journal of Psychology*, 33, 1958, pp. 25-36.

Gani, Abdul: "Socio-economic conditions of workers in Mineral Based Industries of public sector in Jammu and Kashmir State". an unpublished pre-doctoral dissertation, University of Kashmir, 1984.

Gani, A.: "What makes a supervisor: The worker speaks". *Indian Management*, 28(9), 1989, pp. 11-15.

Ganju, M.: *Textile Industries in Kashmir*. Premier Publishing Co. Delhi, 1945.

Ganju, M.K.: Industrial relations in the paper industry of Andhra Pradesh – An unpublished thesis. Nagrajuna University, Nagarjunanagar, Andhra Pradesh, 1978.

Gaur, G.L.: *Trade unionism and industrial relations*. Deep and Deep, New Delhi, 1986.

Ghoshal, Lok Nath: "Industrial Relations in West Bengal". *Indian Worker*, 20(42), 1972, pp. 3-6.

Ghosh, S.: *Trade unionism in undeveloped countries*. Bookland, Calcutta, 1960.

Ghosh, S.N.: "Participative management – Results of some experimental studies". *Indian Journal of Labour*, XVII(6), 1976.

Ghosh, S.N. and S.N. Shukla: "A Study of correlates of job satisfaction of a group of telegraphists". *Indian Journal of Applied Psychology*, 4, 1967.

Giri, V.V.: *Labour problems in the Indian Industry*, Asia, Bombay, 1972.

Glick, William; Mirvis Philip and Hardee Diasn: "Union satisfaction and participation". *Industrial Relations*, 16(2), 1977, pp. 145-51.

Goil, R.M.: "White collar unionism in India with special reference to Madhya Pradesh". *Indian Journal Economics*, Jan.1968.

Golden, C.S. and H.J. Rutterberg: *The dynamics of industrial democracy*. Harper and Bros., New York, 1942.

Gopal, C. Rath and B.S. Murthy: "Participative management – The Indian experience". *The Indian Journal of Social Work*, 36(1), 1975, p. 40.

Gopal, Ji: *Personal management in Indian Industries*. Ashish, New Delhi, 1985.

Govt of India: Ministry of Labour, *Report of the Royal Commission on Labour in India*. New Delhi, 1931.

——.: *Report of the First Seminar on Labour-management Co-operation*, New Delhi, 1958.

——.: *Report of the Second Seminar on Labour-management co-operation*, New Delhi, 1960.

——.: Ministry of Labour, *Attitudes of Employers and Unions to voluntary Arbitration*, 1963.

——.: *Report on the Survey of Labour conditions in Silk Factories in India*. 1964, Labour Bureau.

——.: *Report of the National Commission on Labour*, Manager of Publication, New Delhi, 1969.

——.: *Report of the Occupational wage survey (1958-59)*, VI, Textile Group of Industries, Labour Bureau.

——.: *Third occupational wage survey Report on Textile Industries*, (July to Oct. 1975), Labour Bureau.

——.: *Master Reference Book on Labour Statistics*. Labour Bureau, Chandigarh, 1984.

Govt of Jammu and Kashmir: Department of Information, *Labour in J&K – a new deal*, 1971.

——.: *Chatterjee Wage Commission Report*, 1973.

——.: *Rajan Wage Review Committee Report*, 1980.

——.: Department of Labour, *Labour Laws in Jammu and Kashmir*, III, 1984.

——.: Directorate of Economics and Statistics, *Digest of Statistics, 1983-84*, 1985.

——.: Directorate of Economics and Statistics *Indicators of Economic Development*, 1985-86.

——.: "Planning and Development Department '*Seventh Five-year Plan (1985-90)*, April, 1986.

——.: Department of Labour, *Handbook of Labour Statistics* March, 1986.

Goyal, R.C.: *An Introduction to Industrial Employment, Discipline and Disputes in India*, S. Chand, Delhi, 1969.

Guest, Dand Fatchett, D.: "Worker participation: Individual Control and Performance". Institute of Personnel Management, London, 1974.

Guha, S.R.: "Collective Bargaining and Voluntary Arbitration", *Indian Journal of Social Work*, 20(1), 1959, pp. 7-13.

Guha, T.N.: "Personality Factors and Job Satisfaction Among Shoe Factory Workers", *Indian Journal of Industrial Relations*, 14(1), 1978.

Gupta, Jawahri Lal: "Participation in Decision Making: A Survey of Managers Beliefs", *Indian Management*, 23(2), 1984, pp. 0-12.

Gupta, K. and K.S. Sexena: "Industrial Relations in Public Enterprises in India", *Indian Journal of Commerce*, XXIX, II(107), 1976, pp. 83-94.

Gupta, O.P.: *Commitment to Work of Industrial Workers*, Concept Publishing House, New Delhi, 1981.

Gupta, S.R.: "Industrial Dispute Settlement Machinery", Prateeksha, Jaipur, 1987.

Gurin, G., J. Veroff and S. Feld: *Americans view their Mental Health*, Basic Books, New York, 1960.

Haire, M., E. Ghiselli and L. Porter: *Managerial Thinking: An International Study*, Wiley, New York, 1966.

Halder, Ardhendu Sekhar: "Our Industrial Relations Scenario – Quacks Treating chronics", *Lock-Udyog*, XIX(4), 1985, pp. 11-18.

Harrison, R.: "Cumulative community cluster Analyses of worker's job attitudes". *Journal of Applied Psychology*. 45, 1961, pp. 123-25.

Herzberg, F., B. Mausner, R.O. Peterson and D.F. Capewell, "Job studies: Review of Research and opinion", *Psychological Servicè of Pittusburgh*, Pittsburgh, 1957.

Herzberg, F., B. Mausner and B. Snyderman: *The Motivation to work*, Wiley, New York, 1959.

Hespe, G. and T.D. Wall: "Do Employees participate?" Paper presented at 17th International Congress of Applied Psychology Liege, Belgium, 1971.

——.: "The Demand for participation among Employees", *Human Relations*, 29(-), 1976, pp. 411-28.

Hespe, G.W.A. and A. Little.: "Some aspects of employees participation", in P.B. Warr. (ed.) *Psychological work*, Harmondsworth, Penguin, 1971.

Holter, Harriet: "Attitude towards employee participation in Company Decision Making Process — A study of Non-supervisory Employees in some Norwegian Firms", *Human Relations*, Vol. 18(4), 1965, pp. 297-321.

Hoppock, R.: *Job Satisfaction*, Harper and Brothers, New York, 1935.

Hovels, B.W.M. and P. Nas: Workers councils in the Netherlands — some findings from an empirical survey", *The Netherlands Journal of Sociology*, 13, 1977.

Hullin, C.L.: "Effects of change in job satisfaction levels on employees turnover". *Journal of Applied Psychology*, 52, 1968.

Hullin, C.L. and P.C. Smith: "Sex difference in job satisfaction". *Journal of Applied Psychology*, XLVIII, 1964, pp. 88-92.

Hill, J.M.M. and E.L.A. Trist: "A consideration of Industrial Accidents as a means of withdrawal from the work situation", *Human Relations*, 6, 1953, pp. 357-80.

Hull, R.L. and A. Kilstad: "Moral on the job", in G. Waston (ed.): *Civilian Morale*, Reynal and Hitchcock, New York, 1942.

Huszezo Gergory, E.: "Attitudinal and Behavioural variables related to participation in Union Activities". *Journal of Labour Research*, 1983, pp. 289-97.

I.L.O.: "Payment by Results", studies and reports, Geneva, 1951.

——.: "Trade Union Documentation and Research Services". Report No. WED/s 610 28, Geneva, 1968.

Inderson, J.A.: "Multivariate Analysis of job satisfaction", Doctoral Dissertation, I.I.T., New Delhi, 1973.

Indira, K. and K. Harigopal: "Participative Management", *Indian Management*, 23(3), 1985, pp. 39-44.

Indian Law Institute: "Administrative procedure in conciliation", N.M. Trepathi, Bombay, 1962.

Jalali, P.N.: "Freedom Movement —— Some Glimp", 25 years of progress, Department of Information, Govt. of Jammu and Kashmir, 1972.

James, P.A. and V. Bhaskara Rao: "Unionism in P and T and Audit Departments". *Indian Journal of Industrial Relations*, 7(3), 1972, pp. 465-72.

James, R.: "Politics and Trade Unions in India", *Far Eastern Survey*, 27(3), 1958, pp. 41-45.

Joshi, V.P.: "A Study of Strikes in the Bombay Cotton Textile Industry: University of Poona, Ph.D. thesis, 1966.

Johri, C.K.: *Unionism in a developing economy*, Asia, Delhi, 1967.

Johri, C.K. and S.M. Pandey: "Employment Relations in the Building Industry". *Indian Journal of Industrial Research*, 4(4), 1969, pp. 433-61.

Joseph, Cherian: "Making of a participative forum —— BHEL Experience". *Economic and Political Weekly*, XXII(48), 1987, pp. 143-52.

Joseph Obra Dovice: "Worker's participation. Who Participate?" *Industrial Relations*, 14(1), 1975, pp. 41-43.

Juralewicz, Richard, S.: "An experiment on participation in a Latin American Factory". *Human Relations*, 27(7), 1974, pp. 627-37.

Kacheloffer, G.L.: "Industrial Democracy: Employee participation in Decisions of an undertaking" in S.M. Swnt. (ed.): *Employee participation: Challenge to Management Prerogatives*, UNISA, Pretoria, 1978.

Kahn, R.L.: "Productivity and job satisfaction", *Personnel Psychology*, 13, 1960, pp. 275-87.

Kakar, Sudhir: *Personality and Authority to work.* Somaiya, Bombay, 1974.

Kamath, V.B. and Associates: "A case study of labour-management relation at the Godrej and Boyce MEG. Co. Pvt. Ltd., Bombay Labour Institute, Bombay, 1962.

——.: A case study of Labour-Management Relation at the Central India Spinning, Weaving and Mfg. Co., 1962, Nagpur" Bombay Labour Institute, 1962.

Kananidhi, M.S.: "A study of job satisfaction among drafts women" *Manas*, 19(2), 1972.

Kanappan, S.: "A case study of Labour-Management Relations in Indian Aluminium works Belure, West Bengal", New Delhi, 1958.

——.: "The Tata Steel Strike. Some Dilemmas of Industrial Relations in a developing economy", *Journal of Political Economy*, 67(5), 1959, pp. 489-587.

Kanappan, S. and D. Saran: "Political Strikes and Violence in Labour Disputes". *Indian Journal of Industrial Relations*, 3(3) 1967, pp. 123-27.

Kane, A.R. and P.N. Singh: "An Exploratory Study of workers' participation in Management". *The Indian Journal of Labour Economics*, X(1) 1967, pp. 119-20.

Kanwar Lal: "A study of the Industrial relations in public sector undertakings in India with special reference to Madhya Pradesh". an unpublished thesis of Jiwaji University, Gwalior, 1971.

Kapoor, T.N. (ed.): *Industrial Development in the States of India.* Sterling, Delhi, 1967.

Karim, Bazle: "Industrial Relations in Public undertakings in Jammu and Kashmir". *Indian Journal of Industrial Relations*, 7(2), 1972, pp. 269-74.

Karnik, V.B.: *Indian Trade Unions A Survey.* Allied Publishers, Bombay, 1960.

——.: *Strikes in India*, Manaktalas, Bombay, 1967.

Kathirosan, K.: "Perception towards the specific aspects of job satisfaction : A case study", *Indian Labour Journal*, 28(6), 1987, pp. 781-86.

Katz, D.: "Satisfaction and deprivation, in Industrial Life" in A. Kornhauser, R. Dubin and A.M. Ross, (ed.) *Industrial Conflict*. McGraw-Hill, New York, 1954.

Kartz, H.C., T.A. Kachan and K.R. Gobeille: Industrial relations performance, economic performance and Q.W.L. -- an interplant analysis". *Industrial and Labour Relation Review*, 1, 1983, pp. 3-17.

Kartz, H.C., T.A. Kochan and M.R. Weber: "Assessing the effects of industrial relations systems and efforts to improve quality of working life on organisational effectiveness", *Academy of Management Journal*, 3, 1985, pp. 509-26.

Kartz, R.A., R.S. Barrett and T.C. Parker.: "Job Satisfaction, job performance and situational characteristics". *Journal of Applied Psychology*, 45, 1961, pp. 65-72.

Kendall, L.M., P.L. Smith, C.L. Hulin and E.A. Locke: Cornell Studies of Job satisfaction: IV, unpublished manuscript, 1963 in V.H. Vroom, *Work and Motivation*. John Wiley, London, 1964.

Kennedy, V.D.: "Problems of Indian trade unionism and labour relations", Association of Free Trade Unionists, Bombay, 1954.

——.: "Conceptual and Legislative Framework and Labour and Labour Relations in India", *Industrial and Labour Relations Review*, 2(4), 1958, pp. 487-505.

—.: *Unions, employees and Govt.*, Manaktala, Bombay, 1966.

Kesar, Urvasi.: "Wonders of Sericulture". *Kashmir Today*, IV(9-10), 1980, pp. 14-15.

Khan, A.R.: "Sericulture and Kashmir", *Kashmir Today*, V(12), 1981, pp. 14-16.

Khan, G.H.: "Freedom Movement in Kashmir", *Light and Life*, New Delhi, 1980.

Khullar, L.C.: "Silk Industry in India and its importance". *Indian Journal of Commerce*, XXXIV, II (119), 1979, pp. 89-95.

Khurana, S.K.: "Industrial Relations in Private and Public Sector Industry in India — A Comparative Analysis". *Indian Journal of Industrial Relation* 7(3), 1972, pp. 411-32.

Kohli Geeta: "Labour-management relations in Indian", Airlines — 1970-79", unpublished thesis, University of Delhi, Delhi, 1983.

Knowles, M.C.: "Personal and job factors affecting labour turnover", *Personnel Practice Bulletin*, 20, 1964.

Krech, D. and R.S. Crutchfield.: *Theory and Problems of Social Psychology*, McGraw-Hill, New York, 1948.

Krishna, K.K. Gopala and A. Hafeez: "A study of supervisors' attitudes towards employees and production in relation to some personnel factors", *Indian Journal of Applied Psychology*, 1, 1964, pp. 78-83.

Krishna Murthy, K.S.: "Industrial Relations in India", *Indian Management*, 9(7), 1970, pp. 44-46.

Kudchedkar, L.C.: *Aspects of personnel management and Industrial Relations*. Tata McGraw-Hill, New Delhi, 1979.

Kulkarni, P.D.: "Textile trade unionism in Bombay". *Indian Journal of Social Work*, 7(3), 1946.

Kumar, A.: "Industrial Relations in public sector undertakings in Orissa". *Industrial Journal of Lab. Economics*, XIX (3-4), 1976-77, pp. 65-72.

Kumari, U.: "Self Actualisation and organisational climate — A Study of Indian managers". *Indian Journal of Applied Psychology*, 15, 1978, p. 914.

Kumar, Shrvan: "Industrial Relations in Andhra Pradesh". *Economic Times*, March 31, 1972, p. 11.

Lahiri, D.K.: "Perceived importance of job factors by Government and non-government employees", *Indian Journal of Psychology*, 60, 1965, pp. 37-48.

Lahiri, D.K. and S. Srivastava.: "Determinants of Satisfaction in Middle Management Personnel". *Journal of Applies Psychology*, 51, 1967, pp. 264-65.

Lakshminarayan, H.: "Wage variations in India". Ph.D. thesis, Delhi University, Delhi, 1958.

Laldas, D.K.: "The Dynamics of Industrial Relations in Textile Industries of Indore". Unpublished thesis, Indore University, 1980.

Lal, K.B.: "Worker's Participation in Management: The Case of the Integral Coach Factory, Perambur". *Indian Journal of Industrial Relation*, 19(4), 1984, p. 454-68.

Lawler, E.E. and J.R. Hackman: "Impact of employee participation in the Development of pay incentive plans: A field experiment". *Journal of Applied Psychology*, 53, 1969, pp. 467-71.

Lawrence, Lois, C. and C. Patrica Smith,: "Group decision and employee participation". *Journal of Applied Psychology*, 39(5), 1955, pp. 334-37.

Lawshe, C.H. and B.F. Nagle.: "Productivity and Attitude Towards supervision", *Journal of Applied Psychology*, 37, 1953, pp. 159-62.

Leberman, Susan, M. and Robert Leberman,: "Two Case Studies on Workers' Participation in Management". *Indian Journal of Industrial Relations*. 13(4), 1978, pp.467-510.

Likert, R.: "A technique for the measurement of attitudes". *Archives of Psychology*, 140, 1932.

——.: *New Pattern of Management*, McGraw-Hill, New York, 1961.

Lischeron, J.A. and T.D. Wall.: "Attitude towards participation among local authority employees". *Human Relations*, 28, 1975, pp. 863-84.

——.: "Employee participation : An Experimental field study". *Human Relations*, 28(9), 1975, pp. 863-84.

Lowin, A.: "Participative Decision Making : A model, literature critique and prescriptions for research". Organisational behaviour and human performance, III, 1970, pp. 68-106.

Mahapatra, R.C.: "Industrial relations in public sector in India with special reference to Rourkela Steel Plant", *Indian Journal of Lab. Economics*, Vol. IXI (3-4), 1976-1977, pp. 73-84.

Maier, N.R.F.: *Principles of Human Relations*. Wiley, New York, 1952.

Majumdar Paresh: "An Anatomy of peaceful industrial relations". N.M. Tripathy, New Delhi, 1973.

——.: "Perception of participation in Departmental Decision Making — Its relation with job satisfaction, job effectiveness and personality structure". *Indian Journal of Industrial Relation*, 12(4), 1977, pp. 429-442.

Malhotra, C.S.: "Collective bargaining and bipartite settlements: Review of Leading experience — The Ariline experience". *National Labour Institute Bulletin*, VI (3-4), 1980, pp. 200-7.

Mamoria S.K.: "Personnel Management and Industrial Relations in the textile units of Beawar and Bhilwara (Rajasthan)", unpublished thesis, University of Udaipur, 1978.

Mannan, M.A.: "Workers participation in management", unpublished doctoral dissertation, Delhi University, 1983.

——". Workers influence in Managerial decision-making : A study in Bangladesh". *Indian Journal of Industrial Relation*, 20(2), 1984, pp. 162-76.

——.: "Managerial Attitude towards worker participation in Organisational Decision making : A case study in a State Enterprise in Bangladesh". *Indian Journal of Industrial Relations*, 21(2); 1985; pp. 219-31.

Mann, F.C.: "Cost of disciplinary and adjudication proceedings under labour laws — A case study". *Indian Journal of Industrial Relations*, 3(7), 1971, pp. 60-73.

Mann, F.C.: "A study of work satisfaction as a function of the discrepancy between inferred aspirations and achievement". Unpublished Doctoral dissertation. University of Michigan. Ann. Arbor, 1953.

March, James and Simon Herbert: *Organisations*. John Wiley, New York, 1958.

Marriot, R. and R.A. Denerley.: "A method of interviewing used in studies of workers Attitudes-II, Validity of the method and decision of the results". *Occupational Psychology*, 29, 1955, pp. 69-81.

Mast, M.K.: *Trade Union Movement in Indian Railways*, Minakshi Prakashan, Meerut, 1969.

——.: "Trade Union Movement in Indian Railways. A Survey". *Indian Journal of Labour Economics*, 5(1), 1962, pp. 48-60.

Mathur, A.S. and J.S. Mathur,: *Trade Union Movement in India*. Chaitanya, Allahabad, 1962.

Mathur, A.S. and R. Raman.: "Trade Union Leadership in India". *Agra University Journal of Researches*, 10, 1962.

Mathur, J.S.: *Indian working class movement*. Allahabad, 1964.

——.: "Trade Union Leadership and industrial unrest in India". Industrial Relations, 6, 1965.

Mathur, Kamala: "Settlement of Industrial disputes in India with special reference to Industrial Awards", Ph.D. thesis, Poona University, Poona, 1962.

Mathur, Reeta: "Industrial Relations in Public Enterprises". *Prateeksha*, Jaipur, 1986.

Mathur, R.S. and T.S. Papola: "Growth and practice of white collar unionism (A case study of L.I.C. Employees Union)" *Indian Journal of Labour Economics*, (-), Jan. 1964.

Mattoo, A.R.: "A critical study of Industrial Relations in the Public Sector Units of Kashmir". An unpublished doctoral Dissertation, Aligarh Muslim University, Aligarh, 1976.

Mattoo, A.R. and A. Gani: "Trade unionism in Jammu and Kashmir", Paper presented at the National Seminar on trade unionism and industrial relations, Allahabad University, during 13-15 Oct., 1987, pp. 1-19.

McAllister: "Some requirements of worker representatives on works councils and committees". *Industrial Relations. Journal of South Africa, University of Stellenbosch*, 2(4), 1982, pp. 1-11.

McGregor, Douglas: *The Human side of enterprise*. McGraw-Hill, New York, 1960. pp.

Meher, M.R.: "Industrial Relations in Public Sector: Some Fundamentals considered". *Lock Udyog*, 3(1), 1969, pp. 33-34.

Mehrotra, B.N.: "Industrial Relations in public sector". *Commerce*. Annual, No. 1964: pp. 130-36.

Mehrotra, B.N.: "Collective Agreements in India". *Industrial Relations*, 18(3), 1966, pp. 102-9.

Mehta, Prayag: "From Economism to Democratic commitment. The Role of Worker's participation". *Vikalpa*, 1(4), 1976, pp. 39-46.

—.: "Employees motivation and work satisfaction in a public enterprise". *Vikalpa.*, 11(3), 1977.

—.: "Objective and subjective factors in employees satisfaction in life and work". *Indian Journal of Industrial Relations*, 13(4), 1978, pp. 433-44.

—.: "Participation and negative response", *National Labour Institute Bulletin*, VI, 1980, pp. 231-34.

Mhetras, V.G.: *Labour participation in Management*. Manaktalas, Bombay, 1966.

Mills, Daniel Quinn: *Labour Management Relations*, McGraw-Hill, New York, 1976.

Mills, Ted, "Europe's Industrial Democracy: An American Response". *Harward Business Review*, Nov.-Dec., 1978, pp. 143-52.

Mitra, A.K.: "A study on some aspects of trade union movement among the low paid government employees in India". *Indian Journal of Labour Economics*, (-), Jan. 1968.

Mohan, Dass, Sr.: "Delays in Industrial adjudication — A Study of the Organisations and their behaviour". ICSSR, New Delhi, 1974.

Monga, M.L.: "The worker speaks his mind — A Study of expectations from supervisors and management". *National Labour Institute Bulletin*, 4(2), 1978, pp. 350-56.

Monga, M.L.: "The worker speaks his mind: A study of company and union allegiance". *Indian Labour Journal*. 19(6), 1978, pp. 859-64.

—.: "Trade Union Leader — A study of his background and attitudes". *National Labour Institute Bulletin*, 5(1-2), 1979, pp. 59-65.

—.: "Participative management-workers viewpoint". *Workers Education*, 1979, pp. 19-20.

—.: "Industrial indiscipline: An exploratory survey of its correlates". Report of the Survey Sponsored by ICSSR, National Labour Institute, 1984.

—.: and Ashok Maggu,: *Commitment to Unionism; Productivity"*. XXII (3), 1981, p. 11-18.

Mukherjee, Surya: "The Joint Management Councils in Gujarat: A Study of current practices and performance". *Indian Journal of Industrial Relations*. 19(4), 1984, pp. 443-53.

Morris, M.E.: "Caste and Evolution of the Industrial Work force in India". in B.R. Sharma *Indian Industrial Worker*. Vikas, Delhi, 1960.

—.: "The Emergence of an Industrial Labour Force in India: A study of the Bombay Cotton Mills, 1854-1917", University of California Press, California, 1965.

Morse, N.C.: "Satisfaction in the White Collar Jobs". Ann.Arbor. Survey Research Centre, University of Michigan, Michigan, 1953.

Morse, N.C. and E. Reimer.: "The Experimental change of a major organisational Variable". *Journal of Abnormal and Social Psychology*. 52, 1956, pp. 120-29.

Mukherjee, B.N.: "Importance ranking of job related needs by Indian Textile Mill workers". *Indian Journal of Industrial Relations*, 4(2), 1968, pp. 162-81.

Mukorjoo, Indrani: *Industrial workers in a developing society : A sociological Study*. Mittal Publications, Delhi, 1985.

Mukerjee, Sunil, Kumar: "Collective Bargaining and industrial relations with special reference to selected industries in India". Ph.D. thesis, University of Burdwan, West Bengal, May, 1981.

Mukhpadhay, S.N.: "Labour unrest in tea plantation", *Indian Journal of Social Work*. 7(3), 1946, pp. 180-97.

Mulder, M.: "Power equalisation through participation", *Administrative Science Quarterly*, XVI, 1971.

Mulder, M. and H. Wilke: "Participation and Power equalisation". Organisational behaviour and human performance, 5(-), 1970.

Munsons, F.C.: "Printing unionism in Delhi". *Indian Journal of Industrial Relations*, (-), Jan. 1968.

Munsons Fred C. and A.C. Nanda: "The influence of legal framework on labour leaders and their unions". *Indian Journal of Industrial Relations*, 2(1), 1966, pp. 3-33.

Murphy, Eaman: *Unions in Conflict : A comparative study of Four South Indian Textile Centres*, 1918-1939. (Monograph), Manohar Publications, New Delhi, 1981.

Murthy, B.S.: "Trade unionism in Orissa State: A study of its Growth, Organisation, Structure, Politics and Leadership (1938-1973)", Ph.D. thesis, Berhampur University, Berhampur, 1978.

Murthy, B.S., D.V. Giri and B.P. Rath,: "Conciliation Machinery in Orissa: A Study", *Indian Journal of Industrial Relations*, 21(4), 1986, pp. 428-47.

Myers, C.A. and S. Kanapan,: *Industrial Relations in India.* Asia, Bombay, 1970.

Nagaraju, S.: *Industrial Relations System in India.* Chugh, Allahabad, 1981.

Naik, Haribhau: "Industrial relations in the textile Industry in India". *The Indian Worker*, XXXIII(3), 1985; pp. 6-8.

Nair, K. Ramachandran: *Industrial Relations in Kerala.* Sterling, New Delhi, 1973.

——.: "Collective bargaining: The Kerala experience". *Indian Jr. of Lab. Economics*, XXV(1&2), 1982, pp. 62-71.

Nair, Mohan: "Industrial Relations in Goa". *The Indian Worker*, 21(45-46), 1973, pp. 19-26.

Nanda, S.K.: "Collective bargaining and bipartite settlements: The Airlines experience". *National Labour Institute Bulletin*, VI(3-4), 1980, p. 208.

Narain Laxmi: *Worker's participation in public enterprises*, Himalaya, Bombay, 1986.

Narchal, Renu, Alagh Harveen and Kishore Renu: "Job satisfaction — Some correlates". *Productivity*, XXV(3), 1984; pp. 367-70.

Nath, Santosh: "Industrial relations — A positive approach", *Indian Management*, 9(3), 1970, pp. 17-21.

Natraj, C.L. and A. Hafeez: "A study of job satisfaction among skilled workers". *Indian Journal of Social Work*, 26(1), 1965, pp. 9-12.

Nigam, Gyaneshwar: "Economics of wage determination with special reference to textile industry in Kanpur", Ph.D. thesis, Agra University, Agra, 1960.

Nigam, M.S.: "Trade Union Movement in India — Recent trends and emerging patterns". *Indian Journal of Labour Economics*, XXVI(4), 1984, pp. 419-24.

Ornate, O.: "Indian trade unions since Independence", *Eastern Survey*, 23(8), 1954, pp. 113-21.

——.: *Jobs and workers in India*, Ithaca (N.Y.) Cornell International Industrial and Labour Relations Reports. 1955.

Padmanabhan, R.: "Growth of Trade Unions in India, 1940-1970", *Indian Journal of Industrial Relations*, 16(1), 1980, pp. 125-32.

Pals, H. K.G. Agrawal and T.K. Pachal,: "Industrial Relations in the Engineering Industry : A comparative study of Private and Public Companies". National Labour Institute, New Delhi, 1985.

Pandey, S.M.: "Indian Labour Movement. Growth and Character". *Indian Journal of Labour Economics*, 9(1), 1966, pp. 14-39.

——.. "Govt. Employees Strike — A study in White Collar Unionism in India", Meerut, 1969.

——.: "Conflict in Government Employment Relations : A Case Study". *Indian Journal of Labour Economics*, Jan., 1967.

——.: "Rival unionism in an Industrial Centre : A study of Kanpur", *Indian, Journal of Industrial Relations*, 3(2), 1968, pp. 138-59.

——.: "and C.M. Vikram: "Trade Unionism in Delhi's Building Industry", *Indian Journal of Industrial Relation*, 4(3), 1969, pp. 298-321.

Pande, M.K.: "Labour Organisations in Sholapur city", Ph.D. thesis, University of Poona, Poona, 1960.

Papola, T.S.: "The place of collective bargaining in Indian Industrial relations policy". *Journal of Industrial Relations*, March, 1968.

——.: "Wage determination in the Indian Cotton Textile Industry", *International Labour Review*, Jan., 1969, pp. 21-27.

——.: "Inter-regional variations in manufacturing wages in India: Industrial structure and region effects". *Indian Journal of Industrial Relations*, 7(3), 1972, pp. 355-75.

Patchen, Martin: *Participation, Achievement and Involvement on the job"*. Prentice-Hall, Englewood Cliffs, 1970.

——.: "Participation in Decision Making & Motivations", *Personnel Administration*, XXVII, 1964.

Patil, B.R.: "A study of trade unionism in Karnataka". *Indian Journal of Industrial Relations*, 11(4), 1976, pp. 473-91.

——.: Collective bargaining and conciliation in India". *Indian Journal of Industrial Relations*, 12(1), 1976, pp. 41-60.

——.: *Conciliation in India : A study into its functioning and effectiveness*. Chugh, Allahabad, 1977.

Patel, S.M.: "Work Ethics and labour participation in management". *Indian Management*, 15(2), 1976, pp. 17, 52.

Pestonjee, D.M.: *Organisational Structure and Job Attitude*. The Minerva Associates, Calcutta, 1974.

——.: A.P. Singh and Niyaz Ahmad: "Job satisfaction and accidents". *Ind. Journal of Industrial Relations*, 13(1), 1977, pp. 65-72.

Philip, P.J.: "Adjudication and collective bargaining". *Economic Weekly*, 12(3), 1960, pp. 521, 524.

Pillai, P.N.K.: "Industrial relations in retrospect". *Industrial Relations*, 1, 1968, pp. 149-62.

——.: "Outlook for collective bargaining". *Management Review*, 2(1) Jan., 1962, pp. 23-25.

Pillai, J.K.: "Organisational climate and teacher morale", *Journal of Applied Psychology*, 13, 1978, pp. 47-50.

Poole, M.: *Worker participation in Industry*, Routledge and Kegan Paul, London, 1978.

Pope John XXIII: "Master et Magistra", revised in 1963, in Wall and Lischeron. *Workers Participation — A critique of the literature and some fresh evidences*, McGraw-Hill, London, 1977.

Pradeep Kumar: "The working of the conciliation machinery in Rajasthan", *Indian Journal of Industrial Relations*, 2(1), 1966, pp. 34-49.

Prasad, A.K.: "A study of personality and some personal factors in job satisfaction". *Indian Journal of Psychology*, 40(4), 1965, pp. 147-51.

Punekar, S.D.: *Industrial peace in India — The problem and its solution*. Vora and Co., Bombay, 1952.

——.: "Outside leadership of trade unions: A Bombay Survey", *Economic Weekly*, 1(26, 27, 28), 1958, pp. 877-79.

——.: "The Textile and Cement Wage awards". *Economic Weekly*, 12(2) March, 1960, pp. 493-94.

——.: "The Central Government Employees Strike", *Economic Weekly*, 12(31), 1960, pp. 1202-4.

——.: "Aspects of State Intervention in Industrial Relations in India : An Evaluation" in A.M. Ross (ed.), *Industrial Relations and Economic Development*, London, 1966, pp. 21-44.

—— and S. Madhuri: *Trade union leadership in India*, Lalvani, Bombay, 1967.

——and Manorama Savur: *Management of White Collar Relations*, Bombay, 1970.

Qazi A.D.: "Trade unionism in Textile Industry of Kashmir : A case study", unpublished dissertation, University of Kashmir, 1986.

Raha, N.K.: "Individual dispute as an industrial dispute", *Industrial Relations*, 18, 1966, pp. 10-15.

Raina, N.N.: "Hegemony of the working people — A specific feature of our freedom movement", *Studies of Kashmir Council of Research*, III, 1978, pp. 4-13.

Rajbir and Vasudeva: "Correlates of Job Satisfaction among Industrial workers". *Indian Journal of Social Work*, 37(3), 1976.

Raman Patiabhi, N.: *Political involvement of India's Trade Unions*, Bombay, 1967.

Ramanujan: "From the Babul tree story of Indian Labour". I.N.T.U.C., Delhi, 1967.

Ramaswamy, E.A.: "Politics and organised labour in India". *Asian Survey*, 13, 1973.

——.: *The worker and his union.*' Allied, Bombay, 1977.

Ramsay, H.: "Participation — The shop floor view", *British Journal of Industrial Relations*, 14, 1976, pp. 128-41.

Rao, A.: "Socio-personal correlates of job satisfaction", 1970 in Narchal, Renu *et al.* "Job satisfaction in some correlates" *Productivity*, XXV (3), 1984, pp. 367-700.

Rao, Gomji, Prameshwara,: "Levels of workers' participation in management : An Analytical Framework". *Indian Journal of Industrial Relations*, 12(3), 1977, pp. 305-16.

Rao, G.R.S.: "Socio personal correlates of job satisfaction". *Indian Journal of Applied Psychology*, 2, 1970, pp. 63-70.

Rao, M.G". "Industrial Relations in Indian Railways", Doctoral dissertation Andhra University, Waltair, 1970.

Rao, M. Madhusudhan: "Union leadership profile in Visakhapatnam", *Indian Journal of Industrial Relations*, 19(4), 1984, pp. 502-6.

——.: *Labour-Management Relations and the Trade Union Leadership.* Deep and Deep, New Delhi, 1986.

Rao, Raman, A.V.: "Collective bargaining versus Govt. Regulations Review", *New York Regulations*, Allied, 1964.

Rao V.S.: "Trade Unionism and Union-Management relations — A case study", *Indian Journal of Lab. Economics*, XXVI (4), 1984. pp. 425-34.

Rao, Sarveshwara, G.V.: "Job content and context factors in job satisfaction of female clerical employees", *Indian Journal of Social Work*, 32, 1971, pp. 45-51.

——.: Theoretical and Empirical considerations of the two-factor Theory of Job satisfaction", *Indian Journal of Industrial Relations*, 7(3), 1972, pp. 311-30.

Rao, Sarveshwara, G.V. and T. Gangoli: "Perceived need satisfaction and importance of supervisory and clerical personnel", *Indian Journal of Psychology*, 46, 1971, pp. 31-43.

——.: "Job satisfaction of highly skilled personnel: A test of the generality of the two-factor theory". *Indian Journal of Applied Psychology*, 9, 1972, pp. 26-31.

Rao, Subba, A.V.: "Collective bargaining in Indian industries", *Indian Journal of Social Work*, 22(2), 1961, pp. 81-8.

Rao, T.V.S. Rama Mohan and Acharya Sarthi: "Wage policies in small scale firms and their implications for industrial relations", *Indian Journal of Industrial Relations*, 12(1), 1976, pp. 73-80.

Rao, V. Bhaskara: *Labour-management relations — New perspectives and prospects*, Concept Publishing Company, New Delhi, 1974.

——.: "Trade union awareness and consciousness among public sector employees", *Institute of Public Enterprises Journal*, VIII(1), 1985, pp. 65-74.

Rastogi, J.L.: *Industrial Relations in Uttar Pradesh*, Author, Lucknow, 1965.

Ratnam, C.S. Venkata: "Union-management relations in Indian ports". *Indian Journal of Industrial Relations*, 13(1), 1977, pp. 55-64.

——.: "Trade Union Scenario in India: Some reflection", *Indian Journal of Labour Economics*, XXVI(4), 1984, pp. 435-43.

Razdan, P.N.: "Management of industrial disputes and conflict resolution", *National Labour Institute Bulletin*, VIII(1&2), 1982, pp. 70-9.

Reddy, B. Ramadhar: "Industrial peace — a framework for Indian Business", *Jodhpur Management Journal*, 7, 1979, pp. 61-9.

Reddy, D. Narasimha: "The impact of political party-trade union nexus on bargaining power in public employment : A Case Study". *Indian Journal of Industrial Relation*, (1), 1972, pp. 121-30.

Reddy, Y.R.K.: "Strategic approach to Labour Relations", *Indian Journal of Industrial Relations*, 23(1), 1987, pp. 64-71.

Rees, Albert: "The Economics of trade union participation — A summary of literature". *American Sociological Review*, 25, 1960, pp. 237-44.

——.: *The economics of trade unions*. The University of Chicago Press, Chicago, 1962.

Reindrop, Julian: "Leaders and leadership in the trade unions in Bangalore", The Christian Literature Society, Madras, 1971.

Ridgel, G.T.: "A study of labour movement and industrial relations in the Cotton Textile Industry in Bombay". Doctoral Dissertation, University of Wisconsin, Madison, 1956.

Roach, D.E.: "Dimensions of employee morale", *Personnel Psychology*, 11, 1958, pp. 419-31.

Rose, A.M.: *Union solidarity — The Internal structure of a labour union"*. University of Minnesota Press, Minnesota, 1952.

Ross, A.M. and P.T. Hartman: *Changing Pattern of Industrial Conflict"*, John Wiley, Inc., New York, 1960.

Rosenfield, J.M. and M.J. Smith,: "Participative management — An overview", *Personnel Journal*, 46, 1969, pp. 101-4.

Sahoo, S.C.: "Trade unionism in Orissa". *Indian Journal of Commerce*, XXIV (86), 1977, pp. 73-82.

Sahu, B.: "A study of the dynamics of participative management — Indian Experience", Doctoral Dissertation, Indian Institute of Science, Bangalore, 1980.

——.: "Realities of participation : The case of an engineering industry". *Productivity*, 22(2), 1981, pp. 9-18.

——.: "Participative Management in India: Findings of an empirical study". *Decision*, 10(2), 1983, pp. 69-82.

——.: "Objective of participative management'. *Indian Management*, 24(2) 1985, pp. 9-14.

.: *Dynamics of participative Management: Indian Experience*, Himalaya, Bombay, 1985.

Saini, Debi, S.: "Industrial democracy : Law and challenges in India". *Indian Journal of Industrial Relations*, 19(2), 1983, pp. 191-206.

Saraf, O.P. (ed.): *The Jammu and Kashmir Year Book and Who's Who*. Rambir Publications, Jammu, 1987.

Saran, Jogeshwar: "Labour in Indian Railways". Doctoral Dissertation, Agra University, Agra, 1955.

Saxena, R.C.: *Case Studies in Industrial Relations*. Meerut, 1970.

——.: *Labour problems and social welfare*. Meerut, 1974.

Saxena, S.K.: *Nationalisation and industrial conflicts*. The Hague, Martinus Nejhaff, 1955.

Sayles, L.R. and G. Strause: *The local Union: Its place in the Industrial Plant*. Harper, New York, 1953.

Scheflen, K.G., E.E. Lawler and J.R. Hackman: "Long term Impact of employee participation in the Development of Pay incentive plans: A Field Experiment Revised", *Journal of Applied Psychology*, 55, 1971, pp.182-86.

Schregle, Johannes: "Workers' participation in decision within undertakings". *International Labour Review*, 113(1), 1976, pp.1-15.

Schuster, M.: "The impact of union-management co-operation on productivity and employment". *Industrial and Labour Relations Review*, 3, 1983, pp.415-30.

Schwartz, M.M., E. Jenusaltis and H. Stark: "Motivational factors among supervisors in the utility Industry". *Personnel Psychology*, 16, 1963, pp.45-53.

Semelser, N.: *Theory of collective bargaining*. Free Press, New York, 1968.

Seth, K.G.: "A review of research in Industrial relations in India". *Indian Journal of Industrial Relations*, 1(3), 1966.

Sharma, A.M.: "Comparative perception of labour unrest". *The Indian Journal of Social Work*, April, 1978, pp.47-51.

Sharma, B.: "Union involvement". *Indian Journal of Industrial Relations*, 6(4), 1971, pp.335-56.

——.: "The Indian Industrial worker: His origin, experience and destiny". *Economic and Political Weekly*, 8(23), 1973.

——.: *The Indian Industrial worker: Issues in Perspective*. Vikas, Delhi, 1974.

——.: "Industrial democracy — the Indian experience". *Indian Journal of Industrial Relations*, 22(3), 1987, pp.254-69.

Sharma, G.K.: *Labour movement in India*. Jalandhar, 1963.

Sharma, K.N., V.C. Narawane and S.K. Khandwala: "Job Satisfaction of workers in textile mills". *Productivity*, 5(4), 1964, pp.752-58.

Sharma, M.L.: "School climate and its relationship with principles of effectiveness and teacher satisfaction". *Journal of Psychological Research*, 21, 1975, pp.105-7.

Sharma, P.D.: "Textile Labour Association (role effectiveness and workers perception)". Report of the Research Project sponsored by I.C.S.S.R., 1980.

Sharoff, A.D.: *Conciliation and Arbitration in Industrial Disputes in India*. Popular, Bombay, 1953.

Shervani, R.: "Workers participation in management". *Indian Management*, 15(2), 1976, 11-13.

Sheth, N.R.: "Trade unionism in an Indian Factory: A sociological Analysis", *Economic Weekly*, 12(29-30), 1960.

——.: "Trade unions in India — A sociological approach", *Sociological Bulletin*, 17(1), 1968.

——.: "Workers participation in trade union activity". *Indian Journal of Industrial Relations*, 4(3), Jan., 1969, pp.279-97.

——.: "The Joint Management Council: Problems and Prospects". Sri Ram Centre, 1972.

—— and S.P. Jain: "Workers, leaders and politics: A case study" *Indian Journal of Industrial Relations*, 3(3), 1968.

——.: "The status and the role of local union leader". *Indian Journal of Industrial Relations*, 4(1), 1968, pp.70-89.

Sheth, N.R.: "Dimensions of organisational role: A case study of the supervisor in a textile mill". *Ind. Jr. of Industrial Relations*, 8(4), 1973, pp.579-603.

Shrimali, P.D.: "Industrial relations in Cotton Textile Industry in Kanpur". Labour Research Centre, Lucknow University, Lucknow, 1970.

Shukla, Amaresh Chandra: "Workers participation and industrial democracy". Ph.D. thesis, Lucknow University, Lucknow, 1975.

Shukla, H.N.P.: "The Organisation and Management of trade unions in U.P"., Ph.D. thesis, Agra University, 1960.

——.: "Trade Union Movement in U.P". Agra University, Agra, 1962.

Shukla, N.N.: *Case studies in Industrial Relations*. Bombay, 1968.

Siegel, A.J.: "Method and substance in theorising about worker protest", in H.Gregg Lewis (ed). *Aspects of Labour Economics*, Princeton University Press, 1962, pp.[illegible]9-41.

Singh, A.P.: "Determinants of Industrial Relations. A note", *Indian Journal of Labour Economics*, 14(1-2), 1971.

Singh, Jaspal: *India's Trade Union Leadership*. National, New Delhi, 1980.

Singh, M.K.: "Industrial Relations in Maharashtra". *Indian Journal of Social Work*, XLIV (1), 1983, pp.19-33.

Singh, N.K.: "Workers participation in management in steel industry". *Productivity*, XVII (4), 1977, pp.591-95.

——.: "Collective bargaining and bipartite settlements: Review of Leading experiences". The Steel Experience. *National Labour Institute Bulletin*, VI (3-4), 1980, pp.178-84.

Singh, R.: *Movement of industrial wages in India*. Asia Publishing House, Bombay, 1955.

Singh, R.C.: "Trade union in the Indian posts and telegraphs department". *Indian Journal of Labour Economics*, (-), 1968.

——.: "Determinants of Industrial Relations", *Indian Journal of Labour Economics*, 12(4), 1971, pp.91-7.

——.: "Pattern of Staff Relations in the Indian Civil Services". *Indian Journal of Lab. Economics*, XIX(3-4), 1976, pp.85-103.

Singh, S.: "Leadership pattern of Industrial Relations". *Indian Journal of Commerce*, XXIV(86), 1971, pp.49-56.

Singh, S.P. and A.P. Singh: "The effect of certain social and personnel factors of job satisfaction of supervisors". *Psychological Studies*, 25, 1980, pp.129-32.

Singh, V.B.: *Industrial Labour in India*, Asia, Bombay, 1963.

——.: "Trade union movement in India". in V.B. Singh (ed): *Economic History of India (1857-1956)*, Bombay, 1965.

——.: *Climate for Industrial Relations: A Case Study in Kanpur Cotton Industry*. Allied Publishers, Bombay, 1968.

Sinha, D.: "Job satisfaction and job behaviour", in S.K. Roy and A.S. Menon (eds): *Motivation and organisational effectiveness*. Sri Ram Centre, New Delhi, 1972.

——.: "Job satisfaction and absenteeism". *Indian Journal of Industrial Relations*, 1(1), 1965, pp.1-11.

Sinha, D. and U.N. Agarwalla: "Job Satisfaction and General Adjustment of Indian White Collar Workers". *Indian Journal of Industrial Relations*, 6(4), 1971, pp.357-67.

Sinha, D. and M.U. Pai: "Motivational Analysis of Union membership". *Indian Journal of Social Work*, 23(4), 1963, pp.343-49.

Sinha, D. and R.R. Nair: "A study of job satisfaction in factory workers". *Indian Journal of Social Work*, 26(1), 1965, pp.1-8.

Sinha, D. and K.C. Sharma: "Union Attitude in Indian workers". *Journal of Applied Psychology*, 46, 1962, pp.247-57.

Sinha, G.P.: "Problems of collective bargaining in India". *Industrial Relations*, 16(2), 1964, pp.90-108.

Sinha, J.P.B. and Sinha (-): "A case of reversal in participation management", *Indian Journal of Industrial Relations*, 10(2), 1974, pp.179-89.

Sinha, N.N.: "The history and working of trade unions in the Coal Mining Industry". Doctoral Dissertation Patna University, Patna, 1966.

Sinha, S.: "A Survey of some factors on the question of industrialisation in India". *Indian Journal of Psychology*, 35, 1960, pp.9-16.

Sinha, R.P.: *Social dimension of trade unions in India*. Uppal, New Delhi, 1984.

Sivaprasad, K. and K. Sreeramanumurthy: "Industrial relations in public sector undertakings: A case study of Bharat Heavy Plate and Vessels". *Indian Journal of Lab. Economics*, XIV(3-4), 1976-77, pp.104-10.

Sivayya, K.V.: "*Trade union movement in Visakhapatnam*". Andhra University, Waltair, 1966.

—.: "Industrial relations in Ship Building Industry". Research Programmes Committee, Planning Commission of India, New Delhi, 1967.

—.: *Industrial Relation in Visakhapatnam Port*. Andhra University Press, Waltair, 1968.

—.: *Industrial Relations in selected units of the Sugar Industry of Andhra Pradesh, Waltair*, Andhra University Press, Waltair, 1971.

Smith, P.C. and L.M. Kendalla: "Cornell Studies of Job Satisfaction: Strategy for the development of a general theory of job satisfaction", unpublished manuscript, 1963, in Narchal, *et al.* "Job satisfaction: Some correlates". *Productivity*, XXV(3), 1984, pp.367-70.

Srivastava, A.K.: "Motivation and perception of organisational climate". *Productivity*, XXVI(1), 1985, pp.55-8.

—.: "Need Satisfaction & Job satisfaction of Industrial Employees at Chandigarh", Ph.D. Dissertation, Panjab University, Chandigarh, 1974.

Srivastava, A.K. and Vineta Srivastava: "Job satisfaction — Myth and reality", *Indian Journal of Labour Economics*, XXVI(1-2), 1983, pp.71-85.

Srivastava, B.K.: "Making participation work: Cast study of Implementation of the government scheme" Towards continuing education *(P.F.C.)* Vol. IV (9-12), 1984, 211 27.

Srivastava, G.P.: "A study of some determinants of job satisfaction among underground and group colliery workers". *Indian Journal of Industrial Relations*, 14(1), 1979.

Srivastava, P.K.: "Conciliation and arbitration in U.P.", Doctoral Dissertation Agra University, Agra, 1966.

Srivastava, R.N.: "A perspective view on the industrial relations scene of the future". *Lok Udyog*, 11(2), 1977, 9-14.

Srivastava, Surya Kumar: "Relationship between job satisfaction and organisational climate: A comparative study of private and public sectors". Doctoral Dissertion, University of Roorkee, 1984.

——.: "Achievement motivation in private and public sector employees: A comparative study". *Indian Journal of Industrial Relations*, 19(4), 1984, pp.502-6.

——.: "Motivation and job satisfaction: A study'. *Indian Management*, 24(9), 1985, pp.29-31.

Stagner, R.: "Psychological aspects of industrial conflict: II, Motivation", *Personnel Psychology*, 3, 1950, pp.1-16.

——.: *Psychology of industrial conflict*. John Wiley & Sons, New York, 1956.

Strauss, G.: "Control by the membership in building trade unions". *American Journal of Sociology*, 61, 1956, pp.527-35.

—— and E. Rosenstein: "Workers participation in Management: A critical review". *Industrial Relations*, (2), 1970, pp.197-214.

Subramanian, K.N.: *Labour-Management relations in India*. Asia, Bombay, 1967.

Super, S.D.: "Occupational level and job satisfaction". *Journal of Applied Psychology*, 23, 1939, pp.547-64.

Sutaria, Rupande and Pallavi Shah: "Need fulfilment, job attitudes and job mobility". *Indian Journal of Industrial Relations*, 12(4), 1977, pp.443-52.

Swarson, Charles, R.: "Participation in unions — An analysis of the literature and research agenda". *Journal of Collective Negotiations in the Public Sector*, 10, 1981, pp.1-17.

Tandon, M.L.: "Collective bargaining by Govt. employees in Punjab". *P.U. Management Review*, 1(2), 1978, pp.1-17.

Tandon, P.L.: The statesman, 14 April, 1976. Quoted in Rao Somji Prameshwara, "Levels of workers participation in management: An analytical framework". *Indian Journal of Industrial Relations*, 12(3), 1977, pp.305-16.

Tanic, Tivan: "Workers' participation in Management — Ideal and Reality in India". Sri Ram Centre, New Delhi, 1969.

Tannenbaum, A.S. and F.H. Allport: "Personality structure and group structure: An Interpretative study of their relationship through an Event Structure Hypothesis". *Journal of Abnormal and Social Psychology*, 51, 1956, pp.272-80.

Tannenbaum, A.S. and R.L. Kahan: *Participation in Union Locals — Evenston III*, Row Paterson and Company, 1958.

Terman, L.M. and M.H. Oden: *The gifted group at mid-life — Thirty-five years follow up of the superior child.* Standard University Press, Standardford, 1959.

Thakur, C.P.: "Competitive unionism in a new industrial centre". *Indian Journal of Industrial Relations*, 3(4), 1968, pp.89-104.

——.: "Trade Unions and social science research in India". *Indian Journal of Industrial Relations*, 12(1), 1976, pp.1-26.

—— and F.C. Munson: "Industrial Relations in printing industry: A study in the context of technology and market in Delhi area". Sri Ram Centre, New Delhi, 1969.

—— and K.C. Sethi: "Participative management in public enterprises". *Indian Journal of Industrial Relation*. 7(4), 1974, pp.614-24.

Thakur, G.K.: "Labour problems of Textile Industry". A study of the labour problems of the Cotton Mill Industry in Bombay", Vora, Bombay, 1962.

Thompson, W.A.: "Eleven years after graduation". *Occupations*, 17, 1939, pp.209-714.

Tripathi, K.M.: "Industrial relations in public enterprises — An Analysis", *Lok Udyog*, III(2), 1969.

Tripathi, R.C.:"Relative saiiency of job factors during strike". *Indian Journal of Industrial Relation*, 12(1), 1976, pp.81-5.

Tripathi, Tarak Nath: "Attitudes of workers towards their economic incentives". *Interdiscipline*, 11(2), 1974, pp.122-29.

Turner, A.N.: "What makes a 'Good Foreman'?. The worker speaks his mind". *Personnel*, 32, 1955, pp.382-92.

Twery, R., J. Schmid, Jr. and C. Wrigley: "Some factors in job satisfaction: A comparison of three methods of Analysis". *Education Psychology, Measmt.*, 18, 1958, pp.189-202.

Vaid, K.N.: "Growth and practice of trade unionism: An Area Study". Delhi School of Social Work, Delhi, 1962.

——.: *Trade unionism in India*. Sri Ram Centre, Delhi, 1965. Industrial Relations Statistical Serial No. 4.

——.: "Why workers join unions". *Indian Journal of Industrial Relations*, 1(2), 1965, pp.208-30.

——.: *Papers on Absenteeism*, Asia, Bombay, 1967.

Varkey, N.K.: *A handbook of labour legislation in India*. Lalvani, Bombay, 1968.

——.: *Work and motivation*. John Wiley & Sons. New York, 1964.

Verma, M.K.: "The role of legislation in regulating labour management relations in India". *Labour Law Journal*, 8(4), 1957, pp.257-72.

——.: "Industrial relations in India and abroad: A comparative study", *Productivity*, 13(1), 1972, pp.121-124.

Verma, Pramod: "Industrial conflict in India: A Statistical Analysis", *Vikalpa*, 3(3), July, 1978, pp.119-214.

——.: *Impact of Economic Development on Industrial Relations: An Empirical Analysis*, Academic, Ahmedabad, 1979.

——.: *Managers and workers in Engineering Industries*. Academic, Ahmedabad, 1981.

Virmani, B.R.: *Workers participation in management*. Macmillan, Delhi, 1978.

Viteles, M.S.: *Motivation and Morale in Industry*. Steples Press, London, 1953.

Vroom, V.H.: "Some personality determinants of the effect of participation". *Journal of Abnormal and Social Psychology*. LIX, 1959, pp.322-27.

Walker, C.R. and R.H. Guest: *The man on the Assembly lines*. Harward University Press, Cambridge, 1952.

Walker, Kenneth, F.: "Worker's participation in management: An International Perspective", *Udyog*, 5(12), 1972.

Wall, T.D. and J.A. Lischeron: *Worker participation — A Critique of the literature and some fresh evidences*. McGraw-Hill, London, 1977.

Warrior, S.K.: "Workers participation in Industry". *Management and Labour Studies*, 2(2), 1976, pp.105-14.

——.: "Meaningful participation in management — A new perspective". *Indian Journal of Industrial Relations*, 3(4), 1978, pp.445-66.

Waston, C.: "An evaluation of some aspects of steers and Rhodes Model of employee attendance". *Journal of Applied Psychology*, 66, 1981, pp.385-89.

Webb. W.B. and E.P. Hollander: "Comparison of three morale Measures: A survey, polled group judgement and self-evaluation". *Journal of Applied Psychology*, 40, 1956, pp.17-20.

West, C.: "Relationship between job satisfaction, demographic variables, absenteeism and tenure of workers, in Dilmariva Boiler Processing Plant". *Dissertaion Abstracts International*, 38(4-A), 1977.

Wherry, R.J.: "An orthogonal re-rotation of the Baehr and Ash Studies of SRA employee inventory". *Personnel Psychology*, 7, 1954, pp.365-80.

White, J.K. and A. Ruh: "Effects of Personal Values on the Relationship between Participation and Job attitude". *Administrative Science Quarterly*, 18, 1973, pp.506-14.

Wikert, F.R.: "Neu Entwicklunger der Demorkratic inder Industrie de U.S.A".. *Mensch V. Arbeit*, 6(2-3), 1954, pp.17-43.

Yajnik, K.C.: "Conciliation and industrial development". An operational Analysis with special reference to Gujarat". Ph.D. thesis, Saurashtra University, Gujarat, 1977.

Zechariah, John: "Employee Expectations from a supervisor". *Indian Journal of Social Work*, XLIV(3), 1983, pp.307-10.

Zechariah, John: "Employees' expectations from management", *Indian Management*, 22(12), 1983, pp.19-24.

Zechariah, K.A.: *Industrial Relations and Personnel Problems: A study with particular reference to Bombay*. Asia, Bombay, 1954.

INDEX